ON LINE

CRAFTSMAN

❈ COLLECTION ❈

Design 7483, page 16

HOME PLANNERS, LLC
Wholly owned by Hanley-Wood, Inc.
TUCSON, ARIZONA

Published by Home Planners, LLC
Wholly owned by Hanley-Wood, Inc.
Editorial and Corporate Offices:
3275 West Ina Road, Suite 110
Tucson, Arizona 85741

Distribution Center:
29333 Lorie Lane
Wixom, Michigan 48393

Rickard D. Bailey, *CEO and Publisher*
Cindy Coatsworth Lewis, *Director of Publishing*
Jan Prideaux, *Senior Editor*
Marian E. Haggard, *Editor*
Matthew S. Kauffman, *Graphic Designer*

Design/Photography Credits
Front Cover: Plan W311 by Northwest Home Designing, Inc.
              Photo by Northlight Photography

Back Cover: Plan 7483 by Alan Mascord Design Associates, Inc.
              Exterior photo by David Papazian
              Interior photos by Bob Greenspan

First Printing, February 1999

10 9 8 7 6 5 4 3 2 1

Printed in the United States of America

Library of Congress Catalog Card Number: 98-75295

ISBN softcover: 1-881955-54-0

TABLE OF CONTENTS

ABOUT THE DESIGNERS

HOME PLANNERS

Headquartered in Tucson, Arizona, with additional offices in Detroit, Home Planners is one of the longest-running and most successful home design firms in the United States. With over 2,500 designs in its portfolio, the company provides a wide range of styles, sizes and types of homes for the residential builder.

SELECT HOME DESIGNS

Select Home Designs has 50 years of experience delivering top quality and affordable residential designs to the North American housing market. Since the company's inception in 1948, more than 350,00 new homes throughout North America and overseas have been built from Select's plans. Select's design team is constantly striving to develop the best new plans for today's lifestyles.

DONALD A. GARDNER ARCHITECTS, INC.

The South Carolina firm of Donald A. Gardner was established in response to a growing demand for residential designs that reflect constantly changing lifestyles. The company's specialty is providing homes with refined, custom-style details and unique features such as passive-solar designs and open floor plans.

DESIGN TRADITIONS

Design Traditions was established by Stephen S. Fuller with the tenets of innovation, quality, originality and uncompromising architectural techniques in traditional and European homes. Especially popular throughout the Southeast, Design Traditions' plans are known for their extensive detail and thoughtful design.

DESIGN BASICS, INC.

For nearly a decade, Design Basics, a nationally recognized home design service located in Omaha, has been developing plans for custom home builders. Since 1987, the firm has consistently appeared in Builder magazine, the official magazine of the National Association of Home Builders, as the top-selling designer.

ALAN MASCORD DESIGN ASSOCIATES, INC.

Founded in 1983 as a local supplier to the building community, Mascord Design Associates of Portland, Oregon began to successfully publish plans nationally in 1985. The company's trademark is creating floor plans that work well and exhibit excellent traffic patterns.

LARRY E. BELK DESIGNS

Through the years, Larry E. Belk has worked with individuals and builders alike to provide a quality product. Flowing, open spaces and interesting angles define his interiors. Great emphasis is placed on providing views that showcase the natural environment.

LIVING CONCEPTS HOME PLANNING

With more than twenty years of design experience, Living Concepts Home Planning has built an outstanding reputation for its many award-winning residential designs. Based in Charlotte, North Carolina, the company was founded by partners Frank Snodgrass, Chris Boush, Kim Bunting and Derik Boush. Because of its affinity for glass, and designs that take full advantage of outside views, Living Concepts specializes in homes for golf and lakefront communities.

THE SATER DESIGN COLLECTION

The Sater Design Collection has a long established tradition of providing South Florida's most diverse and extraordinary custom designed homes. This is exemplified by over 50 national design awards, numerous magazine features and, most important, satisfied clients.

LARRY W. GARNETT & ASSOCIATES, INC.

Starting as a designer of homes for Houston-area residents, Garnett & Associates has been marketing designs nationally for the past ten years. A well-respected design firm, the company's plans are regularly featured in House Beautiful, Country Living, Home and Professional Builder.

POLLARD-HOSMAR ASSOCIATES, HOME DESIGNERS, INC.

Pollard-Hosmar Associates is an award-winning firm that was formed in July of 1990 by Steve Pollard and Brad Hosmar. The firm's focus has been in custom home designs, custom neighborhood concepts, cost-effective production housing, stock plans and home additions and remodels. They strive to exceed the expectations of their clients with creativity, integrity, innovation and personal service.

DRUMMOND DESIGNS, INC.

Drummond Designs has been involved in the business of residential architecture since 1973, with over 70,000 satisfied customers. They have achieved this by keeping up with the trends, and sometimes creating them. Their primary goal is to offer consumers top-quality homes that meet or exceed most of the world's building code requirements.

AHMANN DESIGN, INC.

Ahmann Design is a residential design firm specializing in custom residential, stock plan sales, and color rendering. Recognized several times as a finalist in Professional Builder Magazine's "Best of American Living" contest, Ahmann Design, Inc. continues to grow as a leader in the residential design market.

NORTHWEST HOME DESIGNING, INC.

Northwest Home Designing is a family-owned and operated firm that was founded on a simple principle: create custom home designs that are unique to the needs and desires of its customers. The firm's detailed approach has earned them numerous awards for innovation in design.

JAMES FAHY DESIGN

Under the direction of architectural engineer, James R. Fahy, P.E., President, and Douglas R. Bennett, Senior Designer, James Fahy Design has established itself as a leader in residential design, both regionally and nationally. The Fahy design philosophy of developing plans with a diversity of styles and sizes allows the company to better serve clients needs.

THE HOUSING ASSOCIATES

Rodney L. Pfotenhauer opened the doors of The Housing Associates in 1987 as a design consultant and illustrator for the manufactured housing industry. Almost from the beginning, his efforts caught the attention of the public. Pfotenhauer's designs are characterized by carefully composed traditional exteriors with up-to-date interiors.

STUDER RESIDENTIAL DESIGNS, INC.

Studer Residential Designs, Inc was founded in 1971 and specializes in the design of single family custom built homes. The firm enjoys a strong presence in the Greater Cincinnati and Northern Kentucky housing market. In 1992 the decision was made to expand Studer Designs into the national market. Builders enjoy working with a Studer Design because the blueprints are well thought out, easy to read, and simplify the building process.

UNITED DESIGN ASSOCIATES, INC.

United Design offers award-winning Ideal Home Plans to builders and consumers worldwide. "At United Design, we know you've got a lot more to think about than plans, so we make it simple. First and foremost, we design beautiful, intelligent homes that appeal to clients of all interests."

MARK STEWART AND ASSOCIATES, INC.

Founded in 1988, Mark Stewart and Associates was conceived as a perfect format to capitalize on Stewart's strengths and offer the home building industry innovative, practical and popular home designs with timeless character.

The word that is best loved in the language of every nation is home, for when a man's home is born out of his heart and developed through his labor and perfected through his sense of beauty, it is the very cornerstone of his life.

—quote by Gustav Stickley

The Craftsman-Style Home, And Its Cousin The Bungalow

Children of the Arts and Crafts Movement

The word Craftsman is defined by Merriam Webster's Collegiate Dictionary (Tenth Edition) as 1: a worker who practices a trade of handicraft, 2: one who creates or performs with skill or dexterity especially in the manual arts. In architecture, Craftsman refers not to a person, but to a style and philosophy of an era known as the Arts and Crafts Movement.

How do we recognize a Craftsman Home? The term Craftsman usually refers to a 1-½ to 2-story home with the following characteristics:

❈ The house not only complements but makes good use of its surroundings.

❈ The construction of the house uses materials found on the site, and/or natural materials native to the region.

❈ The house designs rely on exposed structural elements, such as rafter tails, for decorative details. The variety of natural materials provides textures for light to play on.

❈ Voids, in the form of recessed porches, entry ways, terraces and pergolas, create heightened visual interest.

❈ Interiors stress form and function. Space is both conservatively and creatively used for living, with design elements using wood and built-ins such as inglenooks, benches and cabinets.

❈ Light fixtures and hardware do double duty as design elements.

❈ More often than not, the interior is designed around a large stone or brick fireplace.

❈ Windows are usually large, some double-hung sash, and many with multiple small panes over a large single pane.

What sets Arts and Crafts architecture apart from any other design form is that it was more than a style: It was a movement concerned as much with questions of social reform as with issues of design aesthetic. The Zen-like quality found in the Arts and Crafts Movement made the style far more complex and encompassing than preceding design ideas. Its mysticism appealed to those who lived outside of the American religious mainstream, but its spirituality, humility, and order also agreed with the teachings of orthodox Catholicism. In America, the Arts and Crafts Movement is in a full revival in the 1990s, and just as it was back at the turn of the nineteenth century, it is again a philosophy as well as a style.

The Arts and Crafts Movement began in 1860s England with the ideas of philosopher John Ruskin and designer William Morris. Ruskin, an art history professor at Oxford

Design 7470, page 43

Design 7473, page 20

University, began a campaign to return England to a simpler way of life in tune with nature. At the same time, Morris, as well as many other artists, writers, philosophers and theologians recognized that people were losing their connection with nature and so banded together to try to re-establish that link. To obtain this goal, these influential thinkers idealized medieval times, and held that society would benefit from a return to an economic system in which workers were valued and natural materials and painstaking handiwork were highly regarded. They were not necessarily anti-technology, but the devaluation of nature and the human touch in favor of progress and production caused great concern. In England, as well as in mainland Europe, groups of artists and craftsmen began producing new objects that conveyed the principles of simplicity and quality.

In 1861 the Arts and Crafts Movement got its biggest boost when Morris founded Morris, Marshall, Faulkner and Co., a furniture, design and decorative accessories company that stressed time-honored craftsmanship and natural materials. The timing was perfect, for in 1862 the London International Exhibition showcased never-before-seen Japanese arts and crafts, which had an immediate effect on design. England quickly grew to like this new look and began shedding the layers of Victorian clutter from its homes. What developed was a single design style based on simplicity, rather than a chaotic hodgepodge of influences. While all of this was happening in Europe, America was going through its own evolution of architectural styling.

There are a number of important issues that made the American Arts and Crafts Movement quite distinct from its English counterpart. Foremost among them was America's lack of national identity and artistic tradition. Throughout the early and mid-1800s, the majority of American architecture had been derived from classic European forms. There was the Victorian style and the Italianate, Gothic Revival and even Egyptian Revival. The era from 1865 to 1900 saw many styles of architecture battling it out for national prominence. The result was a visual mishmash that reflected the nation's own unsettled culture. Often, features of several different styles were incorporated into one structure. The culmination of this practice became known as Queen Anne style. Often lumped into the broad Victorian category, Queen Annes were a visual feast that, while not unpleasant, could be quite overdone.

By the mid-1880s, with the ideas of the European Arts and Crafts Movement beginning to infiltrate the U.S., a more natural architecture evolved from the Queen Anne. New England's Shingle style incorporated many of the exterior features of Queen Annes, however, ornamentation was greatly reduced and the overall look was more subdued. Designers frowned upon the needless collection and display of objects that were not useful or connected to their environment. And, after the excess of the Victorian Age, in

Design 3313, page 157

which people crammed all manner of bric-a-brac and furnishings into their houses regardless of its style, this new simplistic approach was a breath of fresh air. Instead of a contrast of building materials, Shingle-style homes were covered with wooden shingles. Occasionally, rough-hewn stone was used for porch columns, but the color and coarseness was used to compliment the natural texture of the wooden shingles. This use of local building materials, along with the combination of surface texture and material was a first step toward achieving the Arts and Crafts architectural ideal.

Many names are associated with the American Arts and Crafts Movement. For instance, in 1868, Charles Lock Eastlake of England proposed that a single, cohesive style dominate the home, rather than a hodgepodge of influences. This decorative philosophy bore many similarities to the Arts and Crafts style blooming in the U.S.

Around the turn of the century in the Midwest, where bungalows were not as practical, another name came onto the scene. Frank Lloyd Wright and his colleagues produced Prairie School houses, reflecting the flat rolling Midwest prairie. This style is perhaps best exemplified by Wright's Robie House (1908) in Chicago.

Charles and Henry Greene, located in California, began designing homes for a select group of clients in 1901, producing powerful expressions in wood that were married to their landscapes and suited to the hot California climate. The Gamble House (1909) is one of the most famous of the architect-designed Arts and Crafts houses.

An important year for the American Arts and Crafts Movement was 1897, when the Arts and Crafts Societies were founded in Rochester, New York and Chicago. That year also saw the first Arts and Crafts Exhibition in Boston. The success of the

Exhibition and the press coverage of the manufacturers and designs inspired the formation of still more craftsman guilds and societies the next year. 1898 also heralded the founding of Gustav Stickley & Co., in Syracuse, New York. A trained stonemason, furniture maker and metal worker who was born in Wisconsin, Stickley, sometimes referred to as the "American William Morris", set out on a fateful visit to Europe in 1898. There he absorbed what he could of the Arts and Crafts Movement, and brought back to the U.S. the ideas and innovations stemming from the British Arts and Crafts. It was the simple, geometric designs of Gustav Stickley that truly defined the American Arts and Crafts Movement.

Like William Morris and Frank Lloyd Wright, both of whom stressed the need for furnishings to fit the homes they were in, Stickley designed homes to fit the furniture he created. These were simple Craftsman-style

homes—usually no more than a few spacious rooms decorated only with beautiful natural woodwork and room dividers along with a stone or brick hearth. An abundance of windows to let in natural light was also important since sunlight was an entirely different light than gas and electric lights. The Craftsman plans offered the average American family a house that was a home, based on the solid virtues of beauty, simplicity, utility and organic harmony. Stickley firmly believed that the "nesting instinct" was "the most deep seated impulse" of humankind.

The primary inspiration for the Craftsman style was to look to nature, local materials, local (nationalist or native) building traditions and to design and construct after the manner of honest craft traditions: iron and copper blacksmithing, pottery, coarse weaving and rough hewn materials. The reverence for nature inherent in Arts and Crafts philosophy soon gave birth to the environmental movement. The creation of national parks became a priority, and the National Geographic Society and the Sierra Club were born. The Arts and Crafts style depends on simplicity and harmony among the home's many elements. The type of lifestyle it advocates is an holistic and

planet-friendly one, with the environment strongly considered. This is an attitude even more appealing in the 1990s than it was a hundred years ago.

 close cousin to the Craftsman-style home is the Bungalow. The original definition of Bungalow came from India and referred to one-story houses with long, steep, overhanging rooflines that were built to protect British colonists from the heat and harsh sun.

It is considered the first step toward the modern ranch home in several senses. The California Bungalow layout emphasizes the horizontal, rather than multiple stories. It is typically one- to one-and-a-half stories, with a long sloping roofline, and a wide, sheltering overhang that makes the house appear to snuggle down into the earth. This tie to the earth is frequently exaggerated by using a foundation and porch pillars that broaden toward the base. The porch is often wide enough to accommodate furniture, giving it an outdoor-room feeling. The woodwork is still heavy and dark

Design 7475, page 78

like the Craftsman, but it's usually square or simple rather than gussied up in layers or with Victorian-type stylings. According to designer Gustav Stickley, a bungalow was a house reduced to its simplest form.

Bungalows that best exemplified the Movement's philosophy were well crafted, and used materials left as close as possible to their natural state. Cobblestones were used in foundations and broad chimneys, while the rest of the home was constructed of wood or shingles in a natural shade of brown. Due to the Tuberculosis epidemic and health philosophy of the times, many houses were built with "TB rooms" or sleeping porches that were completely surrounded by windows so that fresh "healing" air could circulate freely.

The earliest American examples of the bungalow were the small one-story Queen Anne-style cottages, which were built in profusion in California during the 1880's and '90s. As Craftsman ideas travelled westward, the Queen Anne influences were dropped in favor of less ornate Craftsman, Stick and Japanese design

elements. Granted, different versions of the bungalow can be found throughout the world, but America has made the style its own. It was only a matter of time before the bungalow would be rescued from its long-term obscurity and begin again to be actively recognized for its relationship to the Arts and Crafts Movement by an admiring audience. Within the 1990s, the new bungalow movement also has created a commitment to community, something that has been suffering since our moving out of country hometowns and into big cities. This is because many of these homes can be found in big clusters of similar-type houses, thus creating rewarding places to live.

Although there are many ending dates for the original Arts and Crafts Movement, ranging from 1915 to 1920 (and even up to 1929), it is safe to say that the period had effectively ended by 1916. By 1915 the media had grown tired of the style and started actively searching for the next great trend in design. The Craftsman's popularity had dramatically declined by 1919, however, its design effects were still

felt for some time and homes continued to be built in the style for a good decade, though they were usually modified. In addition, the social changes brought on by America's gearing up for, and eventual entry into World War I served to wake America up from its cocooning, heart-and-home dreaming.

Whichever date one chooses to put on the end of the original era, the influence of the American Arts and Crafts Movement can't be overlooked. An appreciation for the Arts and Crafts-era history helps us redefine the look into a more sophisticated, yet equally eco-friendly style for todays' world. And the idealism, beauty and simplicity it generated has a ring of truth that is as inspiring today as it was 100 years ago. It is clear that the style is not a new fad, but rather a trend that has become a classic.

Design 3315, page 172

Finishings And Furnishings
The Craftsman Interior

Bradbury & Bradbury Art Wallpapers presents an elegant look into the dining room. The ceiling has Circlet Ceiling paper with Oakleaf border and corner blocks. On the wall you'll find Oakleaf Frieze and Avalon wallpaper.

As classic and distinctive as their exteriors were, the primary appeal of Arts and Crafts homes was their open floor plans and the simple, yet beautifully finished and furnished interiors. In the American style of Arts and Crafts furniture that reached its peak popularity from around 1901 to 1915, structure and ornamentation were united in simple, clean design. Home decoration in Craftsman homes always emphasized the importance of wood work in a room. Use of a color that harmonized with the interior wood used set the stage for the rest of the room's decoration also. Various shades of earth tones were most often the choice. Preferred color combinations included gray-green for walls with cream for the ceiling, and golden brown for walls with pale green for the ceiling.

By the spring of 1902, the Arts and Crafts style—or, as it was often called, the "Mission" style—had become the latest decorating fad in the United States. Gustav Stickley, one of the most influential proponents of the Arts and Crafts philosophy, prized designs that expressed honestly, in appropriate materials, the essential qualities of a chair, bed, desk, lamp, etc. Stickley never used the term "Mission" when referring to his own furniture designs. He preferred "Craftsman." No other Arts and Crafts furniture is so widely collected today as the pieces by Stickley. Reproductions of his work are often found in reputable shops, where their goal of simplicity closely follows his own.

The Morris chair, named for William Morris, who designed the first

IWP tries to out do itself with this maple wood door. Covered with a clear finish, shown here with side-lights, this door features architectural, hand-blown glass created by Shelley Jurs. International Wood Products is part of the JELD-WEN family.

chair of this type, is probably the signature piece of the Arts and Crafts period. Their features included rounded spindles or front posts carved with lion or griffin heads.

As common as Morris chairs were in home furnishing of the period, they were actually only a small part of the furniture spectrum. Fireplaces, warm-toned woodwork and built-in bookcases, seating and sideboards all characterize Craftsman-style interiors.

Now that the Arts and Crafts aesthetic is again enjoying popularity, collectors need to educate themselves to the variety of furniture available.

Furniture makers referred to sofas as "settles", a deliberate use of an anachronism no doubt intending to bring to mind an idealized past. Another seating design mentioned before, is the Morris chair, a type of easy chair with a moveable back that could be set at different angles—basically an early example of the recliner.

Tables were varied to meet needs for every room of the house. They ranged in size from 14"-diameter taborets to round tea tables with a convenient bottom shelf, to drop leaf style to massive library tables.

Another style of seating was the inglenook. Usually created by built-in

high-back benches, or in a convenient niche, these seats formed an intimate room within a room beside the fireplace. The fireplace, which serves either as the focal point of the room or as a nostalgic touch, is a must for an Arts and Crafts home. Made with stone or brick, they are often enhanced by ceramic tiles, woodwork and copper hoods.

Incandescent electric lighting was introduced in 1879, when Thomas Edison made the first practical incandescent light bulb. The elimination of the need for oil reservoirs, gas pipes and dangerous open flames inspired designers with new ideas for lamps and lighting fixtures. The Arts and Crafts lights combined ceramic or oak bases with stained-glass or mica shades and iron, copper or brass hardware. The bases of floor and table lamps were works of art themselves. Some were fashioned of quartersawn oak or cherry wood; others were made of art pottery with matte glazes or hand-painted designs. Bases of cast

Two elegant floor lamps, designed by Mica Lamp Company. Shown here are the Mission Floor Lamp and the Torchiere Floor Lamp.

bronze and hand-hammered copper were even more popular than the wood and pottery versions. Arts and Crafts hanging lanterns and floor and table lamps are an inspired choice.

Arts and Crafts ceramics were specifically created to complement the style's architecture and furniture. Again, simplicity was the major application in this medium as well. Conventionalized abstract patterns of flowers, vegetables and occasionally animals began to replace the traditional realistic depictions of nature on a variety of surfaces which included tiles, vases, lamp bases and textiles.

A finishing touch for furniture not usually thought of, is often one that offers the most variety. Hardware for drawers or cabinets can give your Arts and Crafts home that "complete" look. Offered in many materials; brass, copper, wood and ceramic, choosing the right hardware for the home's furniture put the finishing touches on your fine Craftsman home.

The walls of Arts and Crafts rooms can be aptly decorated using Morris-style paper or paint and stencils. At the beginning of the era, it was typical to divide a wall into three parts and then

The Desert Flower Vase and the Bat Vase by Ephraim Faience Pottery Inc. are hand thrown and hand decorated.

Apple Tree Frieze is extended in height by the use of Apple Tree border top and bottom. Border and corner blocks are used to panelize the wall. Room done by Bradbury & Bradbury Art Wallpapers.

This fine oak Library Lamp, by the Mica Lamp Company, is designed after the lamp style by Charles Limber c. 1910 Grand Rapids, Michigan.

treat each part differently. Starting at the floor, the first portion of the wall stopped about waist height. A midsection ended at shoulder height and was surmounted by a top section that went to the ceiling.

On the lowest portion of the wall, a wood paneling was characteristic. Paint in a woodsy brown or leafy yellow-green color or a sturdy wallpaper with an unobtrusive pattern were equally suitable treatments. The midsection of the wall might be covered with a decorative paper or possibly painted. The upper section could be given importance with a stenciled or pictorial border executed in wallpaper, tiles or paint.

Arts and Crafts furniture is both handsome and sturdy; pieces are of versatile design, and look beautiful in combination with many other decorating styles.

Entry hardware by The Craftsman Hardware Company, shown here in the Pacific Knob to Knob Entry set, comes in sets for both interior and exterior.

ABOVE LEFT: Hand crafted, faience stoneware tile with custom Owl Panel adapted from a panel by William DeMorgan sits over a refurbished Wedgewood stove. (Carl Gilman: kitchen designer, contractor, owner. Designs In Tile: tile design and fabrication.)

ABOVE RIGHT: Notting Hill Decorative Hardware presents Prairie Tulips knob and matching pull shown in enamel on brass finish. Other knobs shown are Green Man in verdigris bronze, Dragonfly in antique copper and Cicada in bright nickel antique finish.

BELOW: The Mica Lamp Company presents the Large Onion lamp. This rivet base copper lamp is an original style from the Dirk Van Erp studio. c.1910-1930 San Francisco, CA.

■ DESIGN BY ALAN MASCORD DESIGN ASSOCIATES, INC.

This home, as shown in the photograph, may differ from the actual blueprints. For more detailed information, please check the floor plans carefully.

PLAN 9557

First Floor: 1,371 square feet
Second Floor: 916 square feet
Total: 2,287 square feet

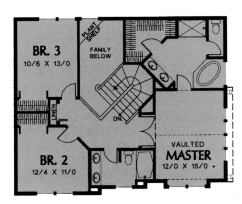

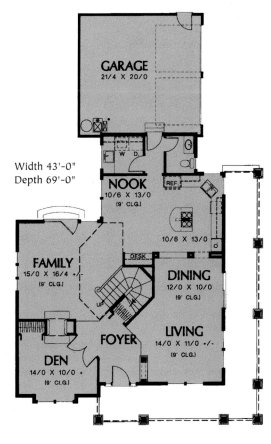

Width 43'-0"
Depth 69'-0"

lassic columns and balusters decorate a charming wrap-around porch on this comfortable home. A secluded den on the first floor offers a through-fireplace to the family room, which opens to the outdoors. The morning nook and L-shaped kitchen, with a cooktop island counter and a built-in writing desk, open through columns to an elegant formal dining room. The second-floor master suite opens through French doors and offers a spacious bath. Two family bedrooms share a full bath.

Exterior photo by David Papazian

This home, as shown in the photographs, may differ from the actual blueprints. For more detailed information, please check the floor plans carefully.

■ DESIGN BY ALAN MASCORD DESIGN ASSOCIATES, INC.

Interior photos by Bob Greenspan

This splendid Craftsman home will look good in any neighborhood, and is sure to become a family favorite. Rafter tails, gabled rooflines, stone-and-siding facade and Craftsman-style windows present this fine four-bedroom home with class. Inside, the foyer offers a beautiful wooden bench to the right, flanked by built-in curio cabinets. On the left, double French doors lead to a cozy study. Here, more built-ins await; a window seat, display shelves and a plate shelf circling the room. A fireplace is available to warm cool evenings, while plenty of windows and a French door to a private deck provide natural light. The formal dining room is complete with 10' beamed ceilings, a built-in hutch with lighting, built-in cabinets and a wall of windows. Formal dinner parties will be a breeze in this room, with its easy access to the large L-shaped kitchen. Note the abundance of wood here, with a long work island/snack bar, plenty of cabinets and drawers for storage and an adjacent sunny nook, open to the kitchen, and perfect for casual meals. Note the spacious sunroom, perfect for plants and early morning

coffee. The nearby two-story great room surely lives up to its name, with a massive stone fireplace, a two-story wall of windows, built-ins and rear yard access. Upstairs, two family bedrooms share a full bath and each have handy built-ins. A guest suite features its own bath. The lavish master bedroom suite is sure to please. Two large walk-in closets, a shower with two shower heads, a spa tub set in a spacious platform, a fireplace and a private deck all combine to completely pamper the homeowner.

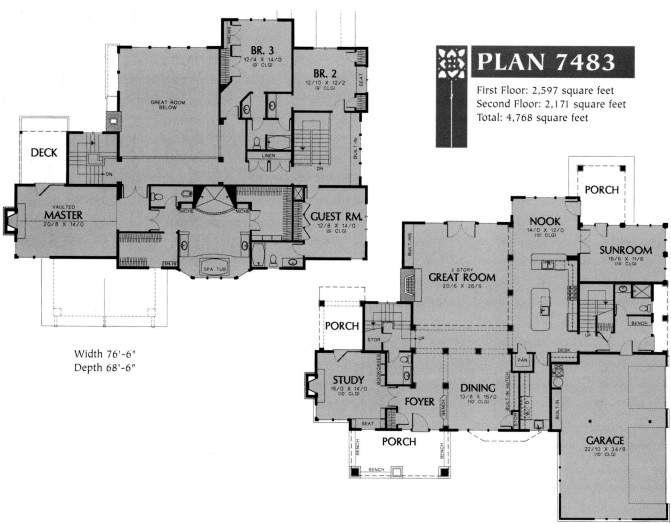

PLAN 7483

First Floor: 2,597 square feet
Second Floor: 2,171 square feet
Total: 4,768 square feet

Width 76'-6"
Depth 68'-6"

Stone-and-siding, gables and rafter tails, window detail and a wonderful floor plan—all elements of a fantastic Craftsman home. With a room for everyone, this two-story, four-bedroom home is designed for today's active family. The foyer is flanked by a spacious living room, with a fireplace, to the right and a cozy den entered through double doors to the left. A curving staircase fills the rest of the foyer and leads to the sleeping zone on the second floor. At the rear of the home, a large family room is perfect for casual get-togethers, offering a corner fireplace and a wall of windows. A huge kitchen is enhanced by tons of counter and cabinet space, a large cooktop work island, a corner sink and an adjacent sunny nook with access to the rear yard. Upstairs, three family bedrooms share a full hall bath, while the master bedroom suite is filled with amenities. A double door leads into this lavish suite, where a wall of windows fills the bedroom with natural light. A hexagonal walk-in closet, a separate shower and corner tub and a dual-bowl vanity complete this sumptuous suite. A three-car garage easily shelters the family fleet.

Photo by Bob Greenspan

PLAN 7473

First Floor: 1,578 square feet
Second Floor: 1,159 square feet
Total: 2,737 square feet

Width 63'-0"
Depth 53'-0"

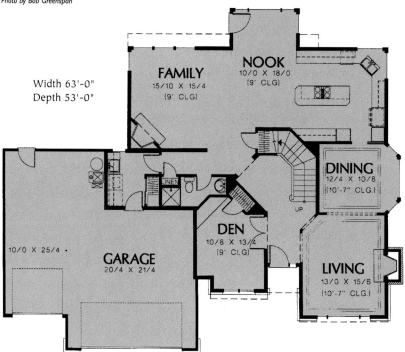

FAMILY
15/10 X 15/4
(9' CLG)

NOOK
10/0 X 18/0
(9' CLG)

GARAGE
20/4 X 21/4

10/0 X 25/4

LINEN

DEN
10/8 X 13/4
(9' CLG)

DINING
12/4 X 10/8
(10'-7" CLG.)

UP

LIVING
13/0 X 15/6
(10'-7" CLG.)

■ DESIGN BY ALAN MASCORD DESIGN ASSOCIATES, INC.

This home, as shown in the photograph, may differ from the actual blueprints. For more detailed information, please check the floor plans carefully.

MASTER
14/10 X 15/10
(9'-8" CLG.)

DN.

BR. 4
13/10 X 10/2

BR. 3
10/0 X 11/10

BR. 2
10/8 X 12/8

FOYER
BELOW

Photo by Northlight Photography

■ DESIGN BY NORTHWEST HOME DESIGNING INC.

tick work, rafter tails, pillars defining a covered porch, Craftsman window detail and a stone-and-siding facade all combine to present this five-bedroom home as a good example of Arts and Crafts-flavored architecture. Not only does it have a great layout, it also offers options for your changing family needs. Inside, the foyer is flanked by the formal dining room and a cozy reading room, each defined by graceful pillars. Beyond the dining room, a large efficient kitchen waits to please the gourmet of the family. Here, a large work island, with a cooktop and snack bar, helps define this spacious workspace. At the rear of the home, up a few steps, a family

room filled with amenities is perfect for casual get-togethers. A fireplace, built-in media center and bookshelves, vaulted ceiling and deck access complete this room. Located on the first floor for privacy, the master bedroom suite is designed to pamper. A beamed ceiling, large walk-in closet and sumptuous bath make this suite pure pleasure. On the second floor, two family bedrooms share a full bath and a balcony, while a third bedroom offers a private bath. A spacious guest suite also has a private bath. A laundry room and two loft areas complete this level. The attic on the third level can be used for a kid's retreat or storage. Take note of the various options offered with this home.

This home, as shown in the photograph, may differ from the actual blueprints. For more detailed information, please check the floor plans carefully.

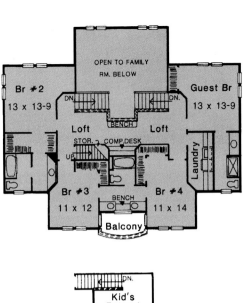

OPEN TO FAMILY RM. BELOW

Br #2
13 x 13-9

Guest Br
13 x 13-9

DN.

DN.

Loft

Loft

STOR.

COMP. DESK

UP

Laundry

Br #3
11 x 12

BENCH

Br #4
11 x 14

Balcony

DN.

Kid's Retreat
12-6 x 13-6

ATTIC

Width 76'-0"
Depth 81'-0"

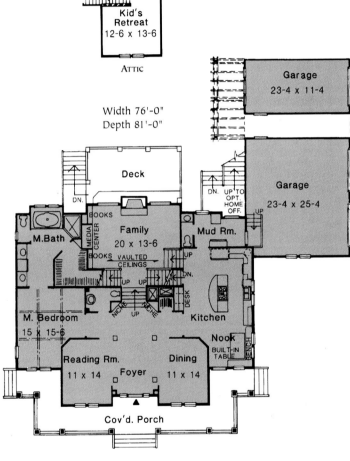

Deck

Garage
23-4 x 11-4

DN.

BOOKS

Family
20 x 13-6

Mud Rm.

Garage
23-4 x 25-4

MEDIA CENTER

BOOKS

VAULTED CEILINGS

DN. UP TO OPT. HOME OFF.

M. Bath

UP

UP

M. Bedroom
15 x 15-6

NICHE

NICHE

DESK

Kitchen

UP

Nook
BUILT-IN TABLE

Reading Rm.
11 x 14

Foyer

Dining
11 x 14

Cov'd. Porch

PLAN W311

First Floor: 2,120 square feet
Second Floor: 1,520 square feet
Total: 3,640 square feet
Optional Basement: 377 square feet
Optional Home Office: 526 square feet
Attic: 183 square feet

UP

Home Theatre Rm.
21 x 12

Cellar

UP

MECH. RM.

BASEMENT

DN.

SLOPE

SLOPE

Home Office

SLOPE

OPTIONAL HOME OFFICE

This home, as shown in the photograph, may differ from the actual blueprints.
For more detailed information, please check the floor plans carefully.

Photo by Bob Greenspan

■ DESIGN BY ALAN MASCORD DESIGN ASSOCIATES, INC.

PLAN 9590

First Floor: 1,205 square feet
Second Floor: 1,123 square feet
Total: 2,328 square feet

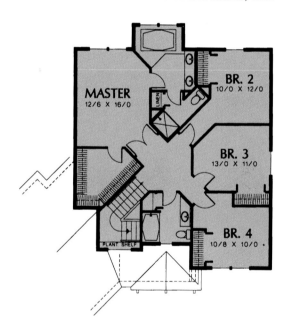

MASTER
12/6 X 16/0

BR. 2
10/0 X 12/0

LINEN

BR. 3
13/0 X 11/0

PLANT SHELF

BR. 4
10/8 X 10/0

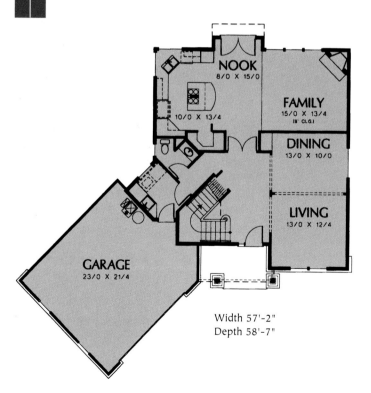

NOOK
8/0 X 15/0

FAMILY
15/0 X 13/4
(9' CLG.)

10/0 X 13/4

DINING
13/0 X 10/0

LIVING
13/0 X 12/4

GARAGE
23/0 X 21/4

Width 57'-2"
Depth 58'-7"

covered porch, multi-paned windows and rafter tails combine to
give this home plenty of curb
appeal. Inside, the foyer is flanked
by the formal living room and an
angled staircase. The formal dining room shares
space with the living room and the kitchen is
accessible through double doors. A large family
room is graced by a fireplace and opens off a
cozy eating nook. The second level presents
many attractive angles. The master suite has a
spacious walk-in closet and a sumptuous bath
complete with a garden tub and separate shower. Three bedrooms share a full hall bath.

PLAN A296

First Floor: 1,661 square feet
Second Floor: 882 square feet
Total: 2,543 square feet

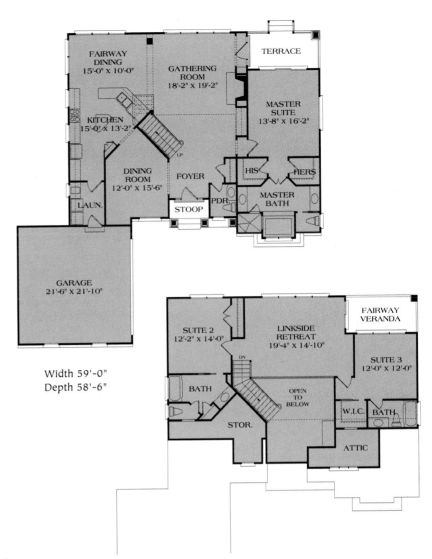

Width 59'-0"
Depth 58'-6"

With rustic rafter tails, sturdy pillars and a siding-and-shingle facade, this welcoming bungalow offers plenty of curb appeal. Inside, the formal dining room is to the left of the foyer, and gives easy access to the angled kitchen. Here, a work island, a peninsula with a sink and plenty of counter and cabinet space are sure to please the gourmet of the family. A spacious gathering room offers a fireplace, built-ins, a wall of windows and access to a covered terrace. Located on the first floor for privacy, the master suite is lavish with its amenities. These include His and Hers walk-in closets, a large corner shower and a bumped-out tub. Upstairs, two suites offer private baths and share a linkside retreat with a covered veranda.

This home, as shown in the photograph, may differ from the actual blueprints. For more detailed information, please check the floor plans carefully.

Photo courtesy of Living Concepts Home Planning

■ DESIGN BY LIVING CONCEPTS HOME PLANNING

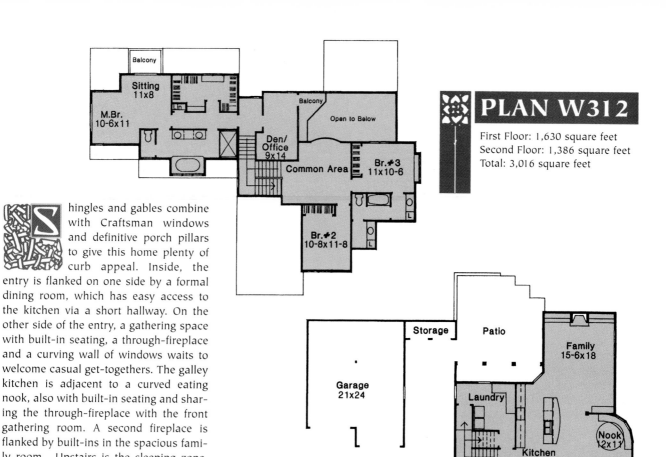

Balcony

Sitting
11x8

M.Br.
10-6x11

Den/Office
9x14

Balcony

Open to Below

Common Area

Br. #3
11x10-6

Br. #2
10-8x11-8

PLAN W312

First Floor: 1,630 square feet
Second Floor: 1,386 square feet
Total: 3,016 square feet

hingles and gables combine with Craftsman windows and definitive porch pillars to give this home plenty of curb appeal. Inside, the entry is flanked on one side by a formal dining room, which has easy access to the kitchen via a short hallway. On the other side of the entry, a gathering space with built-in seating, a through-fireplace and a curving wall of windows waits to welcome casual get-togethers. The galley kitchen is adjacent to a curved eating nook, also with built-in seating and sharing the through-fireplace with the front gathering room. A second fireplace is flanked by built-ins in the spacious family room. Upstairs is the sleeping zone, which consists of two family bedrooms sharing a full bath and a common area. The master suite features a sitting area with a balcony, a huge walk-in closet and a roomy bath. A quiet den/office with a private balcony completes this level.

Storage

Patio

Family
15-6x18

Garage
21x24

Laundry

Nook
12x11

Kitchen

F.P.

Width 73'-0"
Depth 55'-6"

Pantry

Gathering
14x14

Entry

Dining
14x12

Porch

This home, as shown in the photograph, may differ from the actual blueprints. For more detailed information, please check the floor plans carefully.

Photo by James Reuter Photography

■ DESIGN BY NORTHWEST HOME DESIGNING INC.

■ DESIGN BY THE SATER DESIGN COLLECTION

This home, as shown in the photograph, may differ from the actual blueprints. For more detailed information, please check the floor plans carefully.

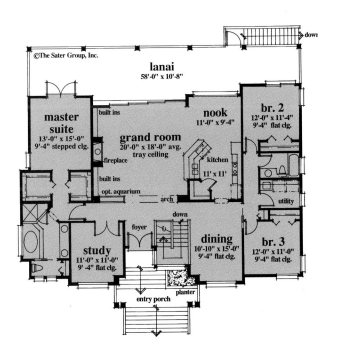

©The Sater Group, Inc.

lanai
58'-0" x 10'-8"

master suite
13'-0" x 15'-0"
9'-4" stepped clg.

built ins

grand room
20'-0" x 18'-0" avg.
tray ceiling

fireplace

built ins

opt. aquarium

nook
11'-0" x 9'-4"

kitchen
11' x 11'

arch

br. 2
12'-0" x 11'-4"
9'-4" flat clg.

utility

down

foyer

study
11'-0" x 11'-0"
9'-4" flat clg.

dining
10'-10" x 15'-0"
9'-4" flat clg.

br. 3
12'-0" x 11'-0"
9'-4" flat clg.

entry porch

planter

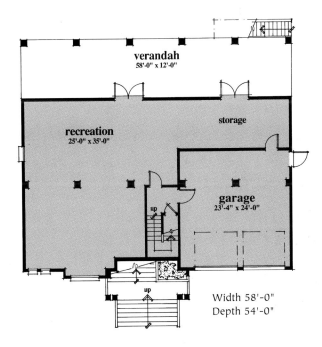

down

verandah
58'-0" x 12'-0"

recreation
25'-0" x 35'-0"

storage

up

garage
23'-4" x 24'-0"

up

Width 58'-0"
Depth 54'-0"

A strikingly simple staircase leads to the dramatic entry of this Contemporary bungalow design. The foyer opens to an expansive grand room with a fireplace and a built-in entertainment center. An expansive lanai opens from the living area and offers good inside/outside relationships. For more traditional occasions and planned events, a front-facing dining room offers a place for quiet, elegant entertaining. The master suite features a lavish bath with two sizable walk-in closets, a windowed whirlpool tub, twin lavatories and a compartmented toilet. Double doors open from the gallery hall to a secluded study that is convenient to the master bedroom. Two additional bedrooms share a private hall and a full bath on the opposite side of the plan.

PLAN 6622

Square Footage: 2,190

■ DESIGN BY R. L. PFOTENHAUER

Innovative architects Charles S. and Henry M. Greene built one of the finest examples of the Craftsman bungalow in 1903. Their goal in designing and building homes was to create an environment that was simple and direct in its function while being beautiful in its appearance.

A quote from Walden Pond by Henry David Thoreau is posted by the elegant front door of this fine, modern-day adaptation. The timber-framed porch and golden wood exterior of this Craftsman-style house would be very much at home in turn-of-the-century Pasadena, California, where the Greene brothers resided.

Upon entering the house, a cathedral-like timber-framed interior fills the eye. Warm woods of all species enhance the great room and kitchen. A beam ceiling in the kitchen ties in with the cabinets and flooring, giving this room a cozy and inviting appeal. A nearby nook is adjacent to the rear deck, providing the opportunity for dining alfresco. The great room is well named, with exposed-wood trusses arching across the ceiling and a magnificent window anchoring one end, framing the outdoors and bringing it inside. A grand stone fireplace sends trails of warmth and light flickering through this gorgeous room.

Photos by Roger Hart

To the right of the foyer, a formal dining room waits, with a beam ceiling and soft lighting to enhance any dinner party. Access to the outdoors is provided, this time to the wraparound covered porch.

Located on the first floor for privacy, the master suite is sprinkled with amenities and charm. A sloped ceiling and plenty of windows are just the start. Two walk-in closets are opposite the bath where a whirlpool tub sits in a bay window. Entry to the sunroom is gained through the master bath or from the great room. A private balcony, perfect for sunset watching, is just steps away from the master retreat.

The second floor is reached via a beautiful staircase off the foyer. An open lounge leads to two bedrooms with vaulted ceilings and a generous second

This home, as shown in the photograph, may differ from the actual blueprints. For more detailed information, please check the floor plans carefully.

PLAN F146

First Floor: 2,078 square feet
Second Floor: 823 square feet
Total: 2,901 square feet

Width 88'-5"
Depth 58'-3"

BALCONY

DECK

GARAGE
22'-10" x 25'-10"

SUNROOM
10'-6" x 12'-5"

GREAT ROOM
16'-10" x 32'-6"

NOOK
13'-4" x 8'-7"

PANTRY D W R

UTILITY

FP

MR. BATH

WIC

SNACK COUNTER

KIT.
13'-4" x 15'-10"

WIC

BALCONY ABOVE

MR. BEDROOM
15'-5" x 15'-5"
(VOLUME CEILING)

ENTRY
16'-10" x 14'-0"

DINING
13'-0" x 13'-7"

PORCH

OPEN TO GREAT ROOM

BEDROOM 2
13'-0" x 16'-6"

LOFT ABOVE

WOOD RAIL

BEDROOM 3
13'-0" x 16'-6"

LOFT ABOVE

LOUNGE
16'-10" x 13'-2"

BATH

WOOD RAIL

OPEN TO ENTRY

DN

TUB/SHWR

LINEN ATTIC

bath. Views from the lounge are breath-taking, looking down into the foyer as well as the graceful great room.

Whether you are a homeowner who wishes to celebrate one of the richest and most enduring themes in American architecture, or live in a home designed to complement nature, this is a fine choice. Perhaps Leslie Bates expressed it best in a poem that accompanied a photograph of Greene and Greene's Tichenor house.

> ...Beauty has builded here
> a soul's design.
> Houses should be like
> this,—home and shrine.

Photo courtesy of Living Concepts Home Planning

■ DESIGN BY LIVING CONCEPTS HOME PLANNING

This home, as shown in the photograph, may differ from the actual blueprints. For more detailed information, please check the floor plans carefully.

BREAKFAST 10'-6" x 8'-0"

GOLF PORCH

MASTER SUITE 14'-6" x 15'-6"

KITCHEN 15'-2" x 15'-6"

GREAT ROOM 15'-0" x 23'-4"

MASTER BATH

W.I.C. LAUNDRY

PDR. BAR

GARAGE 21'-6" x 22'-8"

DINING ROOM 11'-8" x 13'-6"

FOYER

PORCH

STOOP

UP

PLAN A262

First Floor: 1,824 square feet
Second Floor: 842 square feet
Total: 2,666 square feet

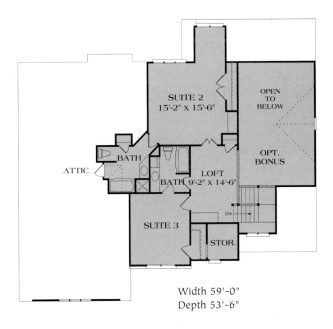

SUITE 2 15'-2" x 15'-6"

OPEN TO BELOW

ATTIC BATH

BATH LOFT 9'-2" x 14'-6"

OPT. BONUS

SUITE 3

STOR.

DN

Width 59'-0"
Depth 53'-6"

his fine Craftsman home exhibits many of the Arts and Crafts-type stylings, such as rafter tails, detailed windows, square pillars defining the porch and a siding-and-stone facade. Inside, the foyer is flanked by a stairway to the right and the formal dining room to the left. A bar separates this room from the kitchen, providing ease in serving. The L-shaped kitchen features a cooktop island and an adjacent sunny breakfast area. The spacious great room offers a fireplace and access to both the front covered porch as well as the rear golf porch. The master suite is lavish with its walk-in closet and pampering bath. Upstairs is the sleeping zone, complete with two suites, each with a private bath and access to a loft with built-ins.

This home, as shown in the photograph, may differ from the actual blueprints. For more detailed information, please check the floor plans carefully.

■ DESIGN BY HOME PLANNERS

Photo by Andrew D. Lautman

Don't be fooled by a small-looking exterior. This plan offers three bedrooms and plenty of living space. Notice that the screened porch leads to a rear terrace with access to the breakfast room. A living room/dining room combination adds spaciousness to the floor plan. Other welcome amenities include: boxed windows in the breakfast room and dining room, fireplace in the living room, planning desk and pass-through snack bar in the kitchen, whirlpool tub in the master bath, an open two-story foyer. The thoughtfully placed flower box, beyond the kitchen window above the sink, adds a homespun touch to this already comfortable design.

Width 34'-1"
Depth 50'-0"

PLAN 3316

First Floor: 1,111 square feet
Second Floor: 886 square feet
Total: 1,997 square feet

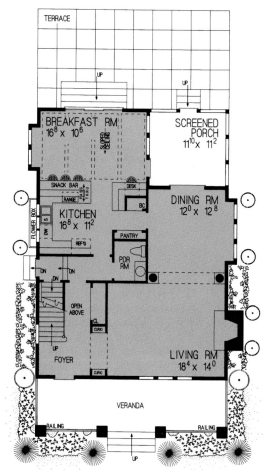

Cost to build? See page 182 to order complete cost estimate to build this house in your area!

■ Design by Alan Mascord Design Associates, Inc.

With rafter-tails, pillars and a combination of stone work and siding, this four-bedroom Craftsman home is sure to please. The two-story foyer is flanked by a formal living room—note the lack of cross-room traffic—and a formal dining room. The spacious family room offers a welcoming fireplace and easy access to the kitchen and nook. The L-shaped kitchen is complete with a large work surface island, a built-in desk for planning meals and paying bills and a nearby pantry. Upstairs, three secondary bedrooms—or make one a cozy den—share a hall bath. A sunny bonus room is also available for a den, office or play room. The master suite presents a vaulted ceiling, large walk-in closet and a sumptuous bath. Note the alternate layout for the master suite which is included in the blueprint set.

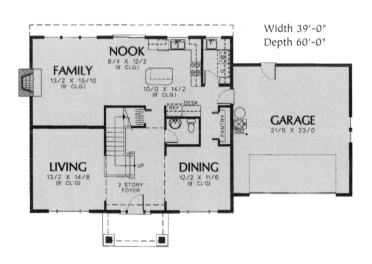

Width 39'-0"
Depth 60'-0"

PLAN 7477

First Floor: 1,216 square feet
Second Floor: 1,078 square feet
Total: 2,294 square feet
Bonus Room: 200 square feet

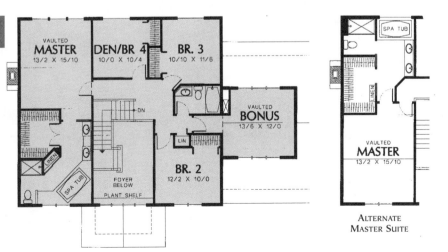

Alternate
Master Suite

Width 41'-0"
Depth 41'-6"

Twin gables, a covered front porch and a wonderful floor plan all combine to give this home plenty of appeal. A bayed den with built-in bookshelves awaits to welcome quiet times just to the right of the foyer. The vaulted great room offers the warmth of a fireplace while also giving access to the rear yard. A U-shaped kitchen is enhanced by a corner sink, a cooktop island and a walk-in pantry. The sleeping zone is upstairs, and includes two family bedrooms sharing a full hall bath, and a vaulted master bedroom suite. Here, the homeowner will be pampered by a huge walk-in closet, a separate tub and shower and a dual-bowl vanity. The two-car garage will easily shelter the family fleet.

PLAN 8875

First Floor: 1,022 square feet
Second Floor: 1,010 square feet
Total: 2,032 square feet

■ DESIGN BY POLLARD-HOSMAR ASSOCIATES

■ DESIGN BY ALAN MASCORD DESIGN ASSOCIATES, INC.

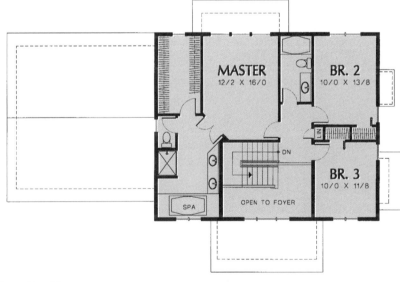

MASTER
12/2 X 16/0

BR. 2
10/0 X 13/8

BR. 3
10/0 X 11/8

SPA

OPEN TO FOYER

DN

PLAN 7471

First Floor: 1,102 square feet
Second Floor: 888 square feet
Total: 1,990 square feet

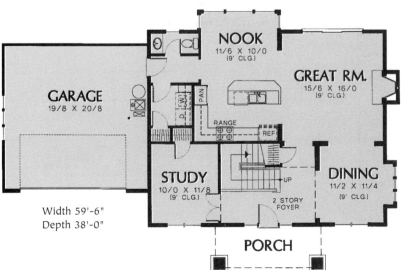

GARAGE
19/8 X 20/8

NOOK
11/6 X 10/0
(9' CLG.)

GREAT RM.
15/6 X 16/0
(9' CLG.)

RANGE
REF

STUDY
10/0 X 11/8
(9' CLG.)

DINING
11/2 X 11/4
(9' CLG.)

UP

2 STORY
FOYER

Width 59'-6"
Depth 38'-0"

PORCH

A shed roof, supported by sturdy pillars, covers the front porch of this fine Craftsman home, while twin gables show off their rafter-tails. Inside, a two-story foyer is flanked by a formal dining room featuring a box-bay window and a cozy study. The L-shaped kitchen is sure to please with a large work surface island and an adjacent nook. The nearby great room offers a fireplace for cool fall evenings, as well as access to the rear yard. The second floor is dedicated to the sleeping zone. Here, two family bedrooms share a full hall bath, while the master bedroom suite is complete with a walk-in closet and a pampering bath.

This split-foyer Craftsman offers many amenities for either a growing family or a family with older children. Of first interest would be the economic design of the home, while still offering an attractive floor plan. Note the three gables, covered porch, siding and shingles that combine to give this home a warm and welcoming attitude. On the main living level, a living room features a fireplace, an L-shaped kitchen has easy access to the dining area and three bedrooms share two full baths. Downstairs, a spacious rec room is further enhanced by access to a patio and laundry room. A fourth bedroom is available for either a grown child, a guest suite or an in-home office.

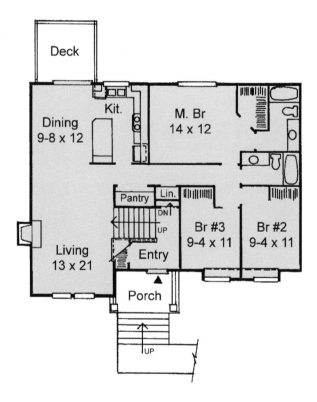

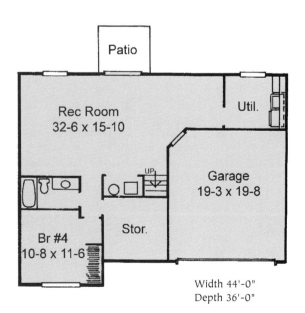

Width 44'-0"
Depth 36'-0"

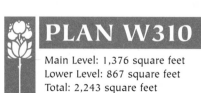

PLAN W310

Main Level: 1,376 square feet
Lower Level: 867 square feet
Total: 2,243 square feet

© 1997 Donald A. Gardner Architects, Inc.

■ DESIGN BY DONALD A. GARDNER ARCHITECTS, INC.

PLAN 7681

First Floor: 1,608 square feet
Second Floor: 657 square feet
Total: 2,265 square feet

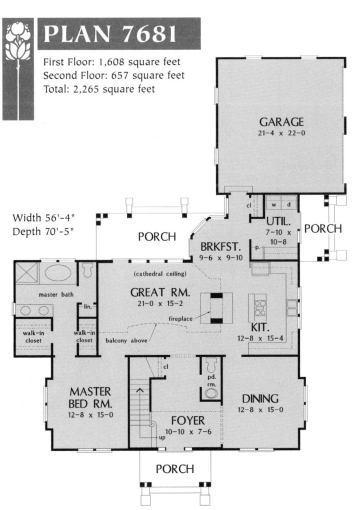

Width 56'-4"
Depth 70'-5"

GARAGE
21-4 x 22-0

PORCH

cl   UTIL.
7-10 x
10-8   PORCH

w d

p.

BRKFST.
9-6 x 9-10

(cathedral ceiling)

master bath

lin.

GREAT RM.
21-0 x 15-2

fireplace

KIT.
12-8 x 15-4

walk-in
closet   walk-in
closet   balcony above

cl

MASTER
BED RM.
12-8 x 15-0

pd.
rm.

DINING
12-8 x 15-0

FOYER
10-10 x 7-6

up

PORCH

© 1997 Donald A Gardner Architects, Inc.

Shingles, window detail, gabled rooflines and an attractively covered front porch all combine to give this home plenty of curb appeal. The floor plan inside is also an eye-catcher, with the U-shaped kitchen featuring a cooktop work island and sharing a through-fireplace with the spacious great room. Here, a cathedral ceiling, a balcony from the second floor and access to the rear porch all enhance an already welcoming ambience. Formal and casual meals are easily taken care of in either the dining room with a box-bay window, or the unique breakfast room. Located on the first floor for privacy, the master suite is full of amenities. Two large second-floor bedrooms, with window seats, share a full bath complete with a dual-bowled vanity.

great room
below

attic storage   railing   attic storage

balcony

cl   cl

BED RM.
12-8 x 16-5   down   BED RM.
12-8 x 16-5

bath

lin.

window
seat   foyer
below   window
seat

■ Design by Alan Mascord Design Associates, Inc.

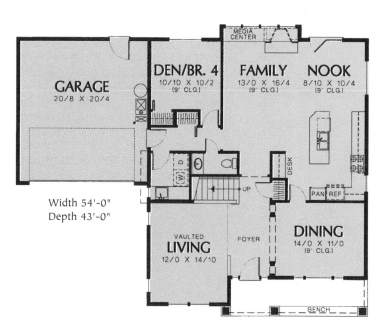

GARAGE
20/8 X 20/4

DEN/BR. 4
10/10 X 10/2
(9' CLG.)

FAMILY
13/0 X 16/4
(9' CLG.)

NOOK
8/10 X 10/4
(9' CLG.)

MEDIA CENTER

Width 54'-0"
Depth 43'-0"

DESK

UP

PAN REF

VAULTED LIVING
12/0 X 14/10

FOYER

DINING
14/0 X 11/0
(9' CLG.)

BENCH

PLAN 7479

First Floor: 1,300 square feet
Second Floor: 933 square feet
Total: 2,233 square feet

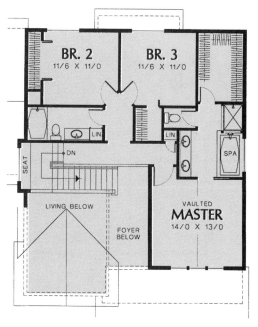

BR. 2
11/6 X 11/0

BR. 3
11/6 X 11/0

LIN

LIN

SPA

SEAT

DN

LIVING BELOW

FOYER BELOW

VAULTED MASTER
14/0 X 13/0

Subtle Craftsman style is evident in this three-bedroom home. From its rafter-tails poking out from under the roof overhang to the pillars supporting the shed roof over the porch, this attractive design is sure to be a favorite. Inside, there is room enough for all family pursuits. Formal entertaining is easy in the formal dining room, with a vaulted living room just across the hall for after dinner conversations. Casual times will be fun in the family room, with a fireplace, built-in media center and nearby L-shaped kitchen and sunny nook. A den—or make it a fourth bedroom—completes this floor. Upstairs, two family bedrooms share a hall bath, while the vaulted master suite features a spacious private bath. Note also the large walk-in closet.

PLAN 8865

First Floor: 1,211 square feet
Second Floor: 867 square feet
Total: 2,078 square feet

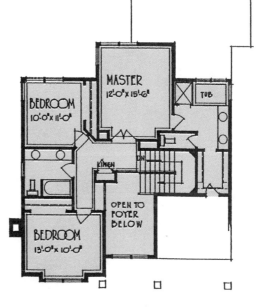

Width 38'-6"
Depth 65'-0"

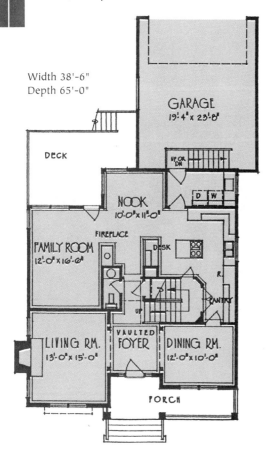

GARAGE
19'-4" x 23'-8"

DECK

UP OR DN

NOOK
10'-0" x 11'-0"

D W

FIREPLACE

FAMILY ROOM
12'-0" x 16'-6"

DESK

R.

PANTRY

UP

LIVING RM.
13'-0" x 15'-0"

VAULTED FOYER

DINING RM.
12'-0" x 10'-0"

PORCH

MASTER
12'-0" x 15'-6"

BEDROOM
10'-0" x 11'-0"

TUB

LINEN

OPEN TO FOYER BELOW

BEDROOM
13'-0" x 10'-0"

UP TO 2,300 SQUARE FEET

Offering plenty of curb appeal, this three-bedroom, two-story Craftsman home is sure to be a favorite of your neighborhood. And with a floor plan as attractive as the facade, this house will be a home for many years. Enter into the vaulted foyer from the covered porch, and you will be greeted by the formal areas first. To the left is the living room, complete with a fireplace. On the right is the formal dining room, which offers a pantry hall to the fine L-shaped kitchen. Casual living takes place toward the rear, in a spacious family room featuring a fireplace it shares with the breakfast nook, as well as access to the rear deck. The sleeping zone is located upstairs for privacy, and includes two secondary bedrooms sharing a hall bath and a comfortable master suite full of amenities.

■ DESIGN BY POLLARD-HOSMAR ASSOCIATES

■ DESIGN BY ALAN MASCORD DESIGN ASSOCIATES, INC.

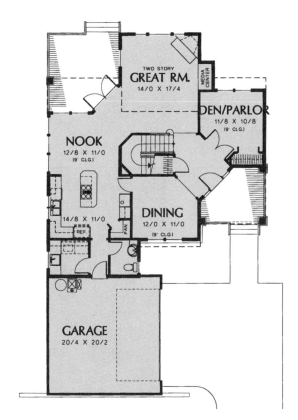

TWO STORY
GREAT RM.
14/0 X 17/4

MEDIA CENTER

DEN/PARLOR
11/8 X 10/8
(9' CLG.)

NOOK
12/8 X 11/0
(9' CLG.)

DINING
12/0 X 11/0
(9' CLG.)

14/8 X 11/0

REF.

PAN.

GARAGE
20/4 X 20/2

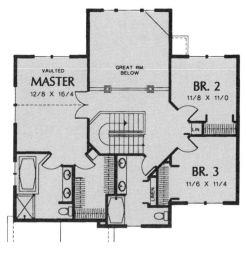

VAULTED
MASTER
12/8 X 16/4

GREAT RM.
BELOW

BR. 2
11/8 X 11/0

LIN.

BR. 3
11/6 X 11/4

LINEN

Width 40'-0"
Depth 64'-0"

PLAN 9591

First Floor: 1,176 square feet
Second Floor: 994 square feet
Total: 2,170 square feet

This home's covered, angled entry is elegantly echoed by an angled door to a rear covered porch, thus setting the style for this amenity-filled design. Flanking the foyer to the left is the formal dining room and to the right, through double French doors, is a cozy den/parlor. The great room opens out into the comfortable breakfast nook, sharing the warmth of its corner fireplace and giving this plan a spacious feeling. Gourmets will enjoy the large island kitchen. Upstairs, the master suite is located away from two secondary bedrooms for privacy and offers a luxurious bath and a walk-in closet.

■ DESIGN BY ALAN MASCORD DESIGN ASSOCIATES, INC.

PLAN 7461

First Floor: 968 square feet
Second Floor: 982 square feet
Total: 1,950 square feet

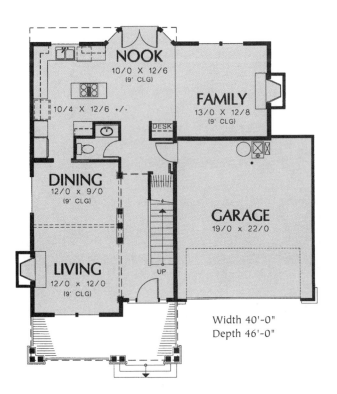

NOOK
10/0 X 12/6
(9' CLG)

FAMILY
13/0 X 12/8
(9' CLG)

10/4 X 12/6 +/-

DESK

DINING
12/0 x 9/0
(9' CLG)

GARAGE
19/0 x 22/0

LIVING
12/0 x 12/0
(9' CLG)

UP

Width 40'-0"
Depth 46'-0"

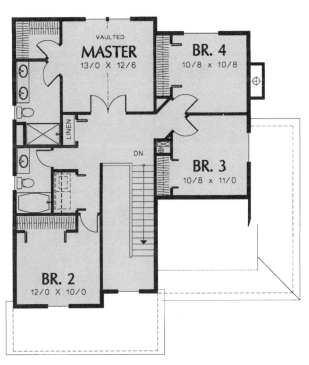

VAULTED
MASTER
13/0 X 12/6

BR. 4
10/8 x 10/8

BR. 3
10/8 x 11/0

LINEN

DN.

BR. 2
12/0 X 10/0

The Craftsman style is subtle, yet sweet, on this two-story home. A covered front porch welcomes family and friends into the two-story foyer. The first of two fireplaces is found in the formal living room, where a dining area resides at one end of the room. The L-shaped kitchen features a cooktop work island as well as plenty of counter and cabinet space. A bayed nook is nearby, offering access to the rear yard. For those casual times, the family room is complete with the second fireplace. Upstairs, the master suite is designed for pampering, with a vaulted ceiling, walk-in closet and a private bath. Three family bedrooms share a full bath and access to the linen closet.

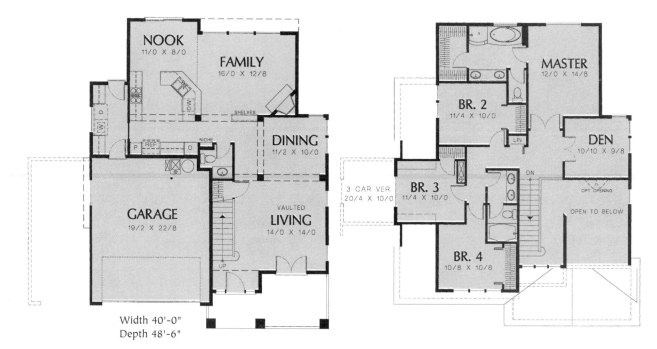

NOOK
11/0 X 8/0

FAMILY
16/0 X 12/8

W D

SHELVES

P REF

NICHE

DINING
11/2 X 10/0

GARAGE
19/2 X 22/8

VAULTED
LIVING
14/0 X 14/0

UP

Width 40'-0"
Depth 48'-6"

MASTER
12/0 X 14/8

BR. 2
11/4 X 10/0

DEN
10/10 X 9/8

3 CAR VER
20/4 X 10/0

LIN

BR. 3
11/4 X 10/0

DN

OPT OPENING

OPEN TO BELOW

BR. 4
10/8 X 10/8

Three pillars support a gabled porch roof on this fine two-story Craftsman home. The foyer opens directly into a vaulted living room, which is defined from the formal dining room by graceful columns. A unique kitchen features a nearby nook and has easy access to the family room. Here, a fireplace waits to warm cool fall evenings, and built-in shelves are available to hold your favorite books. The spacious second floor contains the sleeping zone. Three bedrooms share a full hall bath with a cozy den, while the master suite is designed to pamper. Complete with a walk-in closet, a separate shower and tub and a dual-bowled vanity, this suite is sure to please.

PLAN 7494

First Floor: 1,072 square feet
Second Floor: 1,108 square feet
Total: 2,180 square feet

■ Design by Alan Mascord Design Associates, Inc.

■ DESIGN BY ALAN MASCORD DESIGN ASSOCIATES, INC.

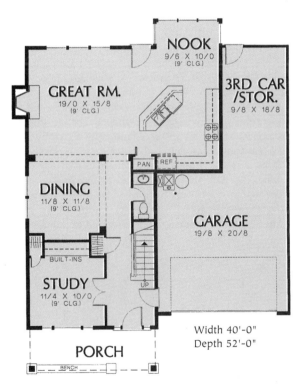

NOOK
9/6 X 10/0
(9' CLG.)

GREAT RM.
19/0 X 15/8
(9' CLG.)

3RD CAR
/STOR.
9/8 X 18/8

PAN   REF

DINING
11/8 X 11/8
(9' CLG.)

GARAGE
19/8 X 20/8

BUILT-INS

STUDY
11/4 X 10/0
(9' CLG.)

UP

Width 40'-0"
Depth 52'-0"

PORCH

BENCH

SPA

VAULTED
MASTER
13/8 X 12/0

BONUS
14/6 X 18/0 +
(9' CLG.)

BR. 2
11/4 X 10/0

DN

LIN

BR. 3
11/4 X 11/0

PLAN 7470

First Floor: 1,082 square feet
Second Floor: 864 square feet
Total: 1,946 square feet
Bonus Room: 358 square feet

This home would look good in any neighborhood. From the covered front porch, with a bench to rest on, to the trio of gables, this design has a lot of appeal. Inside, the Craftsman styling continues in the manner of built-in shelves in the study, a warming fireplace in the great room and plenty of windows to bring in the outdoors. The L-shaped kitchen is open to the nook and great room, and offers easy access to the formal dining area. Upstairs, two family bedrooms share a full bath and access to both a laundry room and a large bonus room. A vaulted master suite rounds out this floor with class. Complete with a walk-in closet and a pampering bath, this suite will be heaven to come home to.

■ DESIGN BY POLLARD–HOSMAR ASSOCIATES

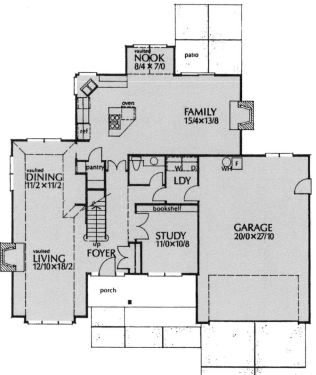

Stick-work adorns two of four gables and a covered porch welcomes friends and family to this fine two-story home. A spacious floor plan awaits inside and features many amenities. The living room and dining room share a vaulted ceiling and the warmth of a fireplace. An L-shaped kitchen offers a corner sink and a cooktop island, with a nearby nook for early morning coffee. The large family room features a second fireplace and access to the rear patio. Note the built-in bookshelves in the cozy study. Located upstairs away from everyday traffic, the sleeping zone is complete with two family bedrooms sharing a bath and a master suite designed to pamper.

PLAN 8863

First Floor: 1,311 square feet
Second Floor: 871 square feet
Total: 2,182 square feet

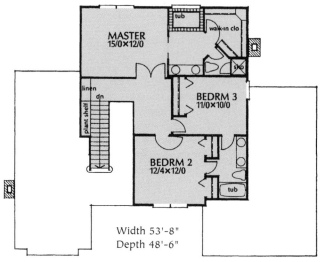

Width 53'-8"
Depth 48'-6"

■ DESIGN BY NORTHWEST HOME DESIGNING INC.

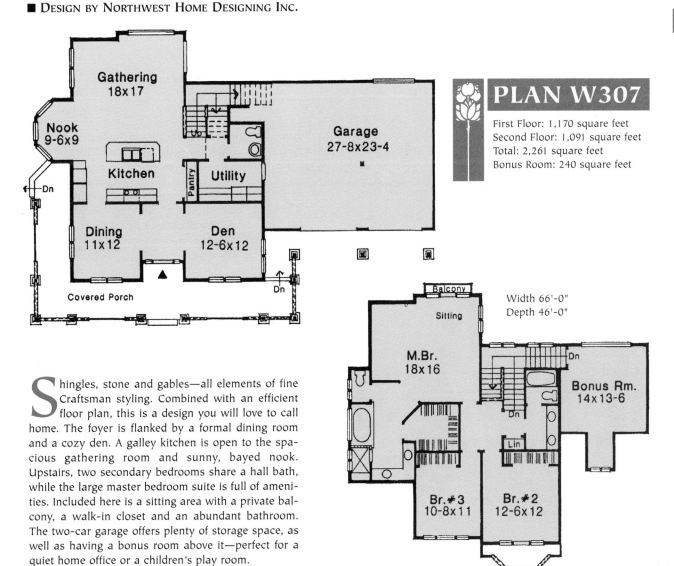

Gathering
18x17

Nook
9-6x9

Kitchen

Dining
11x12

Pantry

Utility

Den
12-6x12

Garage
27-8x23-4

Dn

Covered Porch

Dn

PLAN W307

First Floor: 1,170 square feet
Second Floor: 1,091 square feet
Total: 2,261 square feet
Bonus Room: 240 square feet

Balcony

Sitting

M.Br.
18x16

Bonus Rm.
14x13-6

Lin

Dn

Dn

Br.#3
10-8x11

Br.#2
12-6x12

Width 66'-0"
Depth 46'-0"

Shingles, stone and gables—all elements of fine Craftsman styling. Combined with an efficient floor plan, this is a design you will love to call home. The foyer is flanked by a formal dining room and a cozy den. A galley kitchen is open to the spacious gathering room and sunny, bayed nook. Upstairs, two secondary bedrooms share a hall bath, while the large master bedroom suite is full of amenities. Included here is a sitting area with a private balcony, a walk-in closet and an abundant bathroom. The two-car garage offers plenty of storage space, as well as having a bonus room above it—perfect for a quiet home office or a children's play room.

NOOK
9/0 X 8/0
[9' CLG.]

FAMILY
12/0 X 17/6 +/-
[9' CLG.]

7/6 X 14/4

[8' CLG]

DINING
12/2 X 10/8
[9' CLG.]

GARAGE
20/8 X 21/4

Width 54'-0"
Depth 51'-0"

UP

DEN
12/2 X 10/6 +/-
[9' CLG.]

PARLOR
12/2 X 12/0
[9' CLG.]

PORCH

MASTER
15/6 X 13/6 +/-

DN.

BR. 2
12/2 X 10/8

FOYER
BELOW

BR. 4
11/2 X 10/0

LINEN

BR. 3
11/2 X 12/0

S trong square pillars, a combination of shingles and siding and stylish window detailing dress up this fine Craftsman home. Inside, graceful detail continues, with an angled staircase echoed by the layout of the parlor and formal dining room. This home is designed to accommodate everyone. For quiet studying or working at home, there's the den at the front of the plan. The spacious family room is convenient to the L-shaped kitchen and offers a warming fireplace. Upstairs, three secondary bedrooms share a full hall bath, while the master suite is lavish with its luxuries. Completing this suite are two walk-in closets, a large and pampering bath and plenty of sunshine from the corner windows.

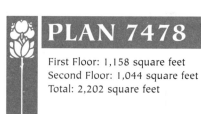

PLAN 7478

First Floor: 1,158 square feet
Second Floor: 1,044 square feet
Total: 2,202 square feet

■ DESIGN BY ALAN MASCORD DESIGN ASSOCIATES, INC.

■ DESIGN BY POLLARD-HOSMAR ASSOCIATES

With rafter-tails, gabled rooflines and a covered front porch supported by sturdy pillars, the Craftsman styling of this home is highly evident. And the floor plan carries out this style, with a fireplace and built-ins in the living room and an open feeling to the family room/dining area/kitchen combination. Upstairs, three secondary bedrooms share a full hall bath, while the master bedroom suite features a bayed sitting area, a walk-in closet and a private bath. The two-car garage will easily shelter the family fleet.

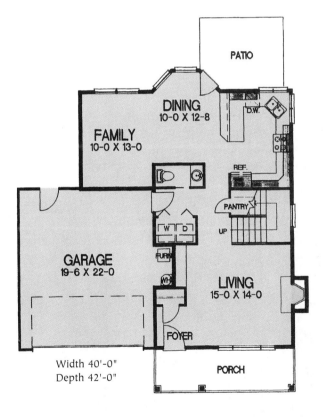

Width 40'-0"
Depth 42'-0"

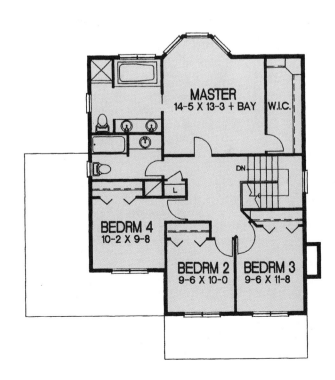

PLAN 8868

First Floor: 911 square feet
Second Floor: 1,006 square feet
Total: 1,917 square feet

■ DESIGN BY POLLARD-HOSMAR ASSOCIATES

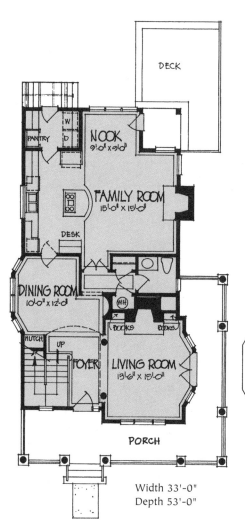

DECK

PANTRY

NOOK
9'-0" x 9'-0"

FAMILY ROOM
15'-0" x 15'-0"

DESK

DINING ROOM
10'-0" x 12'-0"

HUTCH

UP

FOYER

LIVING ROOM
13'-6" x 15'-0"

BOOKS   BOOKS

WH

PORCH

Width 33'-0"
Depth 53'-0"

PLAN 8866

First Floor: 1,117 square feet
Second Floor: 881 square feet
Total: 1,998 square feet

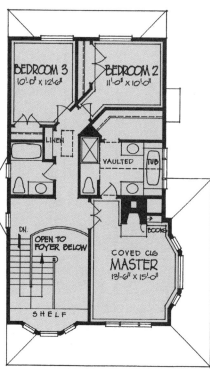

BEDROOM 3
10'-0" x 12'-6"

BEDROOM 2
11'-0" x 10'-0"

LINEN

VAULTED   TUB

DN.

OPEN TO
FOYER BELOW

BOOKS

COVED CLG
MASTER
13'-6" x 15'-0"

SHELF

A wraparound porch supported by pillars, gabled rooflines, two chimneys and Craftsman-style windows all combine to give this home plenty of curb appeal. Inside, the two-story foyer is flanked by an open staircase and a spacious living room. Here, a bay opens to the covered porch and a fireplace is flanked by built-in bookshelves. The kitchen is unique in design, with a nearby pantry, a cooktop work island and a planning desk for paying bills. A huge family room is available for casual get-togethers, and features a second fireplace, access to the sunny nook and wonderful views to the deck and rear yard. Upstairs, the master suite is lavish with its amenities, which include a coved ceiling, a fireplace, built-in bookshelves and a vaulted bath designed to pamper. Two secondary bedrooms and a full bath complete this floor.

■ Design by Northwest Home Designing Inc.

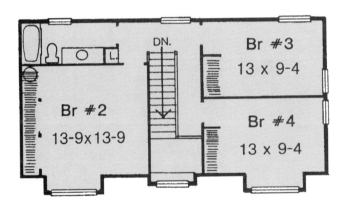

A metal-seamed roof, a trio of gables and a wraparound, covered porch combine with shingles and siding to create a home with a ton of charm. The floor plan is a real charmer, too, with a bayed dining area, a fireplace in the great room and an efficient kitchen with a large work island and plenty of counter and cabinet space. Located on the first floor for privacy, the master bedroom suite is sure to please with a walk-in closet and a private bath. Upstairs, the sleeping zone consists of three family bedrooms, all sharing a hall bath and a linen closet.

PLAN W300

First Floor: 1,033 square feet
Second Floor: 757 square feet
Total: 1,790 square feet

Width 58'-0"
Depth 36'-0"

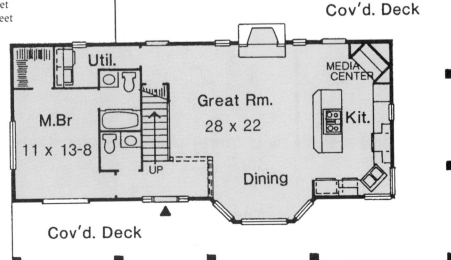

■ DESIGN BY NORTHWEST HOME DESIGNING INC.

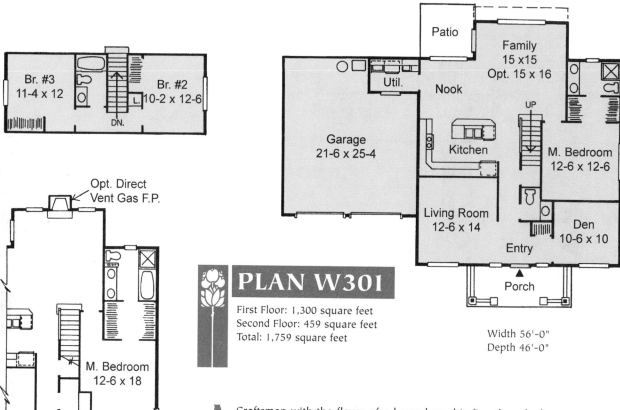

Br. #3
11-4 x 12

Br. #2
10-2 x 12-6

L.

DN.

Opt. Direct
Vent Gas F.P.

M. Bedroom
12-6 x 18

OPTIONS

Patio

Family
15 x15
Opt. 15 x 16

Util.

Nook

Garage
21-6 x 25-4

Kitchen

UP

M. Bedroom
12-6 x 12-6

Living Room
12-6 x 14

Den
10-6 x 10

Entry

Porch

PLAN W301

First Floor: 1,300 square feet
Second Floor: 459 square feet
Total: 1,759 square feet

Width 56'-0"
Depth 46'-0"

A Craftsman with the flavor of a bungalow, this fine three-bedroom home is sure to be a favorite. With options to change both the master bedroom suite as well as the family room, this design will suit any size family. Note the lack of cross-room traffic in the living room. The L-shaped kitchen offers a large cooktop work island and a nearby nook with views to the rear patio. The master suite features a private bath and lots of closet space. Upstairs, two family bedrooms share a full bath. The two-car garage easily shelters the family fleet.

A shed-like dormer, a covered porch with a built-in bench and detailed windows combine to create a wonderful ambience to this fine three-bedroom home. The two-story foyer leads directly to the vaulted living room. To the rear is the formal dining room, with easy access to the L-shaped kitchen. A spacious family room—with a fireplace—is convenient to the kitchen and casual eating nook. A den—or make it a fourth bedroom—finishes off this floor. Upstairs, two family bedrooms share a full hall bath with linen storage. The vaulted master bedroom suite is sure to please, with a large walk-in closet and a private bath with a spa tub.

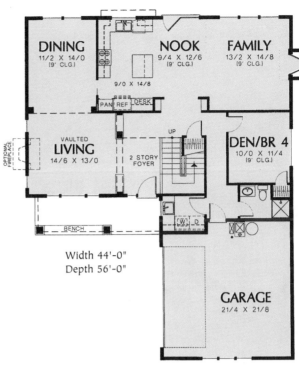

Width 44'-0"
Depth 56'-0"

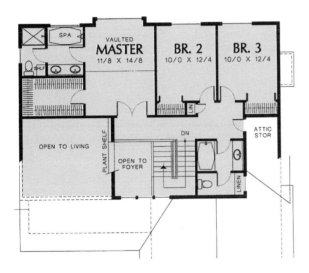

PLAN 7480

First Floor: 1,390 square feet
Second Floor: 865 square feet
Total: 2,255 square feet

■ DESIGN BY ALAN MASCORD DESIGN ASSOCIATES, INC.

■ DESIGN BY POLLARD-HOSMAR ASSOCIATES

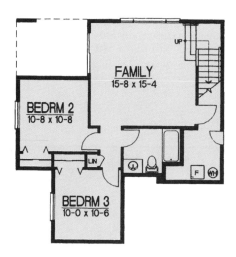

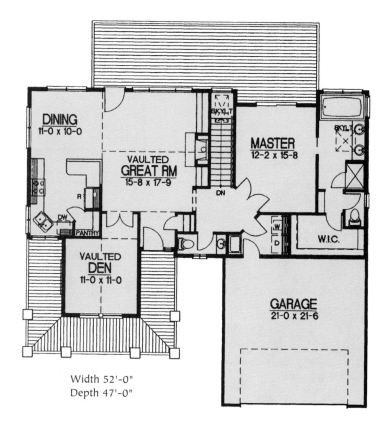

Width 52'-0"
Depth 47'-0"

Sturdy, attractive pillars support a shed-like roof and help to shelter the front porch of this fine Craftsman home. Twin gables, with rafter-tails as accent, further the flavor of the Arts and Crafts era. Inside, the foyer opens to the vaulted great room, which offers a fireplace, built-ins and access to the rear deck. A cozy, vaulted den opens off this room through double doors. The kitchen features a corner sink and a walk-in pantry. Located on the main floor for privacy, the master suite is designed to pamper. Included in this suite is access to the rear deck, a large walk-in closet and a spacious bath. Downstairs, two family bedrooms share a hall bath and have direct access to the family room.

PLAN 8864

Main Level: 1,344 square feet
Lower Level: 777 square feet
Total: 2,121 square feet

■ DESIGN BY POLLARD-HOSMAR ASSOCIATES

PLAN 8869

First Floor: 1,178 square feet
Second Floor: 732 square feet
Total: 1,910 square feet

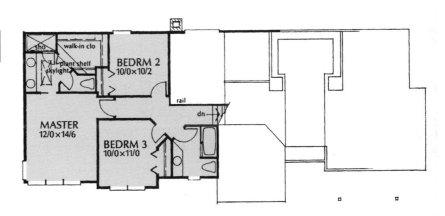

BEDRM 2
10/0×10/2

walk-in clo

sho

plant shelf

skylight

MASTER
12/0×14/6

BEDRM 3
10/0×11/0

rail

dn

Gables, detailed windows and a covered porch all combine to give this home plenty of curb appeal. A wraparound porch welcomes both family and friends to enter in and partake of the comfort within. A vaulted foyer is flanked by a spacious living room to the right and a cozy study to the left. A skylight is situated in just the right spot to shine sunlight into both the foyer as well as the kitchen. The kitchen is sure to please with plenty of counter and cabinet space, and ease of access to both the vaulted formal dining room and to the casual nook. Down a few steps is the vaulted family room, complete with a fireplace and access to the rear deck. The upstairs consists of two family bedrooms sharing a hall bath and a sumptuous master suite.

Width 74'-0"
Depth 28'-6"

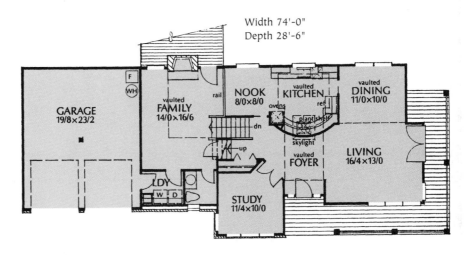

GARAGE
19/8×23/2

F

WH

FAMILY
14/0×16/6
vaulted

rail

NOOK
8/0×8/0

KITCHEN
vaulted

ovens

plant shelf

skylight

DINING
11/0×10/0
vaulted

ref

LIVING
16/4×13/0

FOYER
vaulted

dn

up

LDY

W D

STUDY
11/4×10/0

With shingles and stone, multi-paned windows and a graceful arch over the front door, this home is a good example of being one with its environment, the main philosophy of the Arts and Crafts Movement. Inside, a formal dining room opens just off the foyer, defined by pillars. The spacious great room offers a warming fireplace, built-ins and access to the rear patio. The efficient kitchen is open to this room, as well as to an adjacent bayed breakfast area. The master suite reigns in the left wing, featuring a detailed ceiling, two walk-in closets and a sumptuous bath. Two family bedrooms, located on the opposite side of the home, share a full bath. A large bonus room is found over the garage, and is available for future expansion or as a children's play room.

PATIO

MASTER BED RM.
14-0 x 16-0

GREAT RM.
16-0 x 20-0
(12' ceiling)

BRKFST.
13-4 x 11-0

BED RM.
12-0 x 11-0

walk-in closet

walk-in closet

fireplace

KITCHEN
13-4 x 11-2

bath

cl

lin.

cl

master bath

lin.

UTIL.
6-6 x 6-5

w d

BED RM.
12-0 x 11-7

pan.

cl

FOYER
6-5 x 4-8

DINING
11-11 x 12-2
(12' ceiling)

up

storage

Width 59'-8"
Depth 57'-7"

GARAGE
22-8 x 22-0

(optional door location)

© 1996   Donald A Gardner Architects, Inc.

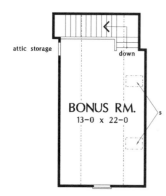

attic storage

down

BONUS RM.
13-0 x 22-0

s

PLAN 7680

Square Footage: 1,888
Bonus Room: 358 square feet

■ DESIGN BY DONALD A. GARDNER ARCHITECTS, INC.

■ DESIGN BY LIVING CONCEPTS HOME PLANNING

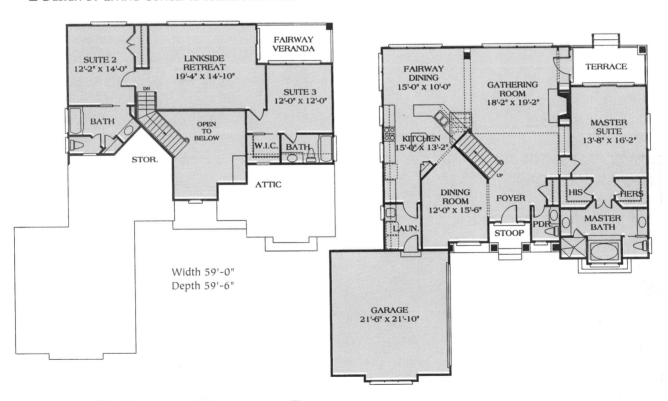

SUITE 2
12'-2" x 14'-0"

LINKSIDE
RETREAT
19'-4" x 14'-10"

FAIRWAY
VERANDA

SUITE 3
12'-0" x 12'-0"

BATH

DN

OPEN
TO
BELOW

W.I.C.

BATH

STOR.

ATTIC

Width 59'-0"
Depth 59'-6"

FAIRWAY
DINING
15'-0" x 10'-0"

GATHERING
ROOM
18'-2" x 19'-2"

TERRACE

KITCHEN
15'-0" x 13'-2"

MASTER
SUITE
13'-8" x 16'-2"

DINING
ROOM
12'-0" x 15'-6"

FOYER

HIS

HERS

UP

LAUN.

STOOP

PDR.

MASTER
BATH

GARAGE
21'-6" x 21'-10"

PLAN A250

First Floor: 1,662 square feet
Second Floor: 882 square feet
Total: 2,544 square feet

Gables, rafter-tails, pillars supporting the shed roof over the porch and window detailing all bring the flavor of Craftsman styling to your neighborhood—with a touch of grace. This spacious home has a place for everyone. The angled kitchen, with a work island, peninsular sink and plenty of counter and cabinet space, will truly please the gourmet of the family. The spacious gathering room offers a warming fireplace, built-ins and access to a rear terrace. Filled with amenities, the first-floor master suite is designed to pamper. Upstairs, two suites, each with a private bath, share an open area known as the linkside retreat. Here, access is available to a small veranda, perfect for watching sunsets.

■ DESIGN BY POLLARD-HOSMAR ASSOCIATES

MASTER
13-0 x 15-0

VAULTED
GREAT RM.
19-0 x 16-0

NOOK
12-0 x 12-0

DW

BATH

PDR.

FOYER

DINING/DEN
12-0 x 12-4

FURN

WH

W.I.C.

GARAGE
21-4 x 21-8

BEDRM 2
13-2 x 10-6

REC. ROOM
18-4 x 14-2

BATH

UP

BEDRM 3
12-4 x 10-6

CRAWL SPACE

Width 55'-0"
Depth 43'-0"

PLAN 8860

Main Level: 1,604 square feet
Lower Level: 796 square feet
Total: 2,400 square feet

A dormer with a shed roof resides over the front porch of this three-bedroom home. Both the foyer and the dining room/den have access to the front porch. The vaulted great room is enhanced by a warming fireplace and multiple windows to the rear yard. The U-shaped kitchen is enhanced by a cooktop work island and an adjacent nook with access to the rear deck. Located on the main level for privacy, the master bedroom suite is designed to pamper. Complete with a large walk-in closet, separate tub and shower and a dual-bowl vanity, this suite will be a welcome haven for the lucky homeowner. On the lower level, two family bedrooms share a full bath as well as easy access to the rec room and the rear patio. A two-car garage will easily shelter the family fleet.

■ Design by Pollard-Hosmar Associates

Twin gables flank a gracefully covered porch, with a shed dormer riding just above. Exhibiting typical Craftsman architecture such as rafter tails, pillars and 9-over-1 sash windows, this fine three-bedroom home is sure to please. Designed for a sloping lot, this house will look good in any neighborhood. A den opens just off the foyer, perfect for a home office or study. The vaulted great room is enhanced by a fireplace, built-ins and two skylights. The U-shaped kitchen features a cooktop work island, with an adjacent dining area nearby. Located on the main level, the master suite is sure to please with a walk-in closet and sumptuous bath. Downstairs, a spacious family room offers access to two family bedrooms as well as outdoors.

Width 57'-0"
Depth 46'-0"

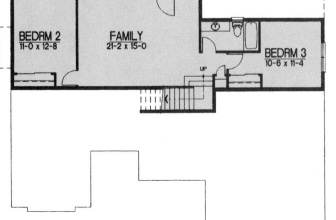

PLAN 8861

Main Level: 1,500 square feet
Lower Level: 852 square feet
Total: 2,352 square feet

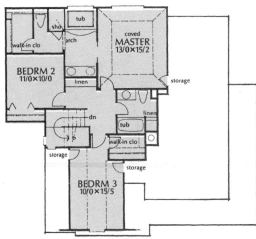

GARAGE
19/4 × 21/4

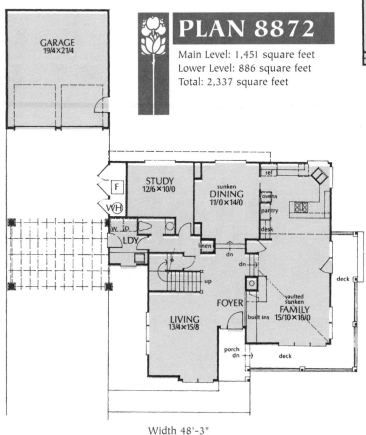

PLAN 8872

Main Level: 1,451 square feet
Lower Level: 886 square feet
Total: 2,337 square feet

Master Level

walk-in clo
sho
tub
coved
MASTER
13/0 × 15/2
arch
storage
BEDRM 2
11/0 × 10/0
linen
dn
linen
tub
walk-in clo
storage
storage
BEDRM 3
10/0 × 15/5

Main Level

STUDY
12/6 × 10/0
F
WH
sunken
DINING
11/0 × 14/0
ref
ovens
pantry
W D
LDY
desk
linen
dn
deck
dn
up
FOYER
vaulted
sunken
FAMILY
15/10 × 16/0
LIVING
13/4 × 15/8
built ins
porch
dn
deck
deck

Width 48'-3"
Depth 41'-6"

With a bit of Craftsman flavor, this fine three-bedroom home will look good in any neighborhood. A covered, wraparound porch welcomes both family and friends, ushering them into the foyer. Here, the living room opens to the left, and offers a design with no cross-room traffic. Down a couple of steps to the right is the spacious vaulted family room, enhanced by built-ins, a fireplace and porch access. Also on this level is the efficient kitchen with easy access to the sunken dining room. A cozy, secluded study finishes out the rooms on this floor. Upstairs, two family bedrooms share a full hall bath, while a lavish master suite features a private bath and a large walk-in closet.

■ DESIGN BY POLLARD-HOSMAR ASSOCIATES

■ DESIGN BY DONALD A. GARDNER ARCHITECTS, INC.

C © 1998 Donald A. Gardner Architects, Inc.

PLAN 7694

First Floor: 1,896 square feet
Second Floor: 692 square feet
Total: 2,588 square feet

attic storage

BED RM.
13-0 x 13-0

dining room below

cl   lin.

bath

skylight   up

great room below   down up

LOFT/ STUDY
13-0 x 12-0

attic storage

BED RM.
12-8 x 11-4

cl

attic storage

STORAGE
15-8 x 11-4

attic storage

Width 84'-10"
Depth 60'-0"

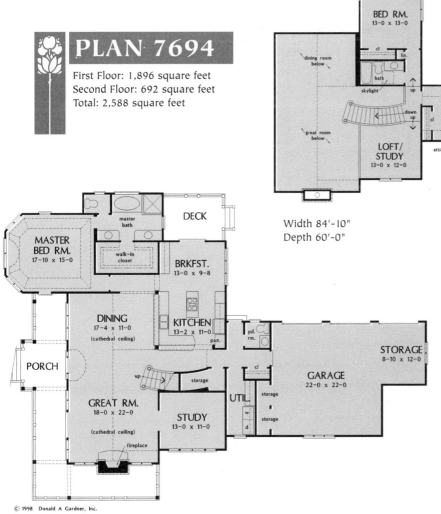

master bath

DECK

MASTER BED RM.
17-10 x 15-0

walk-in closet

BRKFST.
13-0 x 9-8

DINING
17-4 x 11-0
(cathedral ceiling)

KITCHEN
13-2 x 11-0

pan.

pd. rm.

STORAGE
8-10 x 12-0

PORCH

up

storage

cl

GARAGE
22-0 x 22-0

GREAT RM.
18-0 x 22-0
(cathedral ceiling)

STUDY
13-0 x 11-0

UTIL.

storage

w

d

storage

fireplace

C 1998 Donald A Gardner, Inc.

This fine three-bedroom home is full of amenities and will be a family favorite! A covered porch leads into the great room/dining room area. Here, a fireplace reigns at one end, casting its glow throughout the room. A study is tucked away and private, perfect for a home office or computer study. The master bedroom suite offers a bayed sitting area, large walk-in closet and pampering bath. With plenty of counter and cabinet space and an adjacent breakfast area, the kitchen will be a favorite gathering place for casual meal times. The family sleeping zone is upstairs, and includes two bedrooms, a full bath, a loft/study area and a huge storage room.

The Craftsman style is well represented here by exposed rafter tails, an overhanging roof, gabled rooflines and many other details. Inside, the style is evident with the warmth of two fireplaces, open room planning and the open staircase. The spacious kitchen is enhanced by a cooktop work island and easy access to both the formal dining room as well as the cozy eating nook. Upstairs, the coved ceiling of the master bedroom suite is just one of many amenities—others include a large walk-in closet, separate tub and shower and a dual-bowled vanity. Bedrooms 2 and 3 share a bath and access to a linen closet.

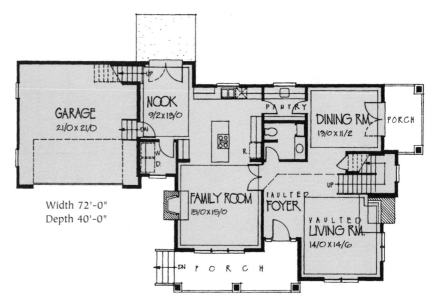

GARAGE 21/0 x 21/0

NOOK 9/2 x 13/0

PANTRY

DINING RM. 13/0 x 11/2

PORCH

Width 72'-0"
Depth 40'-0"

FAMILY ROOM 15/0 x 15/0

VAULTED FOYER

UP

VAULTED LIVING RM. 14/0 x 14/6

DN PORCH

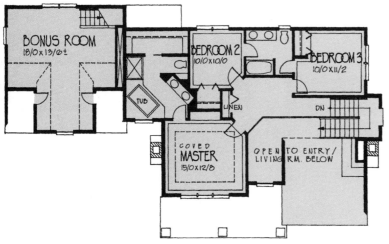

BONUS ROOM 18/0 x 13/0±

BEDROOM 2 10/0 x 10/0

BEDROOM 3 10/0 x 11/2

TUB

LINEN

DN

COVED MASTER 15/0 x 12/8

OPEN TO ENTRY/ LIVING RM. BELOW

PLAN 8858

First Floor: 1,303 square feet
Second Floor: 877 square feet
Total: 2,555 square feet
Bonus Room: 375 square feet

Width 50'-0"
Depth 50'-0"

Shingles, gables, window detail and rafter tails all combine to give this home plenty of curb appeal. The entrance opens right next to the vaulted living and dining area, with a cozy den to the right. The unique kitchen features a peninsula, pantry and easy access to the formal dining room and sunny nook. The nearby family room is warmed by a corner fireplace. Located on the first floor for privacy, the master bedroom suite is complete with a walk-in closet—with built-in shelves—and a pampering bath. The second floor consists of three family bedrooms sharing a full bath and an open study loft with built-ins. Note the abundance of storage in the garage.

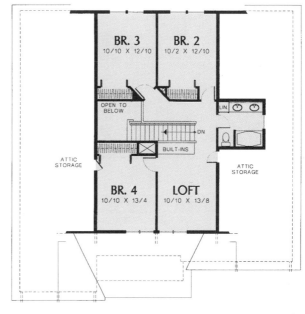

PLAN 7482

First Floor: 1,769 square feet
Second Floor: 893 square feet
Total: 2,662 square feet

■ DESIGN BY ALAN MASCORD DESIGN ASSOCIATES, INC.

PLAN 8859

First Floor: 1,684 square feet
Second Floor: 754 square feet
Total: 2,438 square feet

This fine Craftsman home will be a favorite in any neighborhood. The vaulted entry leads to a formal living room on the right, complete with a warming fireplace. The formal dining room is nearby, and has easy access to the U-shaped kitchen. A vaulted family room is located toward the rear of the home, and offers access to the backyard. Situated on the first floor for privacy, the master bedroom suite is sure to please with its many amenities. These include a walk-in closet, a separate tub and shower, and a dual-bowl vanity. The sleeping zone for the family is upstairs. Here, three bedrooms share a full hall bath and a balcony overlook to the family room below. The two-car garage easily shelters the family fleet.

Width 45'-6"
Depth 66'-3"

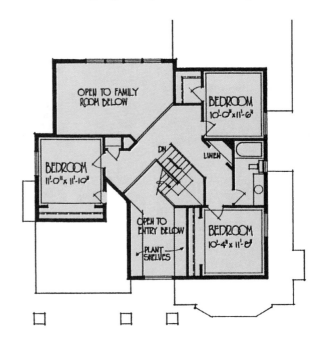

■ DESIGN BY POLLARD-HOSMAR ASSOCIATES

PLAN 8862

First Floor: 1,493 square feet
Second Floor: 833 square feet
Total: 2,326 square feet

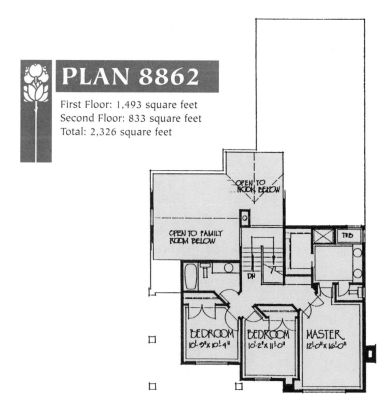

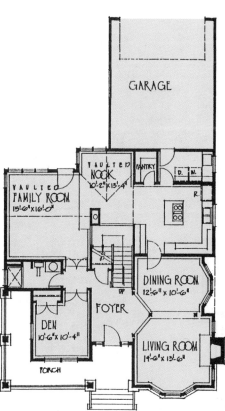

Width 39'-6"
Depth 70'-0"

With elegant window detail, sturdy yet graceful pillars supporting a covered front porch and a shingle-and-siding combination, this home has plenty of curb appeal. Inside, angles help enhance already attractive rooms—the formal living and dining rooms both feature bay windows. The L-shaped kitchen offers a cooktop island, large walk-in pantry and easy access to the vaulted nook nearby. For quiet times, there is the vaulted family room or a cozy den. A full bath is nearby, making the den available as a guest suite. The sleeping zone is upstairs, and includes two family bedrooms sharing a bath, and a spacious master suite with a walk-in closet and lavish bath.

■ DESIGN BY POLLARD-HOSMAR ASSOCIATES

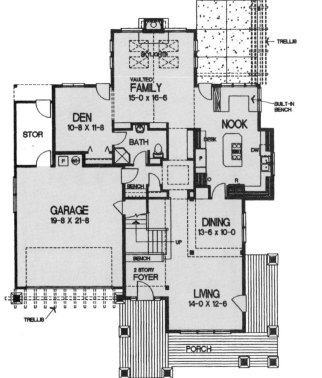

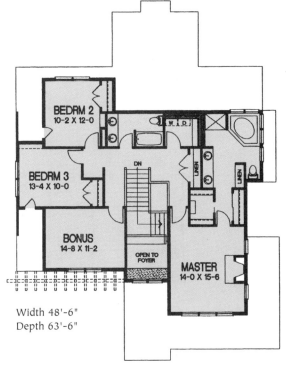

Width 48'-6"
Depth 63'-6"

PLAN 8857

First Floor: 1,421 square feet
Second Floor: 1,273 square feet
Total: 2,694 square feet

Four graceful gables add charm to an already attractive home. Square pillars line a wraparound covered porch, which leads to the two-story foyer. Here, a built-in bench and an open staircase continue the graceful qualities of the Craftsman style. A formal living room is defined from the formal dining room via the use of elegant pillars. A unique kitchen features a cooktop island, a pantry, a built-in desk and an adjacent built-in nook. Four skylights, a fireplace and a vaulted ceiling enhance the family room. A cozy den offers access to the rear yard, as well as to a full bath. Upstairs, the sleeping zone consists of two family bedrooms, a full hall bath, a good sized bonus room and the lavish master suite.

BR. 2
10/2 X 11/0

MASTER
15/0 X 13/8

SPA TUB

PLANT SHELF

BR. 3
10/6 X 10/8

LIVING RM. BELOW

DN

LIN

BR. 4
14/0 X 9/0+

FOYER BELOW

PLANT SHELF

DEN BELOW

PLAN 7476

First Floor: 1,255 square feet
Second Floor: 1,141 square feet
Total: 2,396 square feet

Width 40'-0" with 2 car garage
Depth 50'-0"

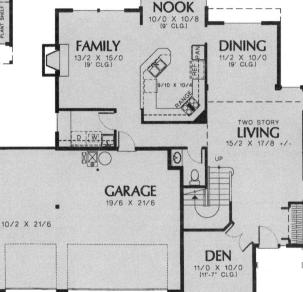

NOOK
10/0 X 10/8
(9' CLG.)

FAMILY
13/2 X 15/0
(9' CLG.)

DINING
11/2 X 10/0
(9' CLG.)

9/10 X 10/4

REF PAN

RANGE

TWO STORY
LIVING
15/2 X 17/8 +/-

D W

UP

GARAGE
19/6 X 21/6

10/2 X 21/6

DEN
11/0 X 10/0
(11'-7" CLG.)

A two-story living room greets family and friends to this fine four-bedroom Craftsman home. A cozy den is isolated toward the front of the home, assuring privacy. The angled kitchen reigns in the center of the home, with easy access to the formal dining room, sunny nook and spacious family room. A fireplace in the family room promises warmth and welcome. Upstairs, three secondary bedrooms share a hall bath, while the master suite features a large walk-in closet, a spa tub and separate shower and a dual-bowl vanity. The three-car garage easily shelters the family fleet.

■ DESIGN BY ALAN MASCORD DESIGN ASSOCIATES, INC.

Shingles, siding, stone and fine detail gives this home plenty of curb appeal. A covered front porch ushers you into the two-story foyer where an open staircase casually divides the home. To the left, a sunken living room waits, encouraging one to relax. To the right of the staircase, a hall leads back to the spacious family room featuring a fireplace, access to the rear patio and an open layout with the kitchen. The second floor contains the sleeping zone. Three family bedrooms share a full bath, and a large bonus room is available for future expansion or as a play room. A comfortable master suite includes a walk-in closet, a private bath and a balcony. The three-car garage is sure to shelter the family fleet.

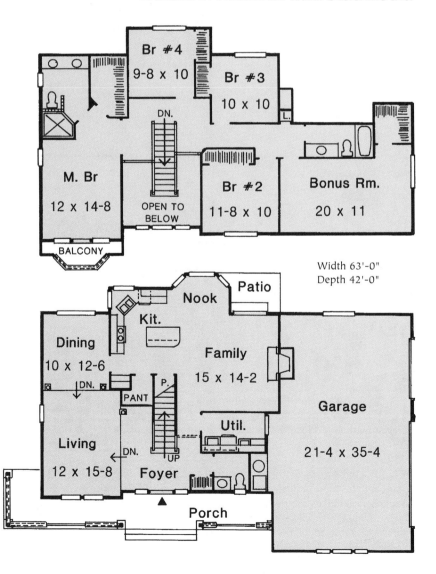

Width 63'-0"
Depth 42'-0"

PLAN W305

First Floor: 1,054 square feet
Second Floor: 1,306 square feet
Total: 2,360 square feet

■ DESIGN BY DESIGN BASICS, INC.

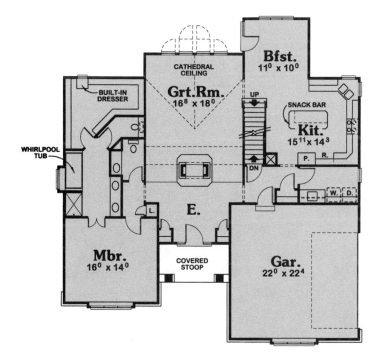

CATHEDRAL CEILING

Bfst.
11⁰ x 10⁰

Grt. Rm.
16⁸ x 18⁰

BUILT-IN DRESSER

UP

SNACK BAR

Kit.
15¹¹ x 14³

DN

WHIRLPOOL TUB

P. **R.**

W. **D.**

L.

E.

Mbr.
16⁰ x 14⁰

COVERED STOOP

Gar.
22⁰ x 22⁴

PLAN 7326

First Floor: 1,640 square feet
Second Floor: 711 square feet
Total: 2,351 square feet

Width 51'-4"
Depth 54'-0"

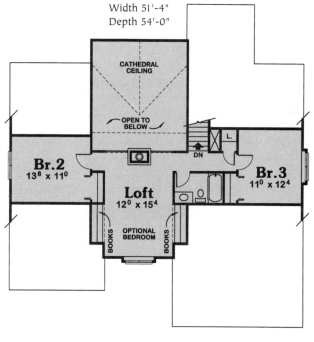

CATHEDRAL CEILING

OPEN TO BELOW

DN

L.

Br. 2
13⁸ x 11⁰

Br. 3
11⁰ x 12⁴

Loft
12⁰ x 15⁴

BOOKS

BOOKS

OPTIONAL BEDROOM

With a shingle-and-stone facade, this Craftsman-flavored home is sure to be a favorite in any neighborhood. The entryway is graced with two closets and shares a through-fireplace with the beautiful great room. This room is further enhanced by a cathedral ceiling and stunning windows. The U-shaped, island kitchen features access to a rear staircase. Located at the top of the stairwell, a loft with bookshelves makes the perfect place for reading or studying. An immense walk-in closet with a built-in dresser, whirlpool tub and dual-sink vanity are enclosed behind French doors adding intimacy to the master suite.

Pillars line the front of a fine covered porch on this attractive two-story home. Craftsman architecture is represented by a smattering of shingles on the second story and the shelter of an overhanging roofline. Inside, a formal dining room has easy access to the efficient kitchen as well as to the front porch. A spacious gathering room features a fireplace, access to the rear patio/deck and shares a snack bar with the kitchen and breakfast room. Located on the first floor for privacy, the master suite is sure to please with its many amenities, which include a large walk-in closet, plenty of windows, a detailed ceiling and a sumptuous bath. Upstairs, two suites share a full bath as well as a large loft—perfect for a study area, computer space or play area. A two-car garage easily shelters the family fleet.

PLAN A301

First Floor: 1,670 square feet
Second Floor: 763 square feet
Total: 2,433 square feet

Width 53'-0"
Depth 54'-0"

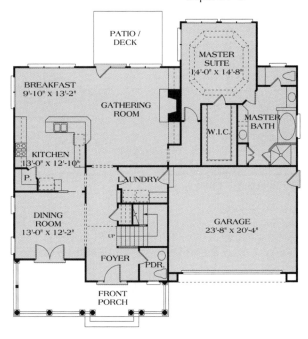

■ DESIGN BY LIVING CONCEPTS HOME PLANNING

■ Design by Alan Mascord Design Associates, Inc.

Acovered front porch introduces this home's comfortable living pattern. The two-story foyer opens to a living room with a fireplace and lots of natural light. The formal dining room looks out over the living room. In the kitchen, an island cooktop, a pantry, a built-in planning desk and a nook with double doors to outside livability aims to please. A spacious family room with another fireplace will accommodate casual living. Upstairs, five bedrooms—or four and a den—make room for all family members and guests. The master bedroom suite exudes elegance with an elegant ceiling and a pampering spa bath. A full hall bath with a skylight and dual lavatories serves the secondary bedrooms.

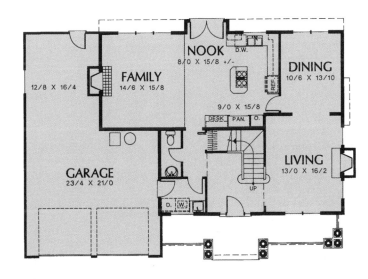

Width 56'-0"
Depth 40'-0"

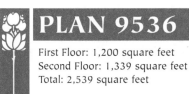

PLAN 9536

First Floor: 1,200 square feet
Second Floor: 1,339 square feet
Total: 2,539 square feet

■ DESIGN BY ALAN MASCORD DESIGN ASSOCIATES, INC.

Shingles and stone combine to give this home plenty of curb appeal, and a multiple gabled roofline furthers the charm found here. Inside, a vaulted den opens to the left of the foyer, and is separated from the main living areas, providing a great place for a home office or quiet study area. The formal dining room shares a fireplace with the vaulted great room, which also offers access to the rear yard. The efficient kitchen will surely please the gourmet of the family, with a corner sink, a pantry, a built-in planning desk and a large cooktop work island. A nearby bayed nook will be perfect for casual meal times. The sleeping zone is upstairs and consists of three secondary bedrooms sharing a full hall bath, and a sumptuous master suite. Here, the homeowner will feel truly pampered, with a walk-in closet, a vaulted ceiling, a spa tub and separate shower and a compartmented toilet.

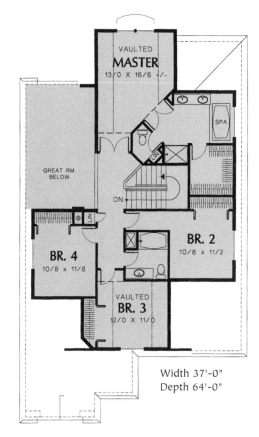

Width 37'-0"
Depth 64'-0"

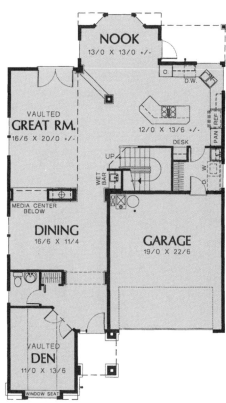

PLAN 7504

First Floor: 1,430 square feet
Second Floor: 1,158 square feet
Total: 2,588 square feet

■ DESIGN BY POLLARD-HOSMAR ASSOCIATES

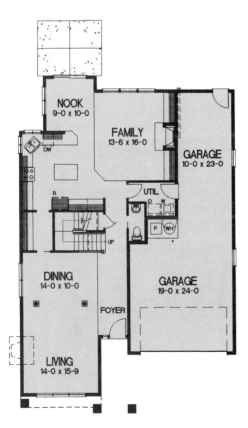

NOOK
9-0 x 10-0

FAMILY
13-6 x 16-0

GARAGE
10-0 x 23-0

UTIL.

DINING
14-0 x 10-0

FOYER

GARAGE
19-0 x 24-0

LIVING
14-0 x 15-9

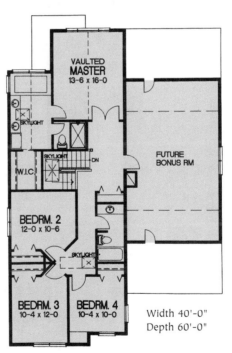

VAULTED
MASTER
13-6 x 16-0

SKYLIGHT

SKYLIGHT

W.I.C.

DN

FUTURE
BONUS RM

BEDRM. 2
12-0 x 10-6

SKYLIGHT

BEDRM. 3
10-4 x 12-0

BEDRM. 4
10-4 x 10-0

Width 40'-0"
Depth 60'-0"

PLAN 8878

First Floor: 1,298 square feet
Second Floor: 1,113 square feet
Total: 2,411 square feet

Two strong pillars support a gabled roof over the front entry of this Craftsman-style home. Adding to the charm are detailed windows and shingle-and-stone work. The foyer opens to a spacious living/dining area to the left, separated from each other by graceful pillars. A large window in the living room provides plenty of natural light. The L-shaped kitchen features a work island and a corner sink. A nearby nook is perfect for casual meals and offers access to the rear yard. A cozy family room is enhanced by a fireplace and built-ins. The second floor is dedicated to the sleeping zone, which consists of three bedrooms sharing a hall bath and a pampering master suite. Amenities here include a walk-in closet, a vaulted ceiling and a lavish bath with a skylight. A huge future bonus room is also available on this level, and could be used as a play room, divided into bedrooms, or as a spacious home office. Note the three-car garage, perfect for sheltering the family fleet.

Floor Plans

Cellar
17-6 x 13

CELLAR

LADDER
Attic
13 x 18
5' WALL   5' WALL

UNFINISHED ATTIC

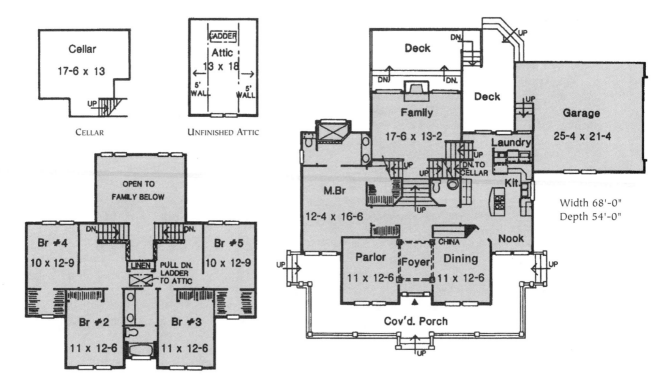

Second Floor:

OPEN TO FAMILY BELOW

Br #4
10 x 12-9

DN.   DN.

Br #5
10 x 12-9

LINEN   PULL DN. LADDER TO ATTIC

Br #2
11 x 12-6

Br #3
11 x 12-6

First Floor:

Deck   DN.   UP

Deck

Family
17-6 x 13-2

Laundry

Garage
25-4 x 21-4

UP   DN. TO CELLAR

M.Br
12-4 x 16-6

Kit.

Nook

Parlor
11 x 12-6

Foyer   CHINA

Dining
11 x 12-6

UP

UP

Cov'd. Porch

Width 68'-0"
Depth 54'-0"

PLAN W315

First Floor: 1,554 square feet
Second Floor: 1,075 square feet
Total: 2,629 square feet

A room for everyone! And in graceful style, too! This fine Craftsman home is sure to please, with multiple gables, pillars on the porch and window detailing. The foyer is flanked by a formal dining room and a formal parlor, defined by more pillars. A built-in china cabinet will add elegance to the dining room. Off to the right is the efficient kitchen and nook. Toward the rear of the home and up a few steps, a spacious family room offers a warming fireplace and access to a sun deck. The master suite is assured privacy by placing it on the first floor. Filled with many amenities, this room will be a homeowners haven. Upstairs, four bedrooms—two with walk-in closets—share a full bath and a linen closet. Note the unfinished attic and the option for a cellar.

■ DESIGN BY NORTHWEST HOME DESIGNING INC.

■ DESIGN BY HOME PLANNERS

Width 86'-7"
Depth 54'-0"

QUOTE ONE®
Cost to build? See page 182
to order complete cost estimate
to build this house in your area!

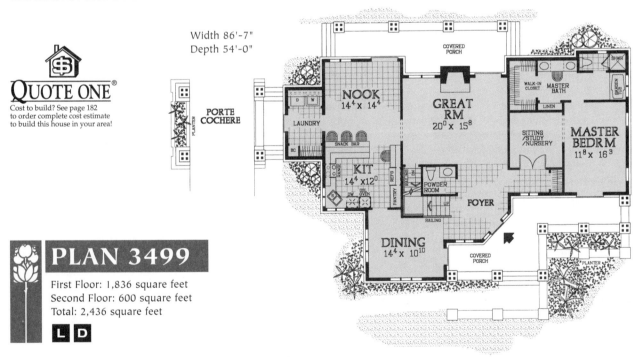

PLAN 3499

First Floor: 1,836 square feet
Second Floor: 600 square feet
Total: 2,436 square feet

L D

Rustic rafter tails and double columns highlight the front covered porch of this slightly rugged exterior, but sophisticated amenities abound inside and out—starting with the unique porte cochere and quiet side entrance to the home. To the left of the foyer, a formal dining room is bathed in natural light from two sets of triple windows. This area is easily served by a well-appointed kitchen with a built-in desk and a snack bar. A secluded master suite is replete with popular amenities: a garden tub with separate shower, knee-space vanity, dual lavatories and an adjoining study or sitting room. Upstairs, a balcony hall connects two additional bedrooms and a full bath—there's even space for a library or study area!

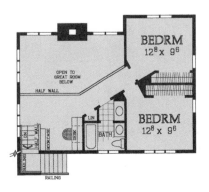

■ Design by Alan Mascord Design Associates, Inc.

This home is designed for lots that slope up from the street. Featuring rafter tails, horizontal siding and stone-work, this is a Craftsman with lots of class. And the floor plan is sure to please also. The foyer opens on the lower level, giving access to a large den, a full bath and a laundry room. Up one flight of stairs and one ends up on the main living level. Here a huge living/dining room awaits and features a fireplace, built-ins and a snack bar into the vaulted galley kitchen. A built-in nook area is to one end of the kitchen, providing space for casual meals. The lavish master suite is also on this level, and offers many amenities, such as a walk-in closet, a private balcony and a pampering bath. Two secondary bedrooms share a full bath on the upper floor.

GARAGE
29/10 X 24/10

DEN
13/0+ X 10/10

FOYER

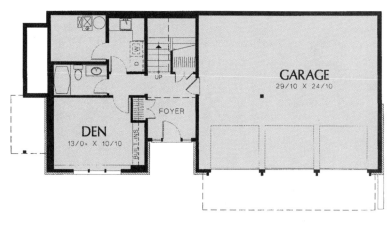

MASTER
16/0 X 13/0
(9' CLG)

OPEN TO BELOW

VAULTED
LIVING/DINING
28/0 X 16/0

VAULTED

NOOK

REF   PAN

PLANT SHELF OVER

STOR

MEDIA CENTER

SPA

BR. 2
10/2 X 11/2

BR. 3
10/8 X 11/2

LIN

DN
DN
DN

PLAN 7518

First Floor: 1,362 square feet
Upper Floor: 400 square feet
Lower Floor: 538 square feet
Total: 2,300 square feet

Width 60'-0"
Depth 26'-0"

■ DESIGN BY LIVING CONCEPTS HOME PLANNING

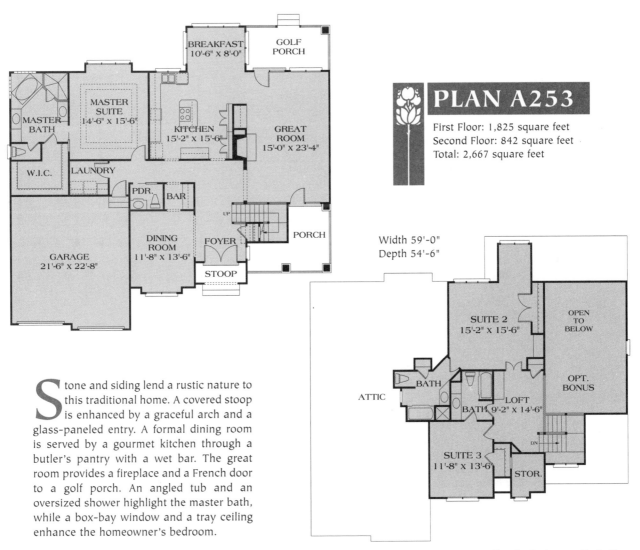

PLAN A253

First Floor: 1,825 square feet
Second Floor: 842 square feet
Total: 2,667 square feet

Width 59'-0"
Depth 54'-6"

Stone and siding lend a rustic nature to this traditional home. A covered stoop is enhanced by a graceful arch and a glass-paneled entry. A formal dining room is served by a gourmet kitchen through a butler's pantry with a wet bar. The great room provides a fireplace and a French door to a golf porch. An angled tub and an oversized shower highlight the master bath, while a box-bay window and a tray ceiling enhance the homeowner's bedroom.

■ Design by Design Basics, Inc.

PLAN 7030

First Floor: 1,823 square feet
Second Floor: 858 square feet
Total: 2,681 square feet

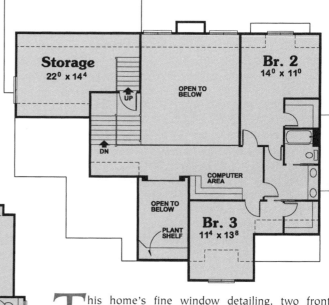

Storage 22⁰ x 14⁴

OPEN TO BELOW

Br. 2 14⁰ x 11⁰

UP

DN

COMPUTER AREA

OPEN TO BELOW

PLANT SHELF

Br. 3 11⁴ x 13⁸

Width 56'-8"
Depth 50'-8"

Gar. 24⁰ x 20⁸

SLOPED CEILING

Grt Rm. 17⁴ x 24⁸

18'-0"HIGH CEILING

Mbr. 14⁰ x 15⁸

UP

DN   UP

WHIRLPOOL

SLOPED CEILING

D. W.

COVERED PORCH

Bfst. 10⁰ x 10⁸

Kit. 14⁰ x 14⁸

R.

PANTRY

E.

BUFFET

Din. Rm. 14⁰ x 11⁰

L.

COVERED PORCH

This home's fine window detailing, two front porches and rafter tails lend the feel of true Craftsman styling. The airiness of the kitchen is enhanced with openings to the second-floor, entry and breakfast area. A built-in buffet and two half railings warmly welcome passerbys into the formal dining room. A tall ceiling in the great room is further dramatized when viewed from an open railing on the second floor. Also of interest in this room is the fireplace centered on the outside wall. A computer area on the second floor accompanies the second-floor bedrooms as a home-work area. A large storage area accessed from the mid-level staircase landing offers a place for a playroom. Note the first-floor master suite with its lavish bath.

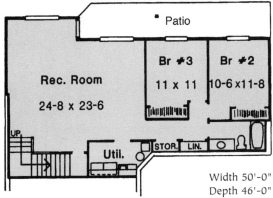

Patio

Br #3
11 x 11

Br #2
10-6 x11-8

Rec. Room
24-8 x 23-6

UP.

Util.

STOR. LIN.

Width 50'-0"
Depth 46'-0"

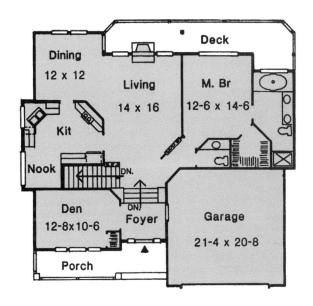

Dining
12 x 12

Deck

Living
14 x 16

M. Br
12-6 x 14-6

Kit

Nook

DN.

Den
12-8x10-6

DN.

Foyer

Garage
21-4 x 20-8

Porch

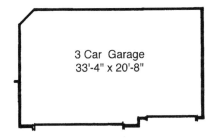

PLAN W320

Main Level: 1,416 square feet
Lower Level: 1,300 square feet
Total: 2,716 square feet

3 Car Garage
33'-4" x 20'-8"

Two gables, supported by pillars and accented with rafter tails, are fine examples of Craftsmanship on this three-bedroom home. Inside, a den opens to the left of the foyer, providing a quiet place for reading. Down a few steps, one comes to the rest of the main floor living space. A living room with a fireplace flanked by windows welcomes casual times. The unique kitchen offers a small, yet cozy, nook as well as ease in serving the dining room. The master suite is also on this floor and features a walk-in closet and a pampering bath. Downstairs, a huge rec room is available for many pursuits. Two secondary bedrooms share a bath and access to the rear patio also.

2,301 TO 2,800 SQUARE FEET

■ DESIGN BY NORTHWEST HOME DESIGNING INC.

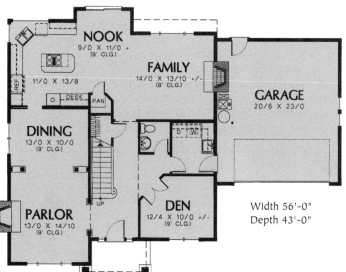

NOOK
9/0 X 11/0 +
(9' CLG.)

FAMILY
14/0 X 13/10 +/-
(9' CLG.)

GARAGE
20/6 X 23/0

DINING
13/0 X 10/0
(9' CLG.)

REF

O. DESK

PAN

PARLOR
13/0 X 14/10
(9' CLG.)

UP

DEN
12/4 X 10/0 +/-
(9' CLG.)

Width 56'-0"
Depth 43'-0"

A grand example of Craftsman-style architecture, this two-story home is sure to please! It offers classic details such as rafter tails, pillars, stone-and-siding, gables and Craftsman windows. Inside, a two-story foyer leads to a formal parlor on the left with a fireplace or a cozy den on the right. The rear of the home is designed for casual times, with a spacious family room featuring a second fireplace, a sunny nook for relaxed meals and an efficient kitchen. The sleeping zone is located upstairs and consists of three family bedrooms sharing a hall bath and access to a large bonus room—perfect for a study or play room. Completing this floor is the lavish master bedroom suite. Amenities included here are a vaulted ceiling, walk-in closet and pampering private bath with a spa tub.

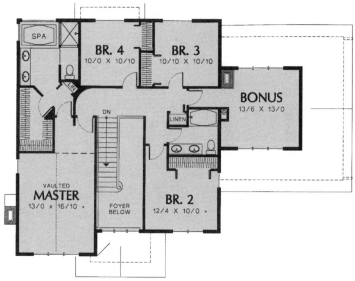

SPA

BR. 4
10/0 X 10/10

BR. 3
10/10 X 10/10

BONUS
13/6 X 13/0

LINEN

DN

MASTER
13/0 x 16/10 +

VAULTED

FOYER
BELOW

BR. 2
12/4 X 10/0 +

PLAN 7475

First Floor: 1,308 square feet
Second Floor: 1,144 square feet
Total: 2,452 square feet
Bonus Room: 214 square feet

■ DESIGN BY NORTHWEST HOME DESIGNING INC.

This home, as shown in the photograph, may differ from the actual blueprints. For more detailed information, please check the floor plans carefully.

Photo by James Reuter Photography

PLAN W306

First Floor: 1,706 square feet
Second Floor: 1,123 square feet
Total: 2,829 square feet

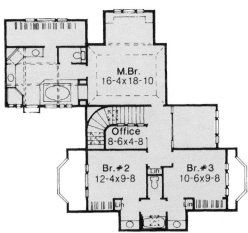

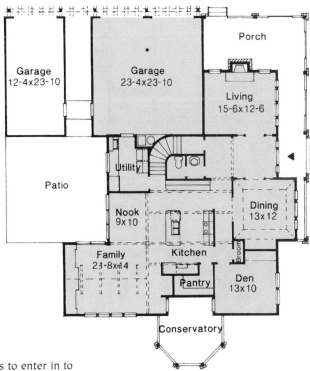

Width 71'-2"
Depth 64'-6"

A welcoming front porch encourages family and friends to enter in to this fine three-bedroom Craftsman home. The foyer is large and is flanked by a delightful living room to the right—complete with a fireplace and plenty of windows—and a formal dining room to the left. The galley kitchen easily serves the dining room, adjacent nook and is open to the spacious family room. Note the roomy walk-in pantry nearby. A secluded den offers privacy, or converts to a perfect home office. Up the curved staircase, two secondary bedrooms share a bath while having their own balconies. The master suite is lavish with its amenities. These include a built-in in the window niche, a walk-in closet and a sumptuous bath with a through-fireplace to the bedroom area.

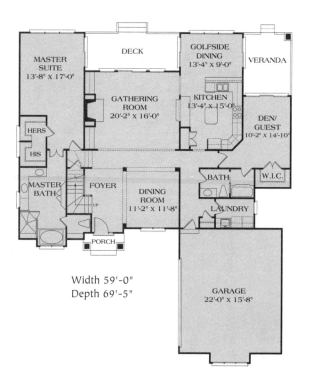

MASTER SUITE
13'-8" X 17'-0"

DECK

GOLFSIDE DINING
13'-4" X 9'-0"

VERANDA

HERS

HIS

GATHERING ROOM
20'-2" X 16'-0"

KITCHEN
13'-4" X 15'-0"

DEN/ GUEST
10'-2" X 14'-10"

MASTER BATH

FOYER

DINING ROOM
11'-2" X 11'-8"

BATH

W.I.C.

UP

LAUNDRY

PORCH

Width 59'-0"
Depth 69'-5"

GARAGE
22'-0" X 15'-8"

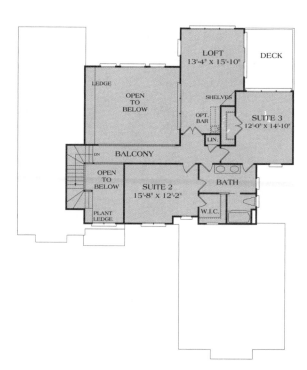

LEDGE

LOFT
13'-4" X 15'-10"

DECK

OPEN TO BELOW

SHELVES

OPT. BAR

SUITE 3
12'-0" X 14'-10"

LIN

DN

BALCONY

OPEN TO BELOW

SUITE 2
15'-8" X 12'-2"

BATH

PLANT LEDGE

W.I.C.

C raftsman-style windows and pillars supporting a shed roof over the porch combine to give this home plenty of curb appeal. The two-story foyer leads to a formal dining room on the right and a spacious gathering room directly ahead, where a fireplace is flanked by built-ins and adds warmth and cheer to the room. The second-floor balcony divides the foyer from the gathering room, while offering beautiful views out the back windows to the rear deck. The master suite is designed to pamper, with His and Hers walk-in closets, a separate tub and shower and a dual-bowl vanity. A den/guest room features a walk-in closet and access to a full bath. Upstairs, across a balcony, two secondary suites share a bath and access to a spacious loft. Note the deck opening off of the loft.

PLAN A186

First Floor: 2,107 square feet
Second Floor: 989 square feet
Total: 3,096 square feet

■ DESIGN BY LIVING CONCEPTS HOME PLANNING

■ DESIGN BY ALAN MASCORD DESIGN ASSOCIATES, INC.

PLAN 7474

First Floor: 2,005 square feet
Second Floor: 689 square feet
Bonus Room: 356 square feet
Total: 3,050 square feet

Shingles and stone combine to present a highly attractive facade on this spacious three-bedroom home. The Craftsman-style influence is very evident and adds to the charm, also. The two-story foyer is flanked by a large, yet cozy, den on the right and on the left, beyond the staircase, is the formal dining room with built-ins. The vaulted great room also offers built-ins, as well as a fireplace. The U-shaped kitchen will surely please the gourmet of the family with its planning desk, corner sink, cooktop island and plenty of counter and cabinet space. The vaulted master suite is complete with a plant shelf, a walk-in closet and a lavish bath. Two secondary bedrooms make up the sleeping zone upstairs, each with a walk-in closet and having access to the full bath. A large bonus room is available for use as a guest suite.

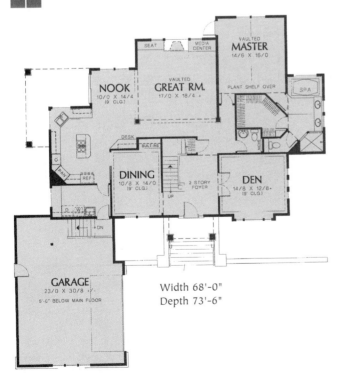

Width 68'-0"
Depth 73'-6"

■ DESIGN BY LIVING CONCEPTS HOME PLANNING

First Floor

MASTER SUITE 13'-8" X 17'-0"

DECK

DINING

VERANDA

HERS

HIS

GATHERING ROOM 20'-2" X 16'-0"

KITCHEN 13'-4" X 15'-0"

P.

DEN/ GUEST 10'-2" X 14'-10"

MASTER BATH

FOYER

UP

DINING ROOM 11'-2" X 11'-8"

BATH

W.I.C.

LAUNDRY

PORCH

Width 59'-0"
Depth 67'-0"

GARAGE

Second Floor

LEDGE

OPEN TO BELOW

LOFT 13'-4" X 15'-10"

DECK

SHELVES

OPT. BAR

LIN.

SUITE 3 12'-0" X 14'-10"

DN

BALCONY

OPEN TO BELOW

SUITE 2 15'-8" X 12'-2"

BATH

PLANT LEDGE

W.I.C.

ATTIC

PLAN A185

First Floor: 2,106 square feet
Second Floor: 984 square feet
Total: 3,090 square feet

With rafter tails peeking out from under an overhanging roof, and pillars supporting a covered porch, this home is truly defined as a Craftsman home. The inside is sure to please also, with a warming fireplace in the spacious gathering room, flanked by built-ins, a large efficient island kitchen and plenty of indoor/outdoor relationships. The first-floor master suite will be a haven for the homeowner, while the family will enjoy their suites on the second floor. A loft is also on the second floor and would be perfect as a media/rec/study room.

MBATH
Dress'g
WI Closet
tray cl'g
MBR
12'6 x 19'6

BR3
11'4 x 13'6
BATH 2

Balcony
Din Rm Below

BR4
11'4 x 11'9

BR2
11'7 x 12'4
Foyer Below

Liv Rm Below

Width 62'-4"
Depth 47'-8"

This four-bedroom Craftsman home, styled with cedar shake siding and stone veneer, has a warm and welcome appeal. The two-story foyer flows into vaulted living and dining areas enjoying a two-sided gas fireplace. U-shaped stairs provide a focal point to the formal area of the home. The study has an adjoining bath which allows versatility—use as a guest bedroom when needed. The kitchen, dinette and family room flow together, providing an ideal gathering area for family living. The second-floor balcony overlooks the entire front living area. The master bedroom has a wide bayed sitting area and tray ceiling. A large walk-in closet and dressing area connects the master bedroom and the master bath, featuring a corner tub and glassed custom shower.

PLAN C119

First Floor: 1,597 square feet
Second Floor: 1,244 square feet
Total: 2,841 square feet

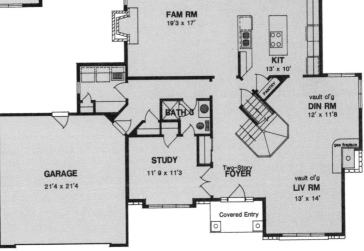

DIN
11'10 x 9'9

FAM RM
19'3 x 17'

KIT
13' x 10'

PANTRY

vault cl'g
DIN RM
12' x 11'8

BATH 3

GARAGE
21'4 x 21'4

STUDY
11' 9 x 11'3

Two-Story
FOYER

gas fireplace

vault cl'g
LIV RM
13' x 14'

Covered Entry

■ DESIGN BY JAMES FAHY DESIGN

■ DESIGN BY LIVING CONCEPTS HOME PLANNING

Craftsman architecture is so distinct that one could hardly miss what the rafter tails, shingles, six-over-one windows and pillars at the front porch are trying to say in this fine four-bedroom home. An efficient kitchen offers a walk-in pantry and easy access to both the formal dining room as well as the sunny breakfast room. In the gathering room, built-ins flank the warming fireplace, while access to the rear deck is nearby. Located on the first floor for privacy, the master suite is full of amenities. These include two walk-in closets, a separate tub and shower and a linen closet. The second floor is complete with three bedrooms, two full baths and an unfinished bonus room with access to unfinished storage. A recreation room finishes off this floor with a flourish, providing space for children to study, play or read.

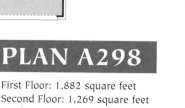

DECK

BREAKFAST
9'-10" X 13'-4"

GATHERING
ROOM
15'-6" X 21'-4"

MASTER
SUITE
16'-2" X 14'-0"

KITCHEN
12'-0" X 15'-6"

LIN.   W.I.C.

W.I.C.   MASTER
BATH

UP

P.

DINING
ROOM
12'-0" X 16'-0"

FOYER

PDR.

LAUNDRY

PORCH

GARAGE
20'-0" X 23'-0"

Width 45'-0"
Depth 66'-10"

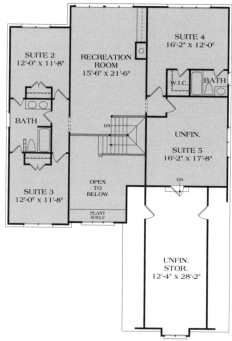

SUITE 2
12'-0" X 11'-8"

RECREATION
ROOM
15'-6" X 21'-6"

SUITE 4
16'-2" X 12'-0"

BATH

W.I.C.   BATH

DN

UNFIN.
SUITE 5
16'-2" X 17'-8"

SUITE 3
12'-0" X 11'-8"

OPEN
TO
BELOW

DN

PLANT
SHELF

UNFIN.
STOR.
12'-4" X 28'-2"

PLAN A298

First Floor: 1,882 square feet
Second Floor: 1,269 square feet
Total: 3,151 square feet
Bonus Room: 284 square feet

■ DESIGN BY LIVING CONCEPTS HOME PLANNING

PLAN A201

First Floor: 2,049 square feet
Second Floor: 1,468 square feet
Total: 3,517 square feet

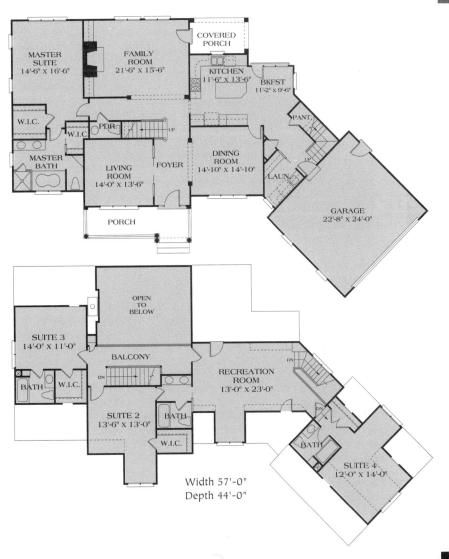

MASTER SUITE 14'-6" x 16'-6"

FAMILY ROOM 21'-6" x 15'-6"

COVERED PORCH

KITCHEN 11'-6" x 13'-6"

BKFST 11'-2" x 9'-6"

W.I.C.

PDR.

W.I.C.

UP

PANT

MASTER BATH

LIVING ROOM 14'-0" x 13'-6"

FOYER

DINING ROOM 14'-10" x 14'-10"

LAUN

UP

GARAGE 22'-8" x 24'-0"

PORCH

SUITE 3 14'-0" x 11'-0"

OPEN TO BELOW

BALCONY

DN

RECREATION ROOM 13'-0" x 23'-0"

DN

BATH

W.I.C.

DN

SUITE 2 13'-6" x 13'-0"

BATH

W.I.C.

BATH

SUITE 4 12'-0" x 14'-0"

Width 57'-0"
Depth 44'-0"

Rafter tails, shingles and stucco and a trio of gables—all can be elements of a fine Craftsman home, and when they're combined, a truly attractive home is the result. A covered front porch welcomes family and friends to enter in and partake of the many amenities found inside. A formal living room opens to the left of the foyer, and can be closed off by sliding doors if need be. A formal dining room is on the right and offers easy access to the island kitchen. A spacious family room resides to the rear and features a fireplace, built-ins and access to a small covered porch. Located on the main floor for privacy, the master suite is enhanced by two walk-in closets and a master bath which includes a tub and separate shower. Upstairs, three comfortable suites—each with a private bath—share access to a large recreation room.

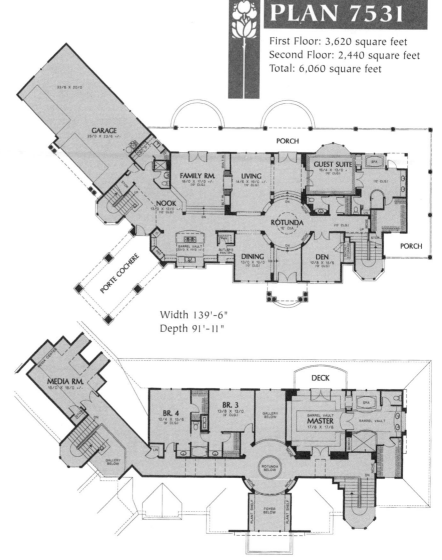

First Floor: 3,620 square feet
Second Floor: 2,440 square feet
Total: 6,060 square feet

If it's space you desire, with a classy facade to further enhance it, this is the home for you! Looking a bit like a resort from the '40s or '50s, this fine Craftsman home is sure to please. Inside, the foyer is flanked by a cozy den to the right and a formal dining room to the left. A lavish guest suite is loaded with amenities and is near the formal living room. The spacious kitchen will please any gourmet, with a cooktop island, walk-in pantry and a nearby sunken family room. Here, a fireplace, shared by the formal living room, will add warmth and charm to any gathering. Upstairs, two large bedrooms—each with walk-in closets and private lavatories—share a bath. A media room is just down the hall and is great for reading, studying or watching movies. The sumptuous master suite is designed to pamper, with such amenities as a walk-in closet, a private deck, a huge shower and a separate spa tub. Note the tremendous amount of storage in the four-car garage.

Width 139'-6"
Depth 91'-11"

■ DESIGN BY ALAN MASCORD DESIGN ASSOCIATES, INC.

■ Design by Alan Mascord Design Associates, Inc.

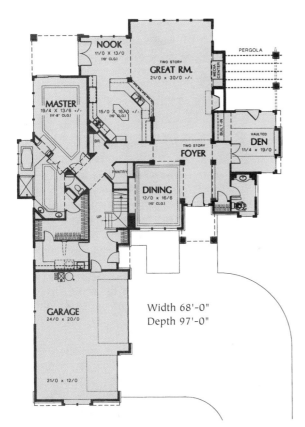

NOOK
11/0 x 13/0
(10' CLG.)

GREAT RM.
21/0 x 30/0 +/-
TWO STORY

PERGOLA

MEDIA CENTER

MASTER
19/4 X 13/6 +/-
(11'-8" CLG.)

15/0 x 16/0 +/-
(10' CLG.)

BR

BUILT IN

DEN
11/4 x 19/0
VAULTED

TWO STORY
FOYER

PANTRY

DINING
12/0 x 16/6
(10' CLG.)

UP

Width 68'-0"
Depth 97'-0"

GARAGE
24/0 x 20/0

21/0 x 12/0

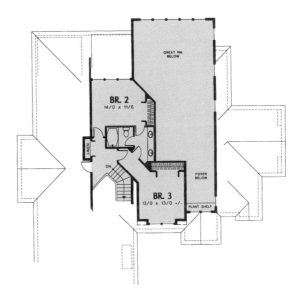

GREAT RM.
BELOW

BR. 2
14/0 x 11/6

LINEN

DN

FOYER
BELOW

BR. 3
12/0 x 13/0 +/-

PLANT SHELF

PLAN 7445

First Floor: 2,943 square feet
Second Floor: 597 square feet
Total: 3,540 square feet

Stone-and-shingles siding, gables and columns framing the front entry all combine to give this home plenty of curb appeal. A two-story ceiling that starts in the foyer and runs through the great room gives a feeling of spaciousness. The great room is further enhanced by a built-in media center, a fireplace and direct access to the kitchen. Double doors lead into a vaulted den which also offers built-ins. Located on the first floor for privacy, the master bedroom suite is designed to pamper the homeowner. Here, amenities such as a huge walk-in closet, separate tub and shower and sliding glass doors to a rear porch make sure the homeowner is comfortable. Upstairs, two secondary bedrooms share a full hall bath.

© 1998 Donald A. Gardner, Inc.

■ DESIGN BY DONALD A. GARDNER ARCHITECTS, INC.

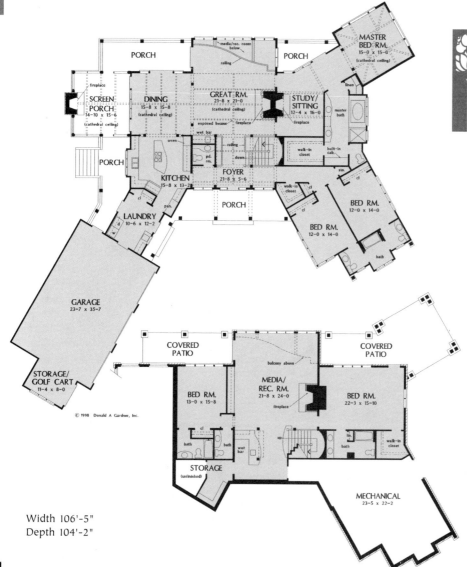

Width 106'-5"
Depth 104'-2"

© 1998 Donald A Gardner, Inc.

PLAN 7707

First Floor: 3,040 square feet
Lower Level: 1,736 square feet
Total: 4,776 square feet

Looking a bit like a mountain resort, this fine Craftsman home is sure to be the envy of your neighborhood. Entering through the elegant front door, one finds an open staircase to the right and a spacious great room directly ahead. Here, a fireplace and a wall of windows accent a cozy welcome. A lavish master suite begins with a sitting room complete with a fireplace, and continues to a private porch, large walk-in closet and sumptuous bedroom area. Two family bedrooms share a bath and have a wing to themselves. The efficient kitchen is adjacent to a large, sunny dining area, and offers access to a screen porch with yet another fireplace! The lower level consists of a huge media room with a fourth fireplace, two spacious bedrooms each with private baths and tons of storage. A three-car garage, with extra space for storage or a golf cart, will be perfect for the family fleet.

■ DESIGN BY DONALD A. GARDNER ARCHITECTS, INC.

© 1998 Donald A. Gardner, Inc.

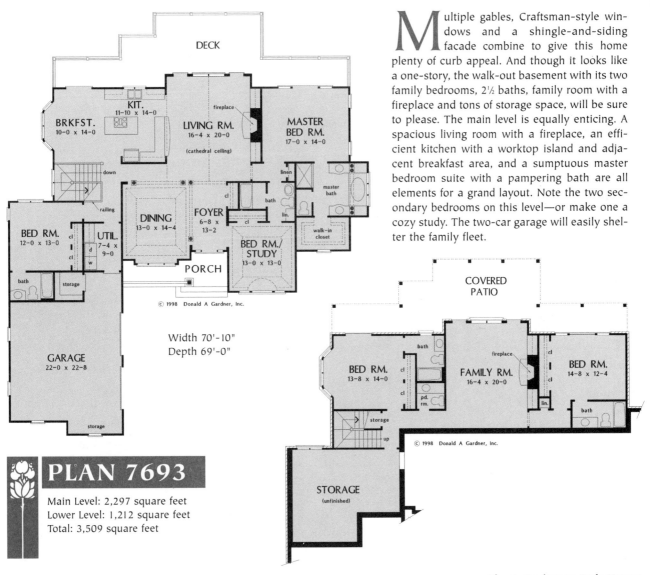

DECK

KIT.
11-10 x 14-0

BRKFST.
10-0 x 14-0

LIVING RM.
16-4 x 20-0
(cathedral ceiling)
fireplace

MASTER
BED RM.
17-0 x 14-0

down

railing

linen

master
bath

cl

bath

DINING
13-0 x 14-4

FOYER
6-8 x
13-2

lin.

BED RM.
12-0 x 13-0

cl
cl

UTIL.
7-4 x
9-0
d
w

BED RM./
STUDY
13-0 x 13-0

walk-in
closet

bath

storage

PORCH

GARAGE
22-0 x 22-8

© 1998 Donald A Gardner, Inc.

Width 70'-10"
Depth 69'-0"

storage

Multiple gables, Craftsman-style windows and a shingle-and-siding facade combine to give this home plenty of curb appeal. And though it looks like a one-story, the walk-out basement with its two family bedrooms, 2½ baths, family room with a fireplace and tons of storage space, will be sure to please. The main level is equally enticing. A spacious living room with a fireplace, an efficient kitchen with a worktop island and adjacent breakfast area, and a sumptuous master bedroom suite with a pampering bath are all elements for a grand layout. Note the two secondary bedrooms on this level—or make one a cozy study. The two-car garage will easily shelter the family fleet.

COVERED
PATIO

bath

fireplace

BED RM.
13-8 x 14-0

cl

cl

FAMILY RM.
16-4 x 20-0

cl

BED RM.
14-8 x 12-4

pd.
rm.

lin.

bath

storage

up

© 1998 Donald A Gardner, Inc.

STORAGE
(unfinished)

PLAN 7693

Main Level: 2,297 square feet
Lower Level: 1,212 square feet
Total: 3,509 square feet

■ DESIGN BY NORTHWEST HOME DESIGNING INC.

A judicious use of shingles and siding combine to give this home a true Craftsman flavor. Pillars support the roof porch and help usher you into the grand foyer. From here, you can see into the sunken living room, the formal dining room and the kitchen. The kitchen has plenty to offer, with a cooktop island and an adjacent nook for casual meals. The family room features a corner fireplace and access to a rear patio. Two secondary bedrooms are nearby and share a full bath. Note the large utility room here. The master suite, at the opposite end of the home, is complete with a walk-in closet, private patio and a sumptuous bath. The three-car garage will easily shelter the family fleet.

PLAN W331

First Floor: 2,765 square feet
Bonus Room: 446 square feet
Total: 3,211 square feet

Width 111'-4"
Depth 77'-1"

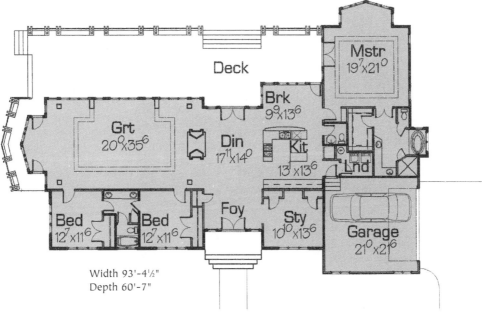

Deck

Mstr
19⁷x21⁰

Brk
9⁹x13⁶

Grt
20⁰x35⁶

Din
17¹¹x14⁰

Kit
13⁰x13⁶

Lnd

Bed
12⁷x11⁶

Bed
12⁷x11⁶

Foy

Sty
10⁰x13⁶

Garage
21⁰x21⁶

Width 93'-4½"
Depth 60'-7"

PLAN V004

Square Footage: 2,927

This is truly a light-filled design—with full and transom windows in many of the interior spaces to give a feeling of connectedness to the outdoors. Double doors open directly to the foyer. At the right is a study with double closets. Ahead is the formal dining area, separated from the great room by a through-fireplace. The island kitchen has an attached nook and nearby powder room. The full-width deck to the rear of the plan can be reached from the dining area, the great room and the master bedroom. Family bedrooms share a full bath with dual sinks. The master bedroom boasts a private bath with garden tub and walk-in closet. A congenial sitting area works well for a chaise or other comfy reading chair.

■ DESIGN BY UNITED DESIGN ASSOCIATES, INC.

© American Home Gallery, Ltd.

■ DESIGN BY DESIGN TRADITIONS

PLAN T176

First Floor: 1,924 square feet
Second Floor: 1,097 square feet
Total: 3,021 square feet

Width 68'-3"
Depth 53'-0"

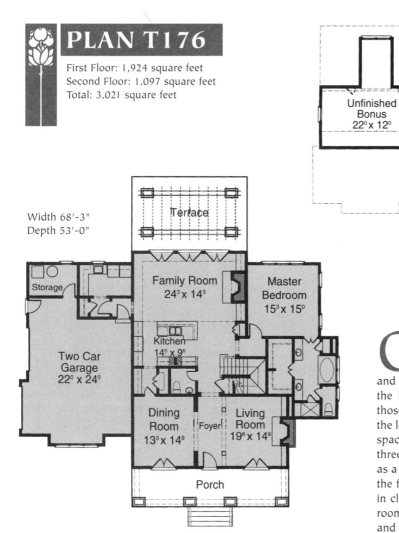

Gables, rafter tails, four sturdy pillars and Craftsman-style windows all combine to give this home the warm feeling of the Arts and Crafts Movement. The foyer opens directly into the living room, where a fireplace waits to warm those cool fall evenings. A formal dining room is to the left, with easy access to the efficient kitchen. The spacious family room at the back of the home offers three sets of French doors to the rear terrace, as well as a second fireplace. The master suite is located on the first floor for privacy and contains a huge walk-in closet and a pampering bath. Upstairs, two bedrooms—each with lots of storage—share a full bath and access to an unfinished bonus room.

■ DESIGN BY SELECT HOME DESIGNS

PLAN Q505

Square Footage: 1,260

This economical-to-build bunga-low works well as a small fam-ily home or a retirement cot-tage. It is available with a basement foundation but could easily be convert-ed to a slab or crawlspace foundation. The covered porch leads to a vaulted living room with fireplace. Behind this living space is the U-shaped kitchen with walk-in pantry and island with utility sink. An attached breakfast nook has sliding glass doors to a rear patio. There are three bedrooms, each with a roomy wall closet. The master bed-room has a private full bath, while the family bedrooms share a main bath. Both baths have bright skylights. A two-car garage sits to the front of the plan to protect the bedrooms from street noise.

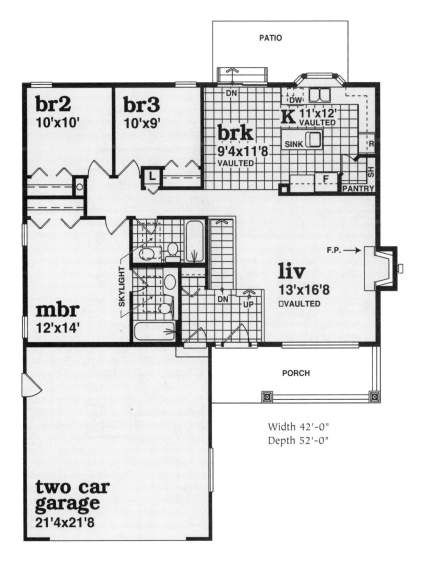

PATIO

br2
10'x10'

br3
10'x9'

DN

K 11'x12'
VAULTED

DW

SINK

brk
9'4x11'8
VAULTED

F

PANTRY

R

L

SKYLIGHT

mbr
12'x14'

DN

UP

F.P. →

liv
13'x16'8
□VAULTED

PORCH

two car
garage
21'4x21'8

Width 42'-0"
Depth 52'-0"

PLAN Q513

Square Footage: 1,293

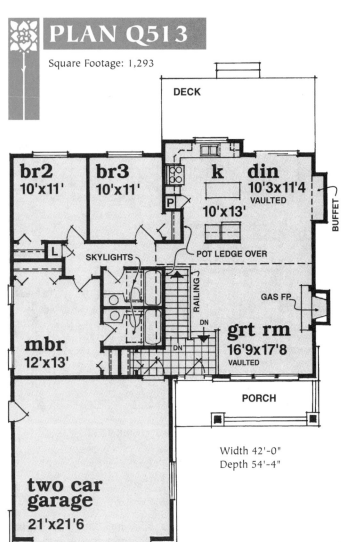

DECK

| br2 10'x11' | br3 10'x11' | k | din 10'3x11'4 VAULTED |

10'x13'

P

L

SKYLIGHTS

POT LEDGE OVER

mbr 12'x13'

RAILING

GAS FP.

DN

DN

grt rm 16'9x17'8 VAULTED

PORCH

Width 42'-0"
Depth 54'-4"

two car garage 21'x21'6

Meeting the needs of first-time homebuilders, this design is, nonetheless, economical to build. Craftsman detailing and a quaint covered porch go a long way to create the charming exterior on the design. Open planning filled with amenities add to the livability on the interior. The foyer opens to a hearth-warmed great room. Vaulted ceilings and a half wall separating the stairs to the basement and the foyer add to the spaciousness. An open island kitchen has an adjoining dining room with sliding glass doors to the deck and box-bay buffet space. The master bedroom adjoins two family bedrooms down the hall. It boasts His and Hers wall closets and a full bath with soaking tub. Family bedrooms—or make one a den—share a full bath.

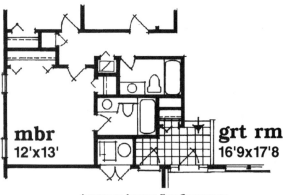

mbr 12'x13'

grt rm 16'9x17'8

ALTERNATE LAYOUT FOR CRAWLSPACE

■ DESIGN BY ALAN MASCORD DESIGN ASSOCIATES, INC.

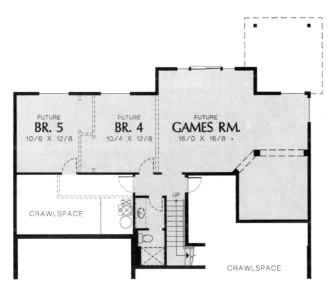

FUTURE
BR. 5
10/6 X 12/8

FUTURE
BR. 4
10/4 X 12/8

FUTURE
GAMES RM.
16/0 X 16/8

CRAWLSPACE

UP

CRAWLSPACE

Width 50'-0"
Depth 50'-0"

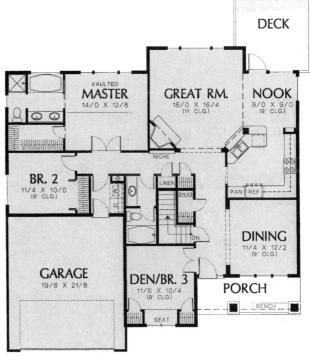

DECK

VAULTED
MASTER
14/0 X 12/8

GREAT RM.
16/0 X 16/4
(11' CLG.)

NOOK
9/0 X 9/0
(9' CLG.)

NICHE

BR. 2
11/4 X 10/0
(9' CLG.)

LINEN

SHLVS

PAN | REF

DN

DINING
11/4 X 12/2
(9' CLG.)

GARAGE
19/8 X 21/8

DEN/BR. 3
11/6 X 10/4
(9' CLG.)

PORCH

SEAT

BENCH

PLAN 7467

Square Footage: 1,632
Unfinished Lower Floor: 1,043 sq. ft.

This petite little bungalow gives the impression of a one-story home, but features a lower level that could be developed when the need arose. The downstairs could accommodate two family bedrooms, a full bath, a huge games room with outdoor access and plenty of storage space. On the main level, a great room offers a corner fireplace, ease of access to the sunny nook and efficient kitchen and a wall of windows. Two bedrooms—or make one a cozy den—share a full hall bath. The vaulted master suite is designed to pamper with a walk-in closet and a private bath.

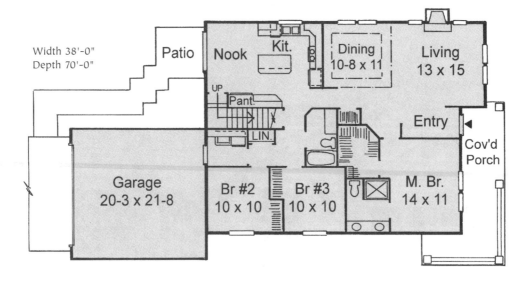

Width 38'-0"
Depth 70'-0"

Patio

Nook

Kit.

Dining
10-8 x 11

Living
13 x 15

UP

Pant.

LIN.

Entry

Cov'd
Porch

Garage
20-3 x 21-8

Br #2
10 x 10

Br #3
10 x 10

M. Br.
14 x 11

Ideal for narrow lots, this fine bungalow home is full of amenities. The entry is just off a covered front porch and leads to a living room complete with a fireplace. The formal dining room is nearby, and works well with the L-shaped kitchen. The sleeping zone consists of a master suite with a walk-in closet and private bath, as well as two family bedrooms sharing a full bath. An unfinished attic waits for future developments while a two-car garage easily shelters the family fleet.

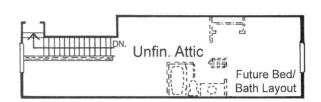

DN.

Unfin. Attic

Future Bed/
Bath Layout

PLAN W318

Square Footage: 1,484
Unfinished Attic: 484 square feet

■ DESIGN BY NORTHWEST HOME DESIGNING INC.

■ DESIGN BY NORTHWEST HOME DESIGNING INC.

PLAN W302

Square Footage: 1,506

This cute little bungalow will not only fit onto a narrow lot, it also features many amenities! With shingles, rafter tails and pillars supporting a covered front porch, Craftsman influence is highly evident. Inside, the foyer opens directly into the living room, where a fireplace adds cheer to any gathering. The formal dining room offers fine ceiling detailing and easy access to the efficient kitchen. Two family bedrooms share a hall bath, while the master bedroom suite is complete with a walk-in closet and a private bath. The attic offers plenty of room for future expansion when it's needed. The two-car garage will easily shelter the family fleet.

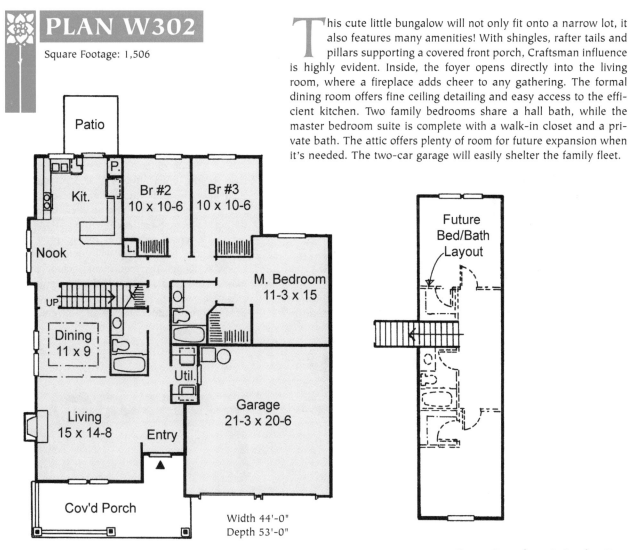

Patio

Kit.

Br #2
10 x 10-6

Br #3
10 x 10-6

Nook

UP

Dining
11 x 9

M. Bedroom
11-3 x 15

Util.

Living
15 x 14-8

Entry

Garage
21-3 x 20-6

Cov'd Porch

Width 44'-0"
Depth 53'-0"

Future
Bed/Bath
Layout

■ Design by Alan Mascord Design Associates, Inc.

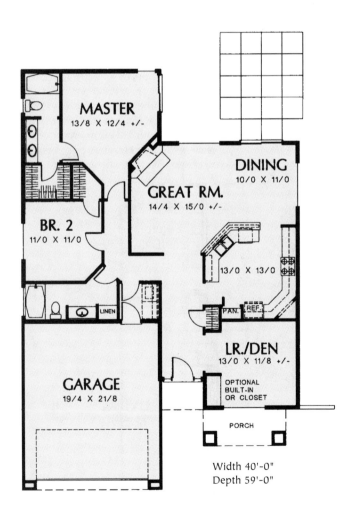

MASTER
13/8 X 12/4 +/-

DINING
10/0 X 11/0

GREAT RM.
14/4 X 15/0 +/-

BR. 2
11/0 X 11/0

13/0 X 13/0

LINEN

PAN. REF.

LR./DEN
13/0 X 11/8 +/-

GARAGE
19/4 X 21/8

OPTIONAL
BUILT-IN
OR CLOSET

PORCH

Width 40'-0"
Depth 59'-0"

This efficient bungalow will look good in any neighborhood. Inside, a living room or den opens to the right of the entry. It offers an optional built-in or closet. In the kitchen, an abundance of counter space and an accommodating layout make meal preparations simple. A great room and dining room connect to this area and will conform to everyday living. Two bedrooms include a master suite with a private bath and ample closet space. The master bedroom also accesses the outdoors for an added treat.

PLAN 9530

Square Footage: 1,420

■ DESIGN BY ALAN MASCORD DESIGN ASSOCIATES, INC.

PLAN 7465

Square Footage: 1,520

A shed roof over a boxed bay window, pillars with stone bases and detailed windows show strong Craftsman-style influence on this three-bedroom bungalow. Perfect for a narrow lot, this home offers many amenities. From the covered porch, the foyer leads you to a spacious living room with a fireplace to add cheer to any gathering. The dining area is large enough for dinner parties, yet small enough for casual family meals. The unique kitchen is sure to be a blessing with plenty of counter and cabinet space and a corner sink. Two family bedrooms share a full hall bath and easy access to the laundry room. The vaulted master suite features such amenities as a box-bay window, walk-in closet and a spa tub.

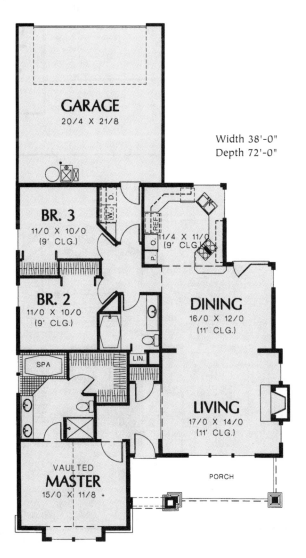

GARAGE
20/4 X 21/8

Width 38'-0"
Depth 72'-0"

BR. 3
11/0 X 10/0
(9' CLG.)

W.D.

REF.
P.O.
1/4 X 11/0
(9' CLG.)

BR. 2
11/0 X 10/0
(9' CLG.)

DINING
16/0 X 12/0
(11' CLG.)

LIN.

SPA

LIVING
17/0 X 14/0
(11' CLG.)

VAULTED
MASTER
15/0 X 11/8 +

PORCH

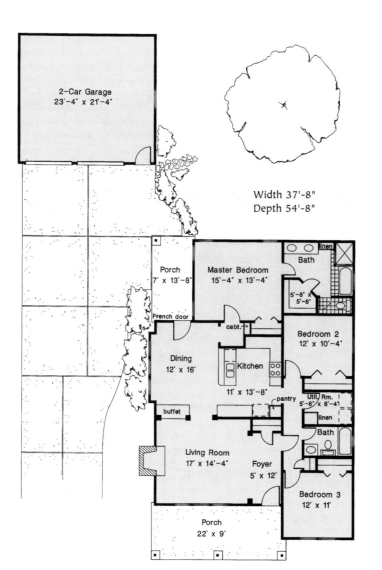

2-Car Garage
23'-4" x 21'-4"

Width 37'-8"
Depth 54'-8"

Porch
7' x 13'-8"

Master Bedroom
15'-4" x 13'-4"

Bath

linen

5'-8" x
5'-8"

French door

cabt.

Dining
12' x 16'

Kitchen
11' x 13'-8"

Bedroom 2
12' x 10'-4"

buffet

pantry

Util. Rm.
5'-6" x 8'-4"

linen

Bath

Living Room
17' x 14'-4"

Foyer
5' x 12'

Bedroom 3
12' x 11'

Porch
22' x 9'

Square columns supported by brick pedestals and a low-pitched roof are reminiscent of the Craftsman style brought to popularity in the early 1900s. Livability is the foremost consideration in this well-designed plan. To the left of the foyer is the cozy living room, warmed by an inviting fireplace. Straight ahead, the dining room shares space with an efficient, step-saving kitchen. A French door provides access to a covered porch for outdoor meals and entertaining. To the rear of the plan rests the master suite. The master bath is highlighted by a tub and a separate shower, a double-bowl vanity, a compartmented toilet and a large walk-in closet. Two family bedrooms, a full bath and a utility room with a linen closet complete this marvelous plan.

■ DESIGN BY LARRY W. GARNETT & ASSOCIATES, INC.

■ Design by Larry W. Garnett & Associates, Inc.

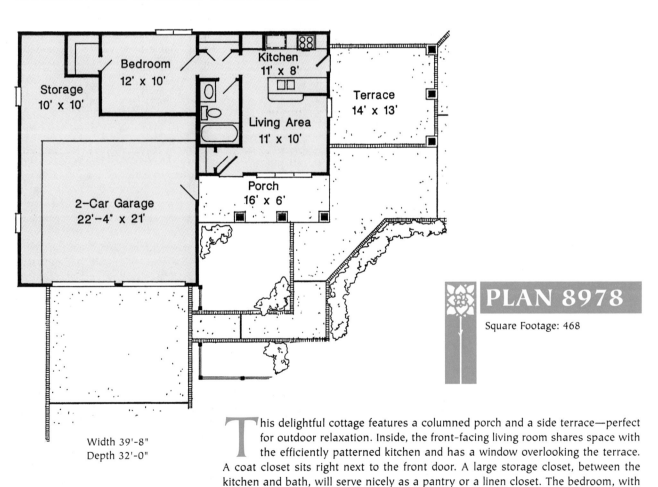

Width 39'-8"
Depth 32'-0"

PLAN 8978

Square Footage: 468

This delightful cottage features a columned porch and a side terrace—perfect for outdoor relaxation. Inside, the front-facing living room shares space with the efficiently patterned kitchen and has a window overlooking the terrace. A coat closet sits right next to the front door. A large storage closet, between the kitchen and bath, will serve nicely as a pantry or a linen closet. The bedroom, with a large walk-in closet, enjoys peace and quiet at the rear of the plan. A step away, the full hall bath is also convenient to living areas. In the two-car garage, a large storage area accommodates all your recreational equipment.

■ DESIGN BY DESIGN BASICS, INC.

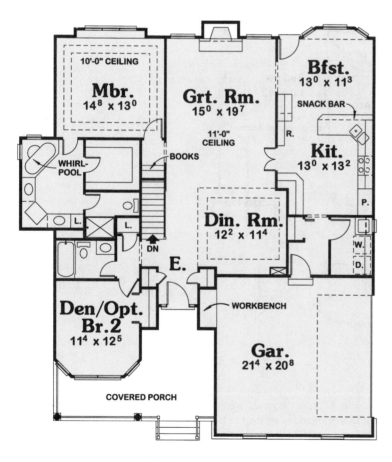

Width 48'-8"
Depth 54'-0"

A front porch reminiscent of the 1920s sets the tone on this charming one-story home. The covered front porch leads to an entry foyer with twin coat closets. The dining room is just beyond, and then the superb great room with a fireplace. The den can be converted to a bedroom and offers a full bath and a bayed window overlooking the front porch. A designer kitchen has an attached breakfast room with another bay window for gracious casual meals. Plenty of extra space in the master bath leaves room for a corner make-up vanity and His and Hers sinks. The two-car garage features workbench space for the family handyman. Note the tray ceilings in both the master bedroom and the dining room.

PLAN 7396

Square Footage: 1,653

■ DESIGN BY ALAN MASCORD DESIGN ASSOCIATES, INC.

With two attractive gables and a covered front porch, this petite bungalow offers plenty of curb appeal. Inside, the foyer opens directly to a living room or den on the right, which can feature either a built-in or a closet. In the angled kitchen, plenty of counter and cabinet space make meal preparation a breeze. The great room and dining room are adjacent to this area and will work well together. The master bedroom suite is designed to pamper, with a walk-in closet and a private bath. A secondary bedroom, also with a walk-in closet, has use of a full hall bath.

PLAN 9529

Square Footage: 1,420

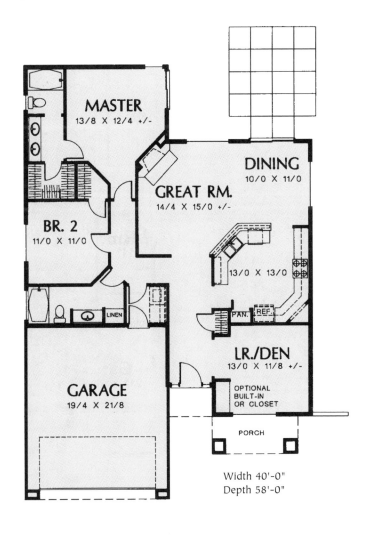

MASTER
13/8 X 12/4 +/-

DINING
10/0 X 11/0

GREAT RM.
14/4 X 15/0 +/-

BR. 2
11/0 X 11/0

13/0 X 13/0

PAN.   REF.

LINEN

LR./DEN
13/0 X 11/8 +/-

GARAGE
19/4 X 21/8

OPTIONAL
BUILT-IN
OR CLOSET

PORCH

Width 40'-0"
Depth 58'-0"

■ DESIGN BY MARK STEWART & ASSOCIATES, INC.

PLAN J155

Square Footage: 1,610

Two covered porches, plus a private master-suite terrace go above and beyond in offering outdoor options for this plan. You'll also have options inside: choose a three-bedroom lay-out, or turn the third bedroom into a cozy den with double doors. The living room/dining room combination to the left of the plan is coun-tered by a large family room with fireplace and porch access. The central kitchen is designed for con-venience. The circular flow of the floor plan makes it very livable and allows for private spaces as well as open living areas. Because all of this is offered in just over 1,600 square feet, this plan is a perfect choice for a starter home, empty nester home or retirement home.

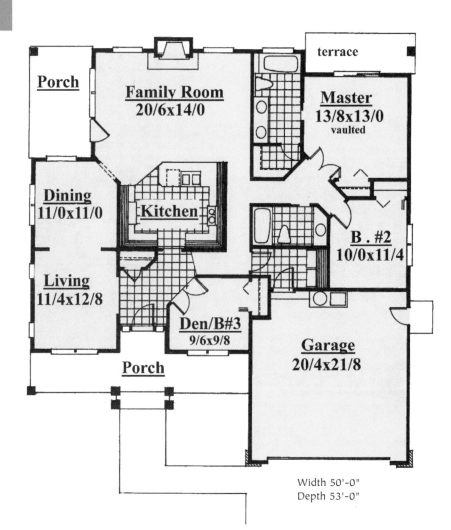

Porch

Family Room
20/6x14/0

terrace

Master
13/8x13/0
vaulted

Dining
11/0x11/0

Kitchen

Living
11/4x12/8

B . #2
10/0x11/4

Den/B#3
9/6x9/8

Porch

Garage
20/4x21/8

Width 50'-0"
Depth 53'-0"

A trio of gables, pillars defining the porch and an efficient floor plan combine to make this a very attractive home. A living room opens to the right of the foyer—or make it a den—and offers the option of either a built-in or a closet. The spacious great room features a corner fireplace and easy access to the dining area and the fantastic kitchen. Here, the abundance of counter and cabinet space will make meal times easy. Note the patio outside of the dining area—perfect for alfresco meals. Two bedrooms include a master suite with a private bath, access to the outdoors and ample closet space. The secondary bedroom has use of a full hall bath.

PLAN 9531

Square Footage: 1,420

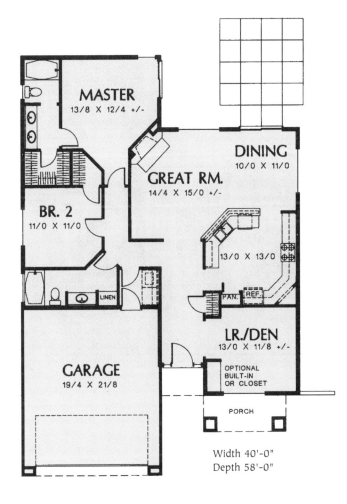

MASTER
13/8 X 12/4 +/-

DINING
10/0 X 11/0

GREAT RM.
14/4 X 15/0 +/-

BR. 2
11/0 X 11/0

13/0 X 13/0

LINEN

LR./DEN
13/0 X 11/8 +/-

OPTIONAL
BUILT-IN
OR CLOSET

PAN. REF.

GARAGE
19/4 X 21/8

PORCH

Width 40'-0"
Depth 58'-0"

Up To 1,700 Square Feet

■ DESIGN BY ALAN MASCORD DESIGN ASSOCIATES, INC.

■ Design by Design Basics, Inc.

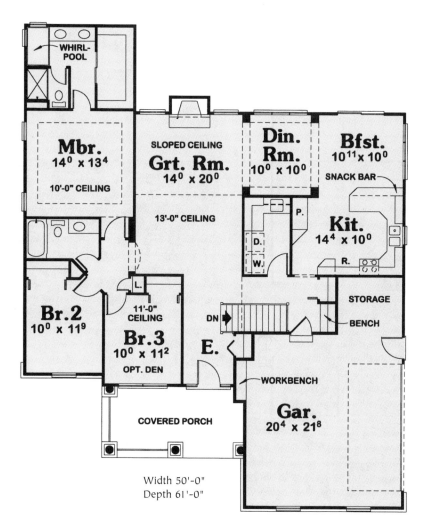

WHIRL-POOL

Mbr.
14⁰ x 13⁴

10'-0" CEILING

SLOPED CEILING
Grt. Rm.
14⁰ x 20⁰

13'-0" CEILING

Din. Rm.
10⁰ x 10⁰

Bfst.
10¹¹x 10⁰

SNACK BAR

Kit.
14⁴ x 10⁰

P.

D.

W.

R.

Br.2
10⁰ x 11⁹

11'-0" CEILING

L.

Br.3
10⁰ x 11²

OPT. DEN

E.

DN

STORAGE

BENCH

WORKBENCH

Gar.
20⁴ x 21⁸

COVERED PORCH

Width 50'-0"
Depth 61'-0"

Brick pedestals anchoring tapered columns and a fine combination of siding and brick give this bungalow plenty of curb appeal. Inside, both the dining room and breakfast area are near the kitchen and readily expand into one another. A boxed ceiling offers beauty in the master bedroom which also features a large walk-in closet and whirlpool tub. The spacious great room features a sloped ceiling and a fireplace flanked by windows. Two bedrooms, or make one a den, share a full hall bath. Note the extra storage space in the two-car garage.

PLAN 7028

Square Footage: 1,679

Photo by Northwest Home Designing, Inc.

■ DESIGN BY NORTHWEST HOME DESIGNING INC.

This home, as shown in the photograph, may differ from the actual blueprints. For more detailed information, please check the floor plans carefully.

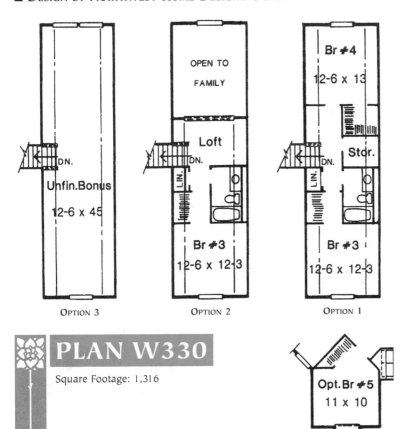

DN.

Unfin.Bonus

12-6 x 45

OPTION 3

OPEN TO FAMILY

Loft

DN.

LIN.

Br #3

12-6 x 12-3

OPTION 2

Br #4

12-6 x 13

Stor.

DN.

LIN.

Br #3

12-6 x 12-3

OPTION 1

Opt.Br #5

11 x 10

PLAN W330

Square Footage: 1,316

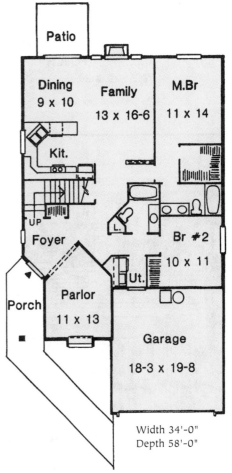

Patio

Dining
9 x 10

Family
13 x 16-6

M.Br
11 x 14

Kit.

UP

Foyer

Porch

Parlor
11 x 13

Ut.

Br #2
10 x 11

Garage
18-3 x 19-8

Width 34'-0"
Depth 58'-0"

The angled foyer of this attractive little bungalow ushers you into a fine floor plan, introducing the parlor and open staircase first. A fireplace waits in the family room to add warmth to any gathering. The U-shaped kitchen is sure to please with serving ease to the dining area. Two bedrooms include a master suite with a walk-in closet and a private bath, while the secondary bedroom has access to a full hall bath. Also note the option for the parlor to be a third bedroom. And talking of options, this plan includes three upstairs options, ranging from 366 square feet to 565 square feet.

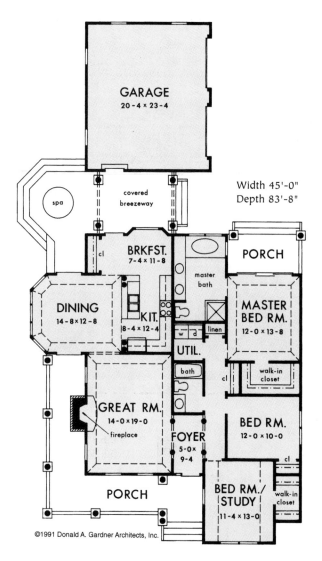

GARAGE
20-4 × 23-4

covered breezeway

spa

cl

BRKFST.
7-4 × 11-8

DINING
14-8 × 12-8

KIT.
8-4 × 12-4

master bath

w d

linen

UTIL.

bath

GREAT RM.
14-0 × 19-0

fireplace

FOYER
5-0 × 9-4

PORCH

BED RM./
STUDY
11-4 × 13-0

PORCH

MASTER
BED RM.
12-0 × 13-8

walk-in closet

cl

BED RM.
12-0 × 10-0

cl

walk-in closet

Width 45'-0"
Depth 83'-8"

©1991 Donald A. Gardner Architects, Inc.

This narrow three-bedroom plan with arched windows and a wraparound porch displays a sense of comfort uncommon to a plan of this size. The great room, dining room and master bedroom all boast tray ceilings, while the front bedroom features a vaulted ceiling to accentuate the arched window. An open kitchen design conveniently services the breakfast area, dining room and deck. The master suite has a private covered porch, a large walk-in closet and a master bath with a whirlpool tub.

PLAN 9637

Square Footage: 1,608

©1991 Donald A. Gardner Architects, Inc.

■ DESIGN BY DONALD A. GARDNER ARCHITECTS, INC.

■ DESIGN BY THE SATER DESIGN COLLECTION

PLAN 6691

Square Footage: 1,288

Welcome home to casual, unstuffy living with this comfortable bungalow design. Asymmetrical lines celebrate the turn of the new century, and blend a current cozy style with vintage panache brought forward from its regional past. The heart of this home is the great room, where a put-your-feet-up atmosphere prevails, and the dusky hues of sunset can mingle with the sounds of crickets chirping. French doors open the master suite to a private area of the covered porch, where sunlight and breezes mingle.

REAR ELEVATION

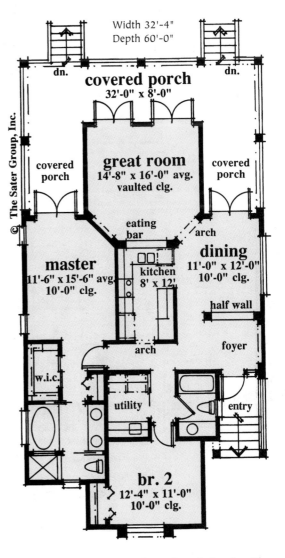

Width 32'-4"
Depth 60'-0"

© The Sater Group, Inc.

dn. **covered porch**
32'-0" x 8'-0" dn.

covered porch **great room**
14'-8" x 16'-0" avg.
vaulted clg. **covered porch**

eating bar arch

master
11'-6" x 15'-6" avg.
10'-0" clg. kitchen
8' x 12' **dining**
11'-0" x 12'-0"
10'-0" clg.

half wall

arch foyer

w.i.c.

utility entry

entry

br. 2
12'-4" x 11'-0"
10'-0" clg.

B. NATHAN

© 1992 Donald A. Gardner Architects, Inc.

■ DESIGN BY DONALD A. GARDNER ARCHITECTS, INC.

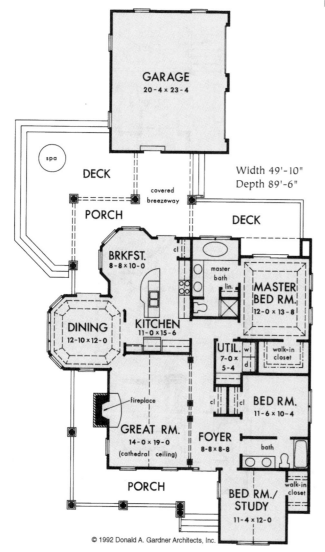

GARAGE
20-4 x 23-4

spa

DECK

covered breezeway

Width 49'-10"
Depth 89'-6"

PORCH

DECK

BRKFST.
8-8 x 10-0

cl

master bath

lin.

MASTER BED RM.
12-0 x 13-8

DINING
12-10 x 12-0

KITCHEN
11-0 x 15-6

UTIL.
7-0 x 5-4

w
d

walk-in closet

fireplace

cl   cl

BED RM.
11-6 x 10-4

GREAT RM.
14-0 x 19-0
(cathedral ceiling)

FOYER
8-8 x 8-8

bath

PORCH

BED RM./
STUDY
11-4 x 12-0

walk-in closet

© 1992 Donald A. Gardner Architects, Inc.

This cozy, three-bedroom plan with arched windows and a wraparound porch displays a sense of elegance uncommon to a plan this size. Cathedral ceilings grace both the great room and the bedroom/study, while tray ceilings appear in the dining room and master bedroom. The open kitchen design allows for a serving island which is convenient to the breakfast area, dining room and rear porch. The master suite has direct access to the deck and also features a large walk-in closet and master bath with double-bowl vanity, shower and whirlpool tub. A covered breezeway connects the garage to the house.

PLAN 9693

Square Footage: 1,677

© 1998 Donald A. Gardner, Inc.

■ DESIGN BY DONALD A. GARDNER ARCHITECTS, INC.

PLAN 7683

Square Footage: 1,307

Graceful stick-work lends a Craftsman-type air to this fine three-bedroom home. The covered front porch ushers you into the spacious great room, where a cathedral ceiling, warming fireplace and built-ins enhance an already attractive room. Adjacent to the great room is the formal dining room, highlighted by a detailed ceiling and access to the rear porch. The U-shaped kitchen is also convenient to the great room, with a serving/snack bar providing a casual eating area. Three bedrooms—or make one a study—include a master suite with a detailed ceiling, walk-in closet and a private bath. Note the storage space in the two-car garage.

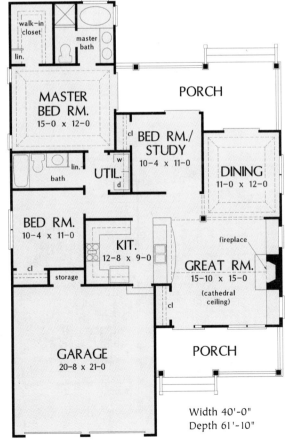

walk-in closet

master bath

lin.

MASTER BED RM.
15-0 x 12-0

PORCH

cl BED RM./ STUDY
10-4 x 11-0

bath lin.

UTIL.

DINING
11-0 x 12-0

BED RM.
10-4 x 11-0

cl

storage

KIT.
12-8 x 9-0

fireplace

cl

GREAT RM.
15-10 x 15-0
(cathedral ceiling)

GARAGE
20-8 x 21-0

PORCH

Width 40'-0"
Depth 61'-10"

© 1998   Donald A Gardner, Inc.

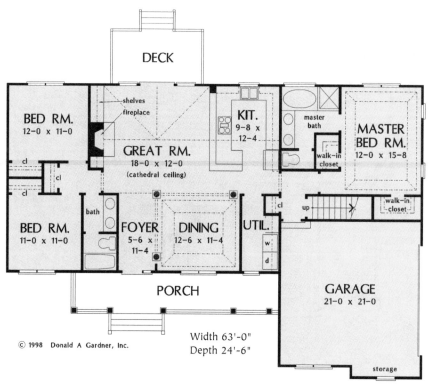

DECK

BED RM.
12-0 x 11-0

shelves
fireplace

KIT.
9-8 x
12-4

master
bath

**MASTER
BED RM.**
12-0 x 15-8

GREAT RM.
18-0 x 12-0
(cathedral ceiling)

walk-in
closet

cl
cl
cl

BED RM.
11-0 x 11-0

bath

FOYER
5-6 x
11-4

DINING
12-6 x 11-4

UTIL.

cl

up

w
d

walk-in
closet

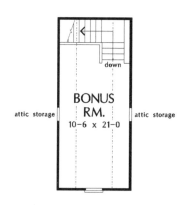

GARAGE
21-0 x 21-0

PORCH

Width 63'-0"
Depth 24'-6"

© 1998 Donald A Gardner, Inc.

storage

down

**BONUS
RM.**
10-6 x 21-0

attic storage   attic storage

A covered front porch, fine stick-work and detailed windows give this home a fine Craftsman-style feeling. The foyer opens to a formal dining room on the right, defined by pillars, and a spacious great room directly ahead. Here, a cathedral ceiling, built-in shelves, a warming fireplace and access to the rear deck enhance the welcome of this house. The kitchen is sure to please with plenty of counter and cabinet space. Two family bedrooms occupy the left side of the home and share a full hall bath. A lavish master suite offers two walk-in closets and a pampering bath with a separate tub and shower. Note the bonus room over the garage, perfect for storage or future expansion.

PLAN 7673

Square Footage: 1,544

© 1998 Donald A. Gardner, Inc.   B. NATHAN

■ DESIGN BY DONALD A. GARDNER ARCHITECTS, INC.

■ Design by Donald A. Gardner Architects, Inc.

©1997 Donald A. Gardner Architects, Inc.

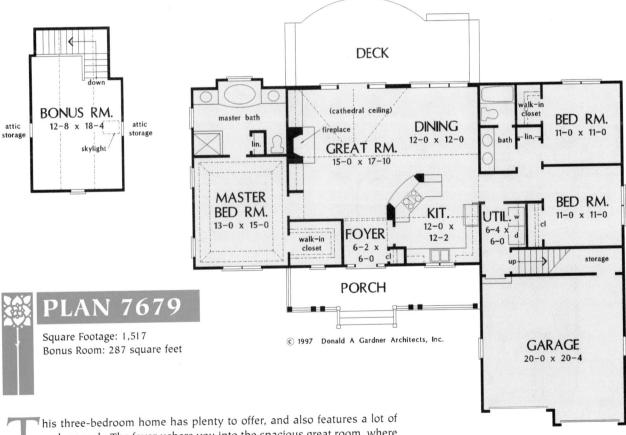

BONUS RM.
12-8 x 18-4

attic storage

attic storage

skylight

down

DECK

(cathedral ceiling)

master bath

lin.

fireplace

GREAT RM.
15-0 x 17-10

DINING
12-0 x 12-0

walk-in closet

bath

lin.

BED RM.
11-0 x 11-0

MASTER BED RM.
13-0 x 15-0

walk-in closet

FOYER
6-2 x 6-0

cl

KIT.
12-0 x 12-2

UTIL.
6-4 x 6-0

w d

cl

BED RM.
11-0 x 11-0

up

storage

PORCH

© 1997 Donald A Gardner Architects, Inc.

GARAGE
20-0 x 20-4

PLAN 7679

Square Footage: 1,517
Bonus Room: 287 square feet

This three-bedroom home has plenty to offer, and also features a lot of curb appeal. The foyer ushers you into the spacious great room, where amenities galore await you. These include a cathedral ceiling, warming fireplace flanked by built-ins and rear deck access. The efficient kitchen also has a lot to offer, with serving ease the main prize. Three bedrooms include two family bedrooms to the right, sharing a full hall bath, and a deluxe master suite to the left. The homeowner will love the ceiling detail, walk-in closet and pampering bath that awaits in this lavish suite. Note the large bonus room over the two-car garage—perfect for storage or future needs.

Width 61'-4"
Depth 48'-6"

■ DESIGN BY NORTHWEST HOME DESIGNING INC.

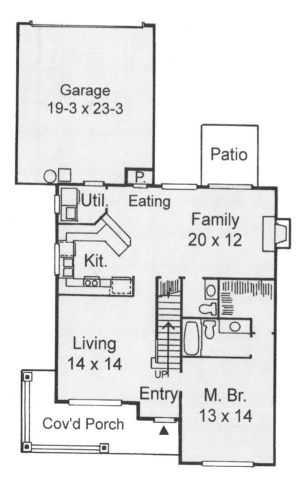

Width 38'-0"
Depth 61'-0"

PLAN W317

First Floor: 1,084 square feet
Second Floor: 461 square feet
Total: 1,545 square feet

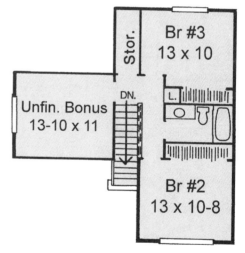

With the flavor of Craftsman-style evident in the pillared porch, shingle-and-siding facade and an attractive floor plan, this three-bedroom home is sure to please. The entry opens to the living room, which has easy access to the unique kitchen. A peninsula separates the kitchen from a sunny eating area and the nearby family room. Here a fireplace and access to a patio provide plenty of welcome. Located on the first floor for privacy, the master suite is designed to pamper. Complete with a walk-in closet and a private bath, this room will surely be a haven for the homeowner. Upstairs, two secondary bedrooms share a full bath and access to storage. An unfinished bonus room completes this level.

■ DESIGN BY POLLARD-HOSMAR ASSOCIATES

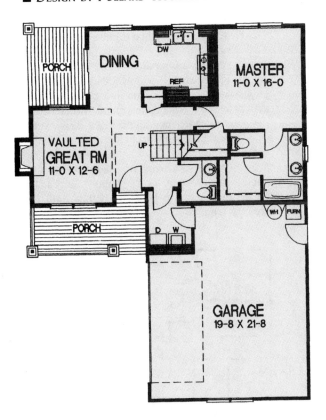

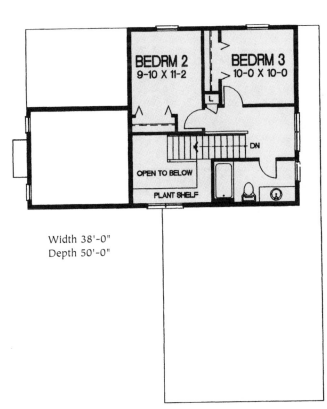

Width 38'-0"
Depth 50'-0"

This petite bungalow shows off its Craftsman roots in the rafter tails and pillared porch, while also presenting a floor plan from that era as well. The entry opens directly into the vaulted great room, where a fireplace and porch access wait to enhance any get-together. The U-shaped kitchen works well with the dining area. A first-floor master bedroom suite is located for privacy and features two walk-in closets and a private bath. The secondary bedrooms upstairs share a full hall bath. A two-car garage easily shelters the family fleet.

PLAN 8870

First Floor: 876 square feet
Second Floor: 437 square feet
Total: 1,313 square feet

■ DESIGN BY DONALD A. GARDNER ARCHITECTS, INC.

PLAN 7700

First Floor: 1,219 square feet
Second Floor: 450 square feet
Total: 1,669 square feet
Bonus Room: 406 square feet

This narrow lot home offers some of the extras usually reserved for wider lots, such as a wraparound porch and a two-car garage. A vaulted ceiling adds volume to the great room, while columns and a bay window add distinction to the dining room. The kitchen is designed for efficiency and offers access to the side porch and rear deck for outdoor dining options. The master suite is located on the first floor, while two secondary bedrooms and a bonus room are upstairs. The bonus room can be turned into a fourth bedroom with a bath for growing families.

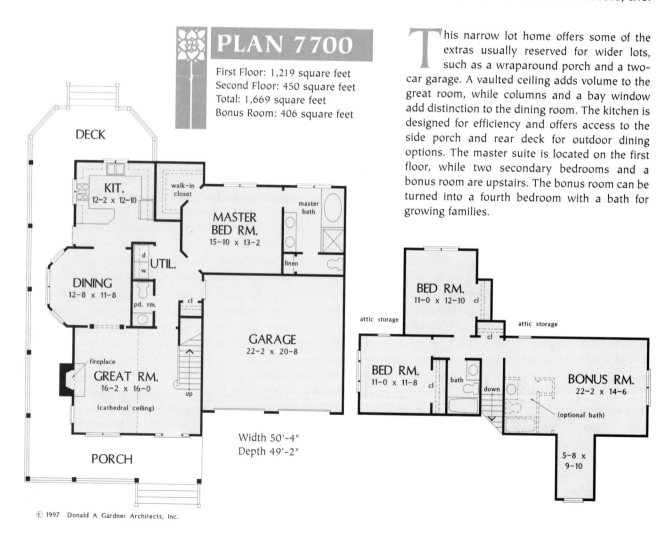

DECK

KIT.
12-2 x 12-10

walk-in closet

MASTER
BED RM.
15-10 x 13-2

master bath

linen

DINING
12-8 x 11-8

UTIL.

d w

pd. rm.

cl

GARAGE
22-2 x 20-8

fireplace

GREAT RM.
16-2 x 16-0

(cathedral ceiling)

up

PORCH

Width 50'-4"
Depth 49'-2"

BED RM.
11-0 x 12-10 cl

attic storage

attic storage

cl

BED RM.
11-0 x 11-8 cl

bath

down

BONUS RM.
22-2 x 14-6

(optional bath)

5-8 x 9-10

PLAN 8874

First Floor: 810 square feet
Second Floor: 696 square feet
Total: 1,506 square feet

Width 38'-0"
Depth 43'-5"

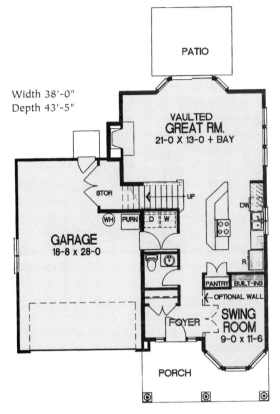

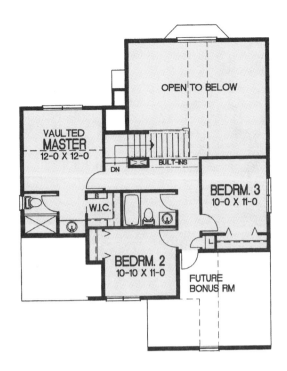

This Craftsman bungalow will look good in any neighborhood. Three graceful pillars define the front porch, while gabled rooflines are highlighted by shingles. Inside, the foyer has a swing room directly to the right—perfect for a home office, a cozy study or a formal dining room. An efficient kitchen offers a snack bar and is open to the vaulted great room. Here, a bay area offers access to the rear patio. A warming fireplace adds cheer to any gathering. The sleeping zone is on the second floor and features two family bedrooms sharing a full bath, and a vaulted master bedroom suite. Here, the homeowner will be pleased with a walk-in closet and a private bath. Note the abundance of storage in the garage.

■ Design by Pollard-Hosmar Associates

Perfect for a narrow lot, this Craftsman-flavored home offers plenty of curb appeal. Strong pillars support the covered porch which leads to an open foyer flanked by a staircase and a formal dining room— or make it a living room. Directly ahead is the gathering room, complete with a welcoming fireplace and rear yard access. The galley kitchen offers an adjacent break-fast room. The sleeping zone is on the second floor and includes two secondary suites, sharing a full hall bath, and a master suite with a walk-in closet and a private bath. The two-car garage easily shelters the family fleet.

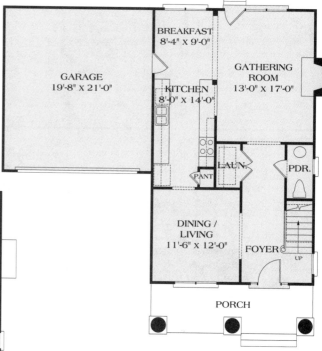

GARAGE
19'-8" x 21'-0"

BREAKFAST
8'-4" x 9'-0"

GATHERING
ROOM
13'-0" x 17'-0"

KITCHEN
8'-0" x 14'-0"

LAUN.

PDR.

PANT

DINING /
LIVING
11'-6" x 12'-0"

FOYER

UP

PORCH

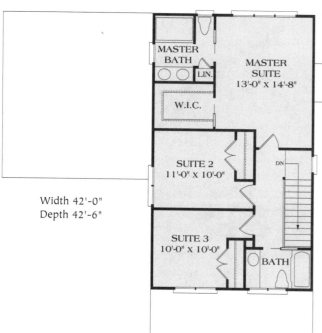

MASTER
BATH

LIN.

MASTER
SUITE
13'-0" x 14'-8"

W.I.C.

SUITE 2
11'-0" x 10'-0"

DN

SUITE 3
10'-0" x 10'-0"

BATH

Width 42'-0"
Depth 42'-6"

PLAN A241

First Floor: 792 square feet
Second Floor: 743 square feet
Total: 1,535 square feet

■ DESIGN BY SELECT HOME DESIGNS

FUTURE FAMILY

D
W

UNFINISHED BASEMENT 468 SQ.FT.

UP

DN

FUTURE BEDROOM

FUTURE DEN

PLAN Q527

Square Footage: 1,108
Unfinished Lower Level: 620 sq. ft.

Craftsman styling and a welcoming porch create marvelous curb appeal while a compact footprint allows construction economy. The kitchen, with generous cabinet space, flows into the dining area to create a casual country atmosphere. The dining area opens to a deck through sliding glass doors. A pampering master suite offers a walk-in closet, three bathrooms and features a bumped-out window. Two additional bedrooms boast boxed-out windows and share a full bath. The unfinished lower level has plenty of expansion potential. Plans include alternative basement and crawlspace foundations below the living area.

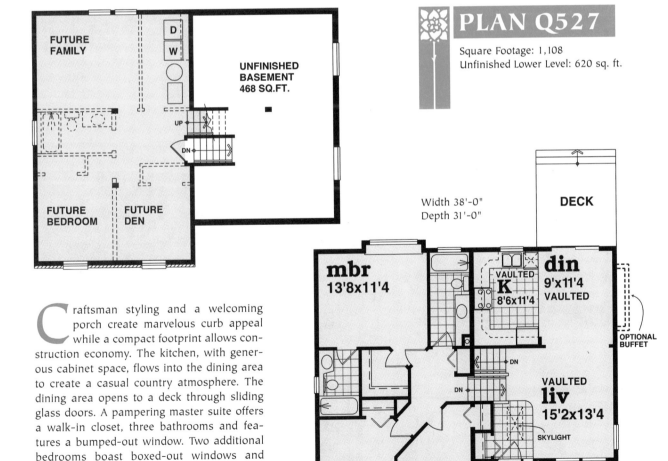

Width 38'-0"
Depth 31'-0"

DECK

mbr
13'8x11'4

VAULTED
K
8'6x11'4

din
9'x11'4
VAULTED

OPTIONAL BUFFET

DN

DN

VAULTED
liv
15'2x13'4

SKYLIGHT

br2
9'4x11'

br3
9'4x12'8

PORCH

DN

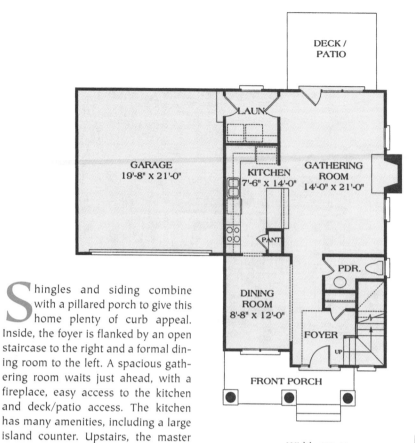

DECK / PATIO

GARAGE
19'-8" x 21'-0"

LAUN.

KITCHEN
7'-6" x 14'-0"

GATHERING ROOM
14'-0" x 21'-0"

PANT.

DINING ROOM
8'-8" x 12'-0"

PDR.

FOYER

UP

FRONT PORCH

Width 43'-4"
Depth 42'-10"

MASTER SUITE
15'-0" x 12'-0"

MASTER BATH

SUITE 2
11'-0" x 9'-6"

W.I.C.

BATH

LIN.

SUITE 3
10'-0" x 10'-6"

DN

OPEN TO BELOW

PLANT LEDGE

S hingles and siding combine with a pillared porch to give this home plenty of curb appeal. Inside, the foyer is flanked by an open staircase to the right and a formal dining room to the left. A spacious gathering room waits just ahead, with a fireplace, easy access to the kitchen and deck/patio access. The kitchen has many amenities, including a large island counter. Upstairs, the master bedroom suite is sure to please with a walk-in closet and a private bath. Two family bedrooms share a full hall bath, completing this level. The two-car garage will easily accommodate the family vehicles.

PLAN A240

First Floor: 774 square feet
Second Floor: 724 square feet
Total: 1,498 square feet

■ DESIGN BY LIVING CONCEPTS HOME PLANNING

■ DESIGN BY NORTHWEST HOME DESIGNING INC.

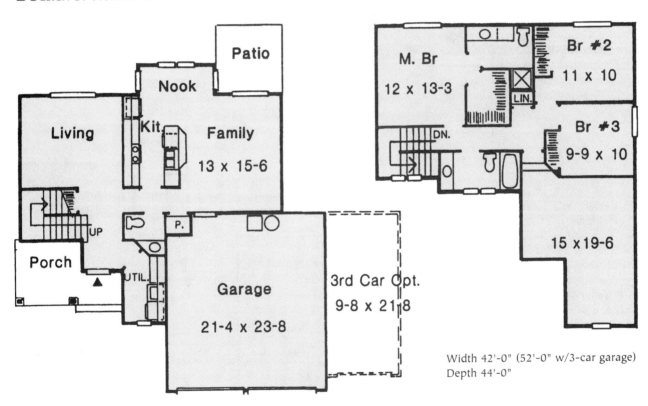

Patio

Nook

Living

Kit.

Family
13 x 15-6

Porch

UP

UTIL.

P.

Garage
21-4 x 23-8

3rd Car Opt.
9-8 x 21-8

M. Br
12 x 13-3

LIN.

Br #2
11 x 10

DN.

Br #3
9-9 x 10

15 x 19-6

Width 42'-0" (52'-0" w/3-car garage)
Depth 44'-0"

A trio of gables adorn this fine three-bedroom bungalow. Accented by shingles and siding, with a welcoming porch, this fine home will dress up any neighborhood. Inside, the efficient kitchen easily serves the sunny nook as well as the family room. Patio access further enhances the appeal of the family room. A separate living room is available for formal gatherings. Upstairs, two family bedrooms share a full hall bath, while the master bedroom suite features a walk-in closet and a private bath. Note the large bonus room on this level—perfect for a play room, study or fourth bedroom. The two-car garage has an option for a 3rd-car bay.

PLAN W314

First Floor: 807 square feet
Second Floor: 709 square feet
Total: 1,516 square feet
Bonus Room: 278 square feet

■ DESIGN BY LIVING CONCEPTS HOME PLANNING

PLAN A244

First Floor: 817 square feet
Second Floor: 759 square feet
Total: 1,576 square feet

Perfect for a narrow lot, this shingle-and-siding home is sure to please. With Craftsman-style influence, this bungalow has plenty to offer. The foyer opens directly into the gathering room, where a fireplace waits to add warmth and cheer to every occasion. The formal dining room is defined by graceful pillars and has a pass-through to the kitchen. U-shaped, the kitchen offers the pleasure of no cross-room traffic, as well as a window over the sink. Upstairs, two family bedrooms—or make one a study—share a full bath. The master bedroom suite offers a walk-in closet and a private bath with a dual-bowl vanity.

GARAGE
19'-8" X 21'-0"

LAUN.

KITCHEN
14'-4" X 11'-0"

PANT

PDR.

DINING
ROOM
9'-8" X 10'-8"

UP

FOYER

GATHERING
ROOM
14'-7" X 17'-4"

PORCH

Width 42'-0"
Depth 45'-6"

SUITE 2
10'-6" X 9'-2"

SUITE 3
10'-6" X 11'-6"

BATH

LIN.

DN

MASTER
BATH

W.I.C.

MASTER
SUITE
14'-7" X 14'-10"

■ DESIGN BY LIVING CONCEPTS HOME PLANNING

PLAN A242

First Floor: 792 square feet
Second Floor: 768 square feet
Total: 1,560 square feet

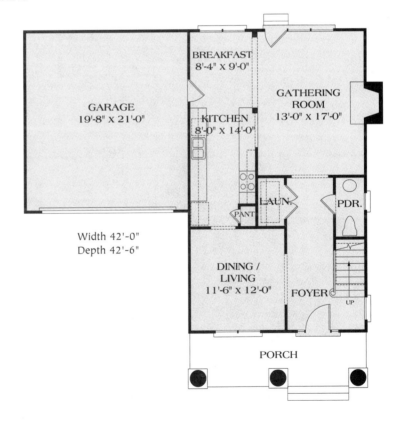

GARAGE
19'-8" X 21'-0"

BREAKFAST
8'-4" X 9'-0"

KITCHEN
8'-0" X 14'-0"

GATHERING
ROOM
13'-0" X 17'-0"

LAUN.

PANT

PDR.

Width 42'-0"
Depth 42'-6"

DINING /
LIVING
11'-6" X 12'-0"

FOYER

UP

PORCH

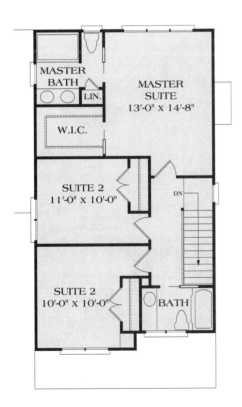

MASTER
BATH

LIN.

MASTER
SUITE
13'-0" X 14'-8"

W.I.C.

SUITE 2
11'-0" X 10'-0"

DN

SUITE 2
10'-0" X 10'-0"

BATH

Three solid pillars support the shed-like roof of this attractive bungalow. Inside, formal and informal gatherings will easily be accommodated. For casual get-togethers, the spacious gathering room with its fireplace and rear yard access is complemented by the nearby availability of the galley kitchen. Formal dinner parties will be a breeze in the dining room at the front of the house—or make it a formal living room if you have the need. Upstairs, two bedrooms share a full hall bath, while the master suite features a walk-in closet and a bath of its own.

PLAN A239

First Floor: 774 square feet
Second Floor: 723 square feet
Total: 1,497 square feet

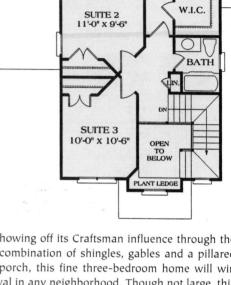

MASTER SUITE
15'-0" x 12'-0"

MASTER BATH

SUITE 2
11'-0" x 9'-6"

W.I.C.

BATH

LIN.

DN

SUITE 3
10'-0" x 10'-6"

OPEN TO BELOW

PLANT LEDGE

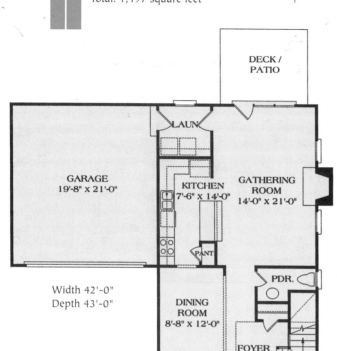

DECK / PATIO

LAUN

GARAGE
19'-8" x 21'-0"

KITCHEN
7'-6" x 14'-0"

GATHERING ROOM
14'-0" x 21'-0"

PANT

Width 42'-0"
Depth 43'-0"

PDR.

DINING ROOM
8'-8" x 12'-0"

FOYER

UP

PORCH

Showing off its Craftsman influence through the combination of shingles, gables and a pillared porch, this fine three-bedroom home will win approval in any neighborhood. Though not large, this two-story home has plenty to offer. A spacious gathering room has a fireplace for those cool fall evenings, while the nearby kitchen features a large work island—creating ease in serving. The formal dining room is pleasant and also has easy access to the kitchen. Up the curving stairs, the sleeping zone awaits. Two secondary bedrooms share a full hall bath and a linen closet, while the master suite includes a walk-in closet and a private bath.

■ DESIGN BY LIVING CONCEPTS HOME PLANNING

■ DESIGN BY ALAN MASCORD DESIGN ASSOCIATES, INC.

PLAN 7464

First Floor: 847 square feet
Second Floor: 845 square feet
Total: 1,692 square feet

Shingles-and-stone, gables and a covered porch—all elements of Craftsman-styling. This petite bungalow is perfect for narrow lots and still provides plenty of amenities for the whole family. The entry opens directly into the vaulted great room. Here, a wood stove, built-ins and an adjacent, vaulted dining room provide fantastic ambience. The C-shaped kitchen features a sink overlooking the great room, a pantry and plenty of counter and cabinet space. A nearby nook offers outdoor access and built-in shelves. Upstairs, the master suite is designed to pamper, with a private balcony, a walk-in closet and a pampering bath. Two secondary bedrooms share a full hall bath with a dual-bowl vanity. The two-car garage enters from the back of the property, hiding it effectively from the road.

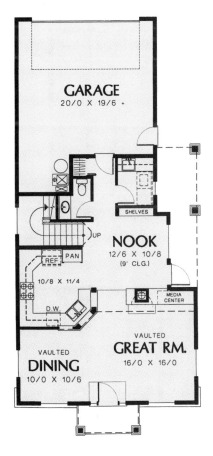

Width 27'-0"
Depth 61'-0"

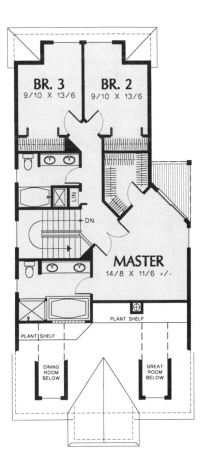

■ DESIGN BY DRUMMOND DESIGNS, INC.

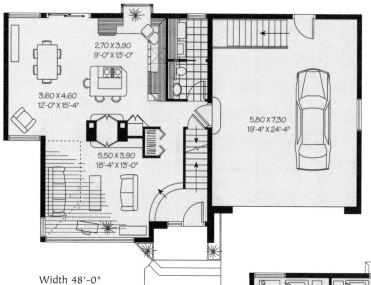

2,70 X 3,90
9'-0" X 13'-0"

3,60 X 4,60
12'-0" X 15'-4"

5,50 X 3,90
18'-4" X 13'-0"

5,80 X 7,30
19'-4" X 24'-4"

Width 48'-0"
Depth 30'-0"

A sturdy and attractive bungalow, this fine three-bedroom home will look good in any neighborhood. The raised foyer overlooks a spacious living room, where a through-fireplace and a wall of windows add to the already abundant charm. In the L-shaped kitchen, a cooktop work island/snack bar benefits from the through-fireplace, while the adjacent dining room offers access and views to the rear yard via sliding glass doors. Upstairs, a small balcony overlooks the living room. Three bedrooms—one with a walk-in closet—share a lavish bath.

PLAN Z052

First Floor: 760 square feet
Second Floor: 792 square feet
Total: 1,552 square feet

3,00 X 3,00
10'-0" X 10'-0"

3,00 X 4,60
10'-0" X 15'-4"

4,20 X 4,60
14'-0" X 15'-4"

■ DESIGN BY HOME PLANNERS

PLAN 3496

Square Footage: 2,033

L

Get more out of your home-building dollars with this unique one-story bungalow. A covered front porch provides sheltered entry into a spacious living room. A bookshelf and a column are special touches. The dining room enjoys a sloped ceiling, a wet bar and direct access to the rear covered patio. In the nearby kitchen, a breakfast bar accommodates quick meals. The adjacent family room rounds out this casual living area. The large master suite pampers with a sitting area, patio access and a luxurious bath which features a corner tub, a separate shower and dual lavatories. Two secondary bedrooms share a full hall bath.

QUOTE ONE®

Cost to build? See page 182
to order complete cost estimate
to build this house in your area!

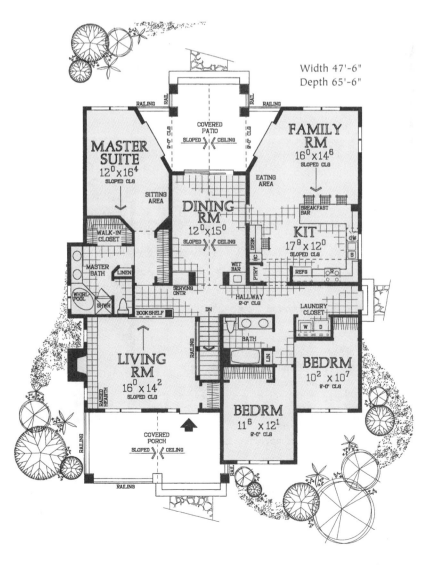

Width 47'-6"
Depth 65'-6"

COVERED PATIO — SLOPED CEILING

MASTER SUITE 12⁰ x 16⁴ SLOPED CLG

SITTING AREA

WALK-IN CLOSET

MASTER BATH

LINEN

WHIRL POOL

SHWR

BOOKSHELF

DINING RM 12⁰ x 15⁰ SLOPED CEILING

FAMILY RM 16⁰ x 14⁶ SLOPED CLG

EATING AREA

BREAKFAST BAR

KIT 17⁹ x 12⁰ SLOPED CLG

DW

REFS

WET BAR

PTRY

DESK

SERVING CNTR

HALLWAY 9'-0" CLG

REFS

LAUNDRY CLOSET

W D

LIVING RM 16⁰ x 14² SLOPED CLG

RAISED HEARTH

DN

RAILING

BATH

LIN

BEDRM 10² x 10⁷ 9'-0" CLG

BEDRM 11⁶ x 12¹ 9'-0" CLG

COVERED PORCH SLOPED CEILING

RAILING

■ DESIGN BY STUDER RESIDENTIAL DESIGNS, INC.

PLAN B510

Square Footage: 1,797

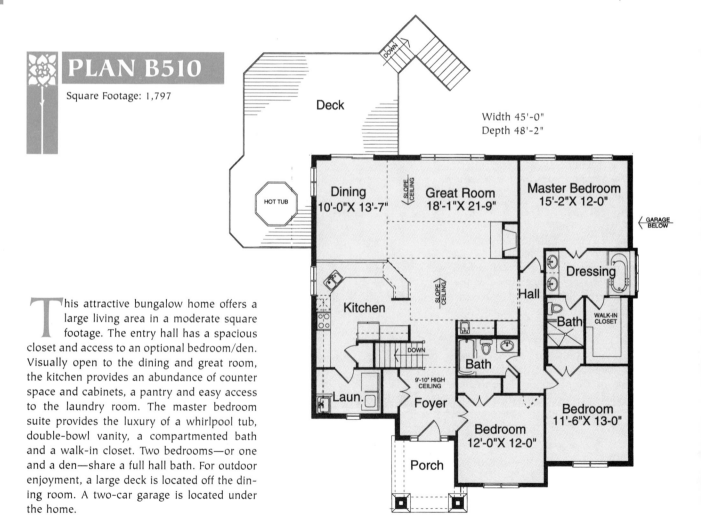

Width 45'-0"
Depth 48'-2"

Deck

HOT TUB

Dining
10'-0"X 13'-7"

SLOPE CEILING

Great Room
18'-1"X 21-9"

Master Bedroom
15'-2"X 12'-0"

GARAGE BELOW

Dressing

Kitchen

SLOPE CEILING

Hall

Bath

WALK-IN CLOSET

DOWN

Bath

Laun.

Foyer

9'-10" HIGH CEILING

Bedroom
12'-0"X 12'-0"

Bedroom
11'-6"X 13-0"

Porch

This attractive bungalow home offers a large living area in a moderate square footage. The entry hall has a spacious closet and access to an optional bedroom/den. Visually open to the dining and great room, the kitchen provides an abundance of counter space and cabinets, a pantry and easy access to the laundry room. The master bedroom suite provides the luxury of a whirlpool tub, double-bowl vanity, a compartmented bath and a walk-in closet. Two bedrooms—or one and a den—share a full hall bath. For outdoor enjoyment, a large deck is located off the dining room. A two-car garage is located under the home.

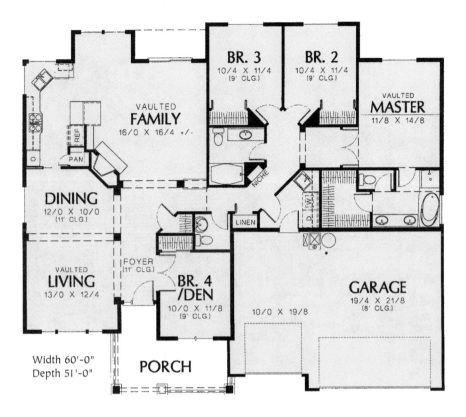

VAULTED
FAMILY
16/0 X 16/4 +/-

BR. 3
10/4 X 11/4
(9' CLG.)

BR. 2
10/4 X 11/4
(9' CLG.)

VAULTED
MASTER
11/8 X 14/8

DINING
12/0 X 10/0
(11' CLG.)

NICHE

LINEN

GARAGE
19/4 X 21/8
(8' CLG.)

VAULTED
LIVING
13/0 X 12/4

FOYER
(11' CLG.)

**BR. 4
/DEN**
10/0 X 11/8
(9' CLG.)

10/0 X 19/8

Width 60'-0"
Depth 51'-0"

PORCH

1,701 To 2,100 Square Feet

Craftsman styling is highly evident in this fine three-bedroom bungalow. From its rafter tails, detailed windows, stone and shingles and gabled rooflines, this home is sure to win in any neighborhood. The foyer is flanked by a vaulted living room and a den or fourth bedroom. A formal dining room is defined by pillars and has easy access to the efficient kitchen. A vaulted family room features a corner fireplace and sliding glass doors to the outdoors. Two family bedrooms share a hall bath, while the vaulted master bath offers a walk-in closet and a private bath. The three-car garage will easily shelter the family fleet.

PLAN 7466

Square Footage: 1,997

■ DESIGN BY ALAN MASCORD DESIGN ASSOCIATES, INC.

PLAN 3314

Square Footage: 1,959

L

This bountiful bungalow is an owner's paradise with a luxurious master suite that far exceeds its Craftsman-style roots. The large gathering room is joined to the dining room and is accented with a large brick fireplace. The galley kitchen has an abundance of cabinet space, a walk-in pantry and a full-sized snack bar from the sunny breakfast room. A lovely screened porch that is accessed from both the dining room and the breakfast room adds an extra measure of charm to casual living. Two secondary bedrooms include one that can double as a den with a foyer entrance and another that is romanced with an expanse of corner windows and a wrap-around flower box.

Cost to build? See page 182
to order complete cost estimate
to build this house in your area!

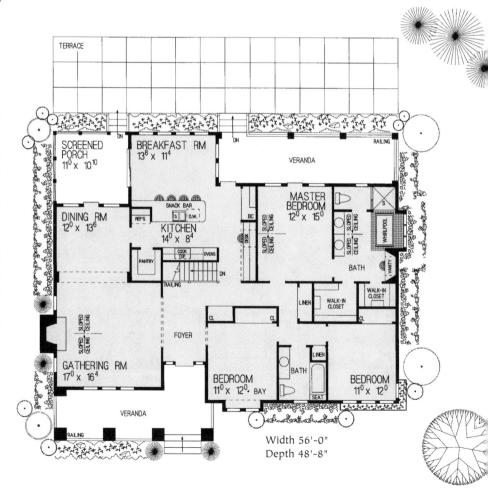

Width 56'-0"
Depth 48'-8"

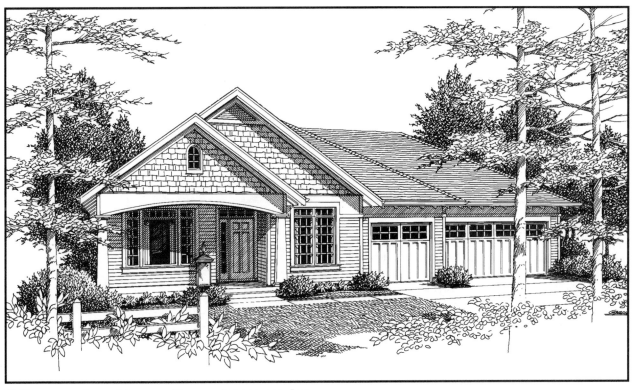

■ DESIGN BY ALAN MASCORD DESIGN ASSOCIATES, INC.

1,701 To 2,100 Square Feet

PLAN 7468

Square Footage: 1,999

Width 60'-0"
Depth 52'-0"

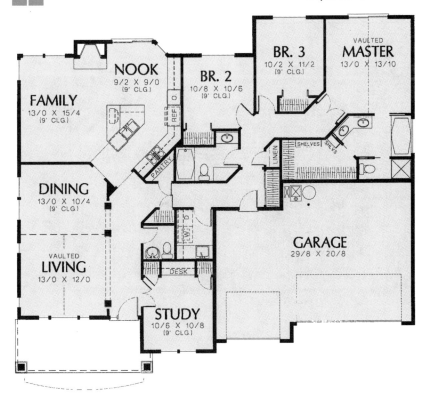

There's room for all in this fine Craftsman bungalow home. An attractively covered front porch welcomes family and friends into a vaulted living room. A formal dining room at one end works well with this space, providing a good place for entertaining. The angled kitchen features plenty of cabinet and counter space and shares a worktop snack bar with the nook as well as the family room. A warming fireplace becomes a tie to these three rooms, adding cheer to any gathering. A study at the front of the house offers a built-in desk, flanked by closets. The sleeping zone consists of two family bedrooms sharing a hall bath and a vaulted master suite complete with a walk-in closet and a pampering bath. A three-car garage is perfect to shelter one's cars.

The cozy atmosphere of this delightful bungalow is warm and inviting. The impressive view from the foyer includes the great room with a fireplace and triple windows across the rear. The formal dining room adds dimension to the entry and is conveniently located to the kitchen. French doors and skylights flood the breakfast area with natural light and a recessed alcove provides for efficient furniture placement. Split bedrooms offer privacy to the master bedroom suite with a large walk-in closet and a lavish bath. Two secondary bedrooms and a full basement expand this home to create a home perfect for the empty-nester or the growing family.

PLAN B511

Square Footage: 1,980

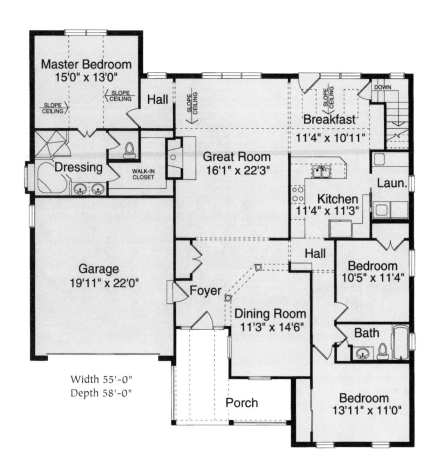

Master Bedroom 15'0" x 13'0"

SLOPE CEILING   SLOPE CEILING

Hall

SLOPE CEILING

SLOPE CEILING   DOWN

Breakfast 11'4" x 10'11"

Dressing   WALK-IN CLOSET

Great Room 16'1" x 22'3"

Laun.

Kitchen 11'4" x 11'3"

Garage 19'11" x 22'0"

Hall

Bedroom 10'5" x 11'4"

Foyer

Dining Room 11'3" x 14'6"

Bath

Width 55'-0"
Depth 58'-0"

Porch

Bedroom 13'11" x 11'0"

■ DESIGN BY STUDER RESIDENTIAL DESIGNS, INC.

■ DESIGN BY THE SATER DESIGN COLLECTION

Exposed rafters, lattice panels and a deep covered porch make a strong Arts and Crafts architectural statement. The covered entry porch runs the width of the home, creating an outdoor haven for cozy family gatherings and leisurely chats with neighbors. Inside, decorative arches and columns make a grand entrance to the living and dining areas. The gourmet kitchen provides a pass-through to the formal dining room, while a focal-point fireplace warms the great room. A secluded master suite nestles to the back of the plan, with private access to a sundeck and French doors to the covered porch. The bayed sitting area offers space for reading and sunlight to the homeowner's retreat. His and Hers walk-in closets provide plenty of storage, while a garden soaking tub enjoys a bright, bumped-out bay in the master bath. The plan includes pier and crawlspace foundation options.

PLAN 6694

Square Footage: 1,792

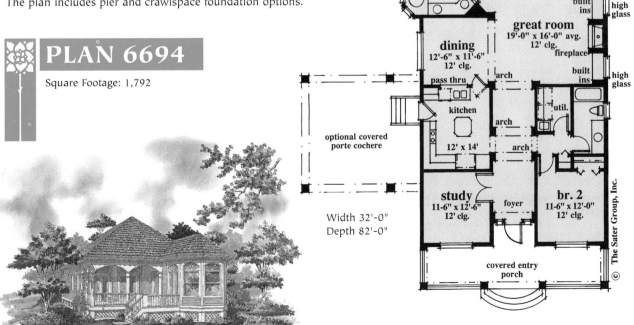

REAR ELEVATION

Width 32'-0"
Depth 82'-0"

master
12'-0" x 16'-6"
12' clg.

sundeck

his

hers

covered porch
19'-0" x 16'-0" avg.

built ins

high glass

great room
19'-0" x 16'-0" avg.
12' clg.

fireplace

dining
12'-6" x 11'-6"
12' clg.

pass thru

arch

built ins

high glass

kitchen
12' x 14'

arch

util.

arch

optional covered porte cochere

arch

study
11'-6" x 12'-6"
12' clg.

foyer

br. 2
11'-6" x 12'-0"
12' clg.

covered entry porch

© The Sater Group, Inc.

■ DESIGN BY AHMANN DESIGN, INC.

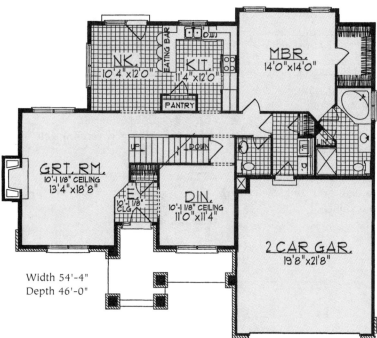

Width 54'-4"
Depth 46'-0"

PLAN U212

First Floor: 1,365 square feet
Second Floor: 518 square feet
Total: 1,883 square feet

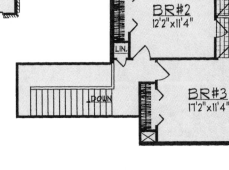

Pillars, gables, shingles and stone—all elements of fine Craftsman style. This comfortable one-and-a-half story home is sure to look good in any neighborhood. The entry is flanked by a formal dining room to the right and a spacious great room on the left. Here, a warming fireplace adds cheer to any gathering. The U-shaped kitchen features a snack bar, large pantry and an adjacent nook with rear yard access. Located on the first floor for privacy, the master bedroom suite is designed to pamper. Complete with a walk-in closet and a sumptuous bath, this suite guarantees relaxation. Upstairs, two family bedrooms share a full bath.

■ DESIGN BY LARRY E. BELK DESIGNS

A thoughtful mix of Arts and Crafts elements lends charm to this modern traditional home. The foyer opens to formal rooms, which feature lovely tray ceilings, through arches and columns. A fireplace is flanked by built-ins in the living room, where access to the rear patio is another bonus. A gourmet kitchen features a food prep island with a snack counter and easily serves the dining room through a butler's pantry. The master retreat has its own door to the patio, and a deluxe bath.

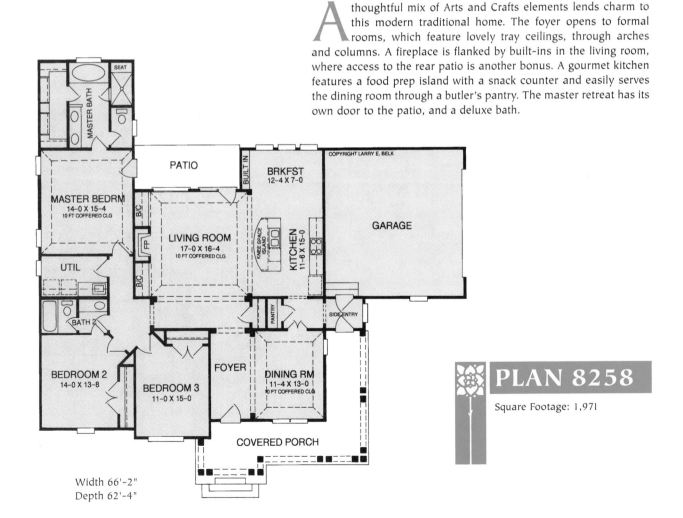

Width 66'-2"
Depth 62'-4"

PLAN 8258

Square Footage: 1,971

■ DESIGN BY NORTHWEST HOME DESIGNING INC.

PLAN W309

First Floor: 1,454 square feet
Second Floor: 627 square feet
Total: 2,081 square feet

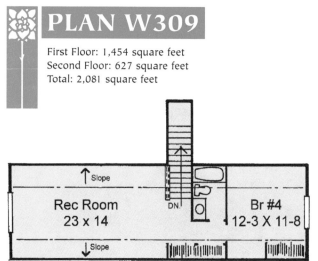

Rec Room
23 x 14

Br #4
12-3 X 11-8

Slope

Slope

DN

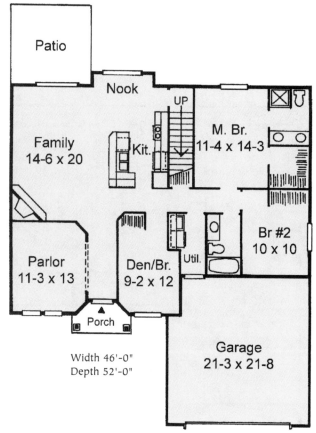

Patio

Nook

Family
14-6 x 20

Kit.

UP

M. Br.
11-4 x 14-3

Parlor
11-3 x 13

Den/Br.
9-2 x 12

Util.

Br #2
10 x 10

Porch

Width 46'-0"
Depth 52'-0"

Garage
21-3 x 21-8

Craftsman style is recognized from its various elements, and this bungalow certainly has them. From the pillars at the front door, and the gabled rooflines, to the rafter tails and shingles, this home is sure to be a favorite in any neighborhood. The entryway presents a formal yet cozy parlor, then leads back to the spacious family room. Here, a corner fireplace casts its cheer throughout the room and into the kitchen, where a snack bar does double duty as a work surface island. A patio is available nearby, for dining alfresco. Two bedrooms complete this floor, one a pampering master suite with a walk-in closet and a private bath. Upstairs, a huge rec room is available for more casual pursuits, with a fourth bedroom and a full bath nearby.

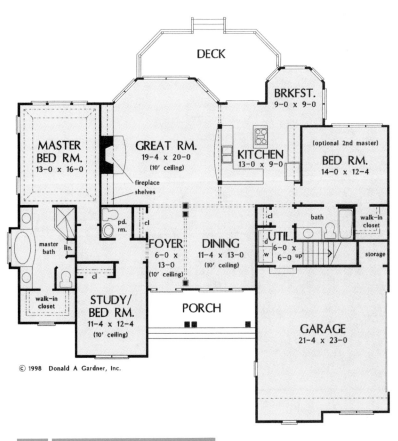

DECK

BRKFST.
9-0 x 9-0

MASTER
BED RM.
13-0 x 16-0

GREAT RM.
19-4 x 20-0
(10' ceiling)

KITCHEN
13-0 x 9-0

(optional 2nd master)
BED RM.
14-0 x 12-4

fireplace
shelves

master
bath

lin.

walk-in
closet

pd.
rm.

cl

FOYER
6-0 x
13-0
(10' ceiling)

DINING
11-4 x 13-0
(10' ceiling)

cl

UTIL.
6-0 x
6-0

bath

walk-in
closet

storage

STUDY/
BED RM.
11-4 x 12-4
(10' ceiling)

PORCH

GARAGE
21-4 x 23-0

© 1998   Donald A Gardner, Inc.

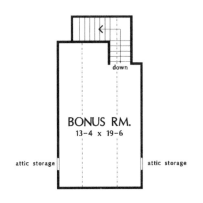

BONUS RM.
13-4 x 19-6

down

attic storage

attic storage

PLAN 7695

Square Footage: 1,966
Bonus Room: 355 square feet

Width 62'-6"
Depth 56'-10"

Shingles, gables, stick-work and pillars all combine to give this home plenty of curb appeal, with Craftsman 9-over-1 windows adding the finishing touch. Inside, the foyer is flanked by a formal dining room and the hall to the study and master suite. Defined by pillars, the dining room has easy access to the efficient kitchen. A bayed breakfast room provides a pleasant place to have an early morning coffee break. The spacious great room, with a 10-foot ceiling, a warming fireplace and built-in shelves will be a favorite place to gather together. The master suite is lavish with its amenities, which include a walk-in closet, a separate tub and shower and two vanities. An optional second master suite is located on the right side of the home, and it offers a walk-in closet and access to a full bath.

© 1998 Donald A. Gardner, Inc.

■ DESIGN BY DONALD A. GARDNER ARCHITECTS, INC.

© 1998 Donald A. Gardner, Inc.

B. NATHAN

■ DESIGN BY DONALD A. GARDNER ARCHITECTS, INC.

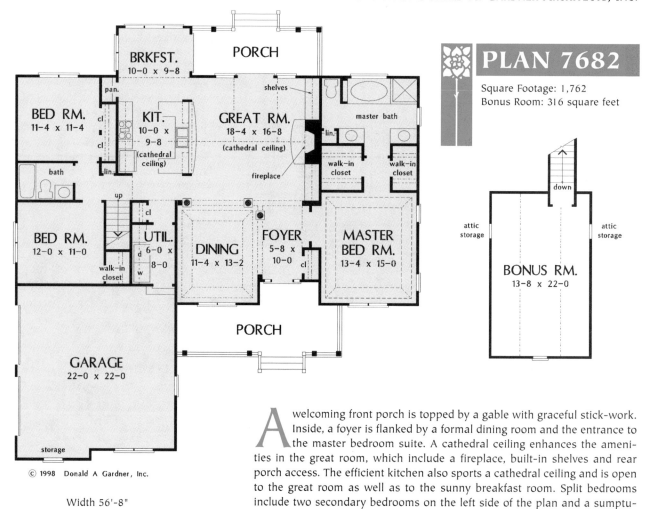

© 1998 Donald A Gardner, Inc.

Width 56'-8"
Depth 59'-0"

PLAN 7682

Square Footage: 1,762
Bonus Room: 316 square feet

A welcoming front porch is topped by a gable with graceful stick-work. Inside, a foyer is flanked by a formal dining room and the entrance to the master bedroom suite. A cathedral ceiling enhances the amenities in the great room, which include a fireplace, built-in shelves and rear porch access. The efficient kitchen also sports a cathedral ceiling and is open to the great room as well as to the sunny breakfast room. Split bedrooms include two secondary bedrooms on the left side of the plan and a sumptuous master suite on the right. Here, the homeowner will feel well pampered with two walk-in closets, a separate tub and shower and two vanities. Note the large bonus room over the garage—perfect for future expansion.

■ DESIGN BY NORTHWEST HOME DESIGNING INC.

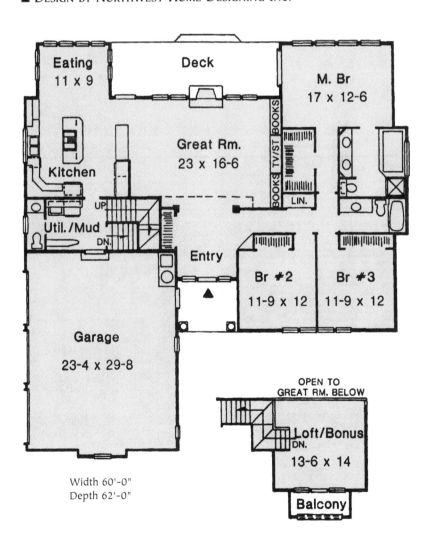

Width 60'-0"
Depth 62'-0"

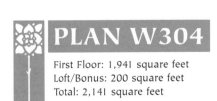

Craftsman style is very evident on this fine bungalow home. From its shingles, gabled rooflines, detailed windows and definitive pillars to its grand layout, this home is sure to please. A spacious great room features a fireplace flanked by windows, a wall of built-ins and easy access to the L-shaped kitchen. Adjacent to the kitchen is a sunny eating area, perfect for early morning coffee. In the sleeping zone, two family bedrooms share a full hall bath, while the master suite is full of amenities. Complete with a walk-in closet, a wall of windows and a sumptuous bath, this suite will be a haven for any homeowner. A loft/bonus area overlooks the great room, and offers a private outdoor balcony.

PLAN W304

First Floor: 1,941 square feet
Loft/Bonus: 200 square feet
Total: 2,141 square feet

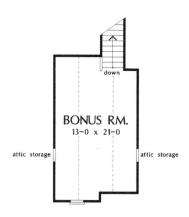

BONUS RM.
13-0 x 21-0

down

attic storage   attic storage

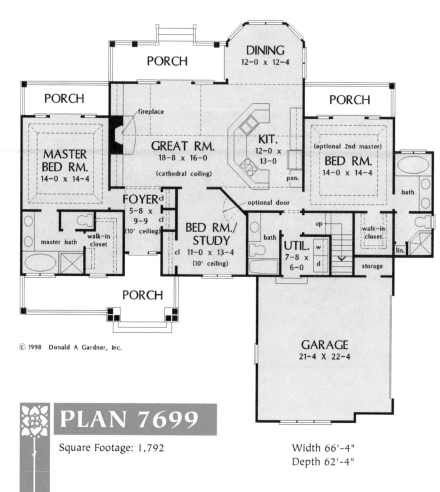

PORCH

DINING
12-0 x 12-4

PORCH

PORCH

PORCH

fireplace

MASTER
BED RM.
14-0 x 14-4

GREAT RM.
18-8 x 16-0
(cathedral ceiling)

KIT.
12-0 x
13-0

(optional 2nd master)

BED RM.
14-0 x 14-4

bath

pan.

master bath

walk-in
closet

FOYER
5-8 x
9-9
(10' ceiling)

cl

cl

BED RM./
STUDY
cl 11-0 x 13-4
(10' ceiling)

optional door

bath

UTIL.
7-8 x
6-0

up

w
d

walk-in
closet

lin.

storage

PORCH

© 1998   Donald A Gardner, Inc.

GARAGE
21-4 X 22-4

Stucco, stone and shingles combined with Craftsman windows, rafter tails and a pillared porch give this home plenty of curb appeal. A great room features a fireplace, built-ins, access to the rear porch and a cathedral ceiling. The unique kitchen offers tons of counter and cabinet space and has easy access to the bayed dining area. Two full bedroom suites could serve as separate master suites, or one as a fine guest suite. A bedroom/study is available for an in-home office or unexpected guests. Note the large bonus room over the two-car garage.

PLAN 7699

Square Footage: 1,792

Width 66'-4"
Depth 62'-4"

©1998 Donald A. Gardner, Inc.

■ DESIGN BY DONALD A. GARDNER ARCHITECTS, INC.

■ DESIGN BY NORTHWEST HOME DESIGNING INC.

PLAN W313

Square Footage: 1,933

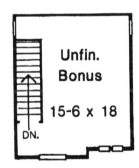

Unfin.
Bonus

15-6 x 18

DN.

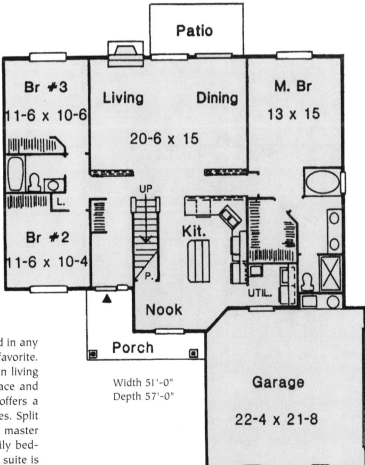

Patio

Br #3
11-6 x 10-6

Living

Dining

M. Br
13 x 15

20-6 x 15

L.

UP

Br #2
11-6 x 10-4

Kit.

P.

UTIL.

Nook

Porch

Width 51'-0"
Depth 57'-0"

Garage

22-4 x 21-8

This fine Craftsman bungalow will look good in any neighborhood and will surely be a family favorite. Entertaining will be a breeze with the open living and dining area, which is highlighted by a fireplace and access to the rear patio. The L-shaped kitchen offers a large island and an adjacent nook for casual times. Split bedrooms ensure privacy, with the sumptuous master suite on the right side of the home and two family bedrooms on the left, sharing a full bath. The master suite is designed with amenities, including a walk-in closet and a separate tub and shower. The unfinished bonus space is available for future use as a home office, a playroom for kids, a media room or a guest suite, it's your choice!

■ DESIGN BY ALAN MASCORD DESIGN ASSOCIATES, INC.

Width 40'-0"
Depth 47'-0"

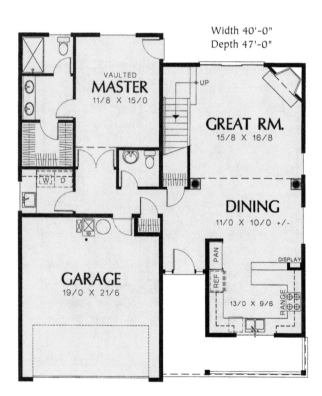

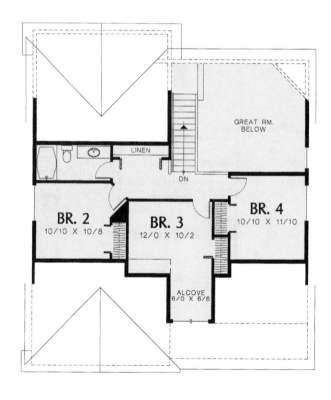

PLAN 7497

First Floor: 1,198 square feet
Second Floor: 673 square feet
Total: 1,871 square feet

This petite bungalow would be perfect for either empty-nesters or those just starting out. The charm of the exterior is echoed inside, where a comfortable floor plan is very accommodating with its layout. A G-shaped kitchen has no cross-room traffic and serves the dining room with a pass-through. The spacious great room features a corner fireplace and sliding glass doors to the rear yard. The vaulted master bedroom, on the first floor, offers a walk-in closet and private bath. Upstairs, three secondary bedrooms are available—one with an alcove—and share a full hall bath and a large linen closet.

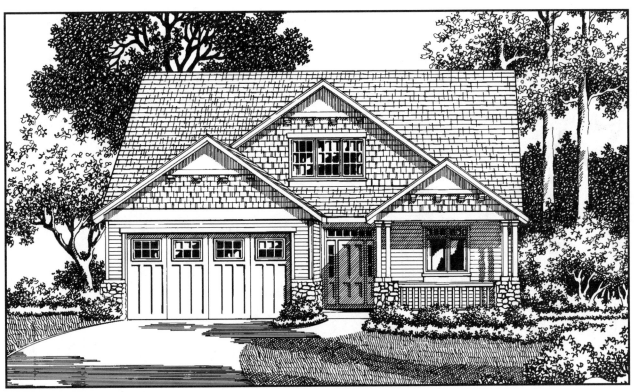

■ DESIGN BY ALAN MASCORD DESIGN ASSOCIATES, INC.

PLAN 7472

First Floor: 1,198 square feet
Second Floor: 668 square feet
Total: 1,866 square feet

Width 40'-0"
Depth 47'-0"

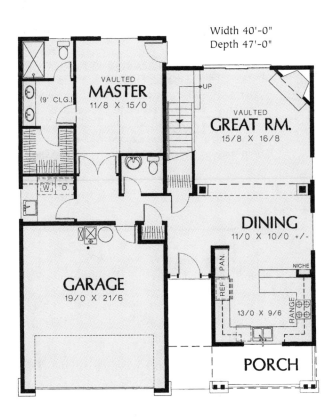

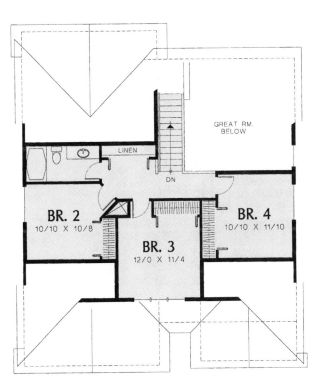

A fine example of a Craftsman bungalow, this four-bedroom home will be a delight to own. The efficient kitchen offers a serving island into the dining area, while the glow from the corner fireplace in the great room adds cheer to all the area. Located on the first floor for privacy, the vaulted master suite features a walk-in closet, a private bath with a dual-bowl vanity and access to the rear yard. Upstairs, three secondary bedrooms share a full hall bath and a large linen closet. The two-car garage will easily shelter the family fleet.

■ DESIGN BY DESIGN TRADITIONS

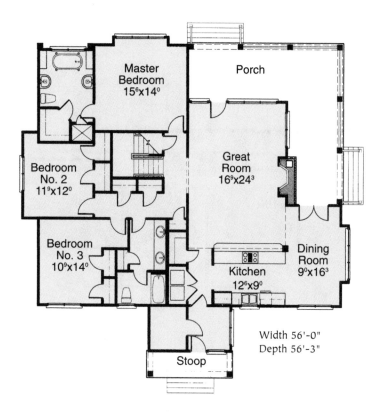

Width 56'-0"
Depth 56'-3"

PLAN T183

Square Footage: 2,019
Loft: 363 square feet

This design takes inspiration from the casual fishing cabins of the Pacific Northwest and interprets it for modern livability. It offers three options for a main entrance. One door opens onto a mud porch, where a small hall leads to a galley kitchen and the vaulted great room. Two French doors on the side porch open into a dining room with bay-window seating. Another porch entrance opens directly into the great room, which is centered around a massive stone fireplace and is accented with a beautiful wall of windows. The secluded master bedroom features a master bath with a clawfoot tub and twin pedestal sinks, as well as a separate shower and walk-in closet. Two more bedrooms share a spacious bath. Ideal for a lounge or extra sleeping space, an unfinished loft looks over the great room.

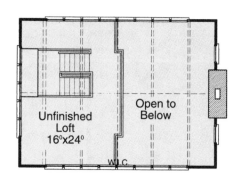

PLAN 3318

First Floor: 1,557 square feet
Second Floor: 540 square feet
Total: 2,097 square feet

Details make the difference in this darling two-bedroom (or three-bedroom if you choose) bungalow. From covered front porch to covered rear porch, there's a fine floor plan. Living areas are to the rear: a gathering room with through-fireplace and pass-through counter to the kitchen and a formal dining room with porch access. To the front of the plan are a family bedroom and bath and a study. The study can also be planned as a guest bedroom with bath. Upstairs is the master bedroom with a through fireplace to the bath and a gigantic walk-in closet.

QUOTE ONE®

Cost to build? See page 182
to order complete cost estimate
to build this house in your area!

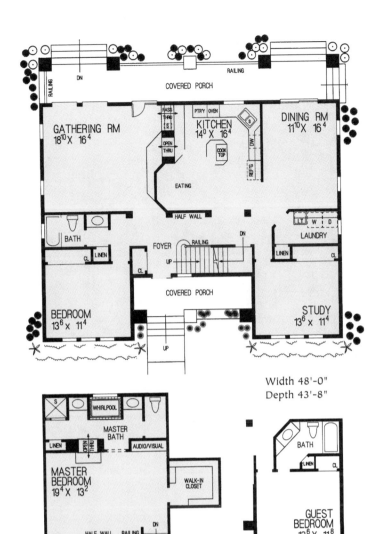

Width 48'-0"
Depth 43'-8"

OPTIONAL FIRST FLOOR PLAN

1,701 To 2,100 Square Feet

■ DESIGN BY HOME PLANNERS

■ DESIGN BY ALAN MASCORD DESIGN ASSOCIATES, INC.

The combination of rafter tails, stone-and-siding and gabled rooflines give this home plenty of curb appeal. The Craftsman styling on this three-bedroom bungalow is highly attractive. Inside, a cozy vaulted den is entered through double doors, just to the left of the foyer. A spacious, vaulted great room features a fireplace and is right near the formal dining room, providing entertaining ease. The kitchen offers an octagonal island, a corner sink with a window and a pantry. Up the angled staircase is the sleeping zone. Here two secondary bedrooms share a hall bath, while the master suite is enhanced with a private bath and a walk-in closet. The three-car garage easily shelters the family fleet.

MASTER
11/10 X 14/4

DN

BR. 3
9/10 X 11/10

BR. 2
11/8 X 12/0

Width 50'-0"
Depth 45'-0"

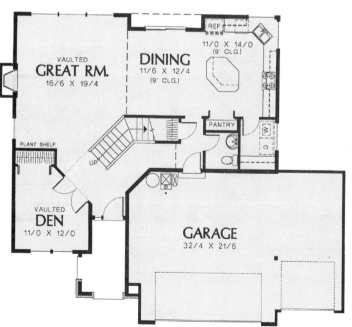

VAULTED
GREAT RM.
16/6 X 19/4

DINING
11/6 X 12/4
(9' CLG.)

REF

11/0 X 14/0
(9' CLG.)

PANTRY

W
D

PLANT SHELF

UP

VAULTED
DEN
11/0 X 12/0

GARAGE
32/4 X 21/6

PLAN 7521

First Floor: 1,097 square feet
Second Floor: 807 square feet
Total: 1,904 square feet

■ DESIGN BY POLLARD-HOSMAR ASSOCIATES

PLAN 8877

First Floor: 1,155 square feet
Second Floor: 930 square feet
Total: 2,085 square feet

Craftsman details abound on this fine four-bedroom home. From stick work, rafter tails and pillars, to stone, shingles and siding, this design will look good in any neighborhood! Inside, a living/dining area offers a fine area for formal entertaining—note the option for a fireplace in the living area. Casual living takes place at the rear of the home, with a large family room featuring a warming fireplace and built-ins. The open kitchen assures that the cook won't miss out on any of the fun. Upstairs, three family bedrooms share a full hall bath, while the master suite pampers the homeowner. A huge future bonus room is also on this level and offers many possibilities. The three-car garage will easily shelter the family fleet, or provide tons of work space.

Width 40'-0"
Depth 50'-0"

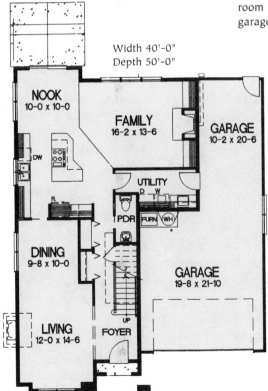

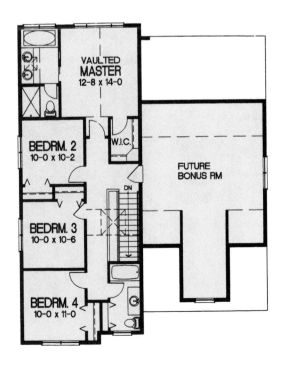

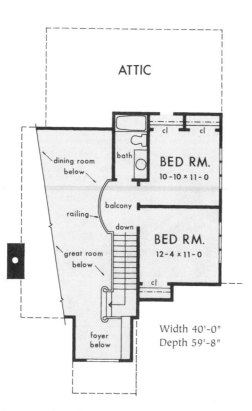

ATTIC

bath

cl   cl

BED RM.
10-10 × 11-0

dining room below

balcony

railing

down

great room below

BED RM.
12-4 × 11-0

cl

foyer below

Width 40'-0"
Depth 59'-8"

PLAN 9641

First Floor: 1,292 square feet
Second Floor: 423 square feet
Total: 1,715 square feet

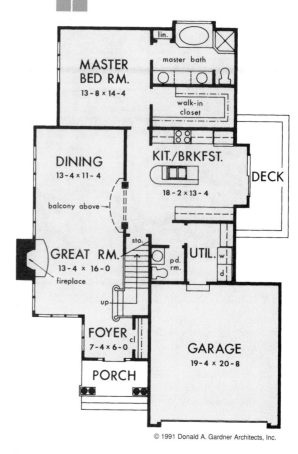

lin.

MASTER
BED RM.
13-8 × 14-4

master bath

walk-in closet

DINING
13-4 × 11-4

balcony above

KIT./BRKFST.
18-2 × 13-4

DECK

GREAT RM.
13-4 × 16-0
fireplace

sto.

p.d. rm.

UTIL.

w

d

up

FOYER
7-4 × 6-0   cl

GARAGE
19-4 × 20-8

PORCH

© 1991 Donald A. Gardner Architects, Inc.

This narrow-lot plan is highlighted by an entrance with a barrel vaulted ceiling and flanking detailed pillars. The great room and dining room share a vaulted ceiling to the second level. A spacious kitchen boasts an island and convenient breakfast area leading to the deck. The master bedroom on the main level has a large walk-in closet and complete master bath including a double-bowl vanity, whirlpool tub, shower and linen storage. The second level accommodates two bedrooms, a full bath and a balcony as well as attic storage. The plan is available with a crawlspace foundation.

© 1991 Donald A. Gardner Architects, Inc.

■ Design by Donald A. Gardner Architects, Inc.

■ DESIGN BY THE SATER DESIGN COLLECTION

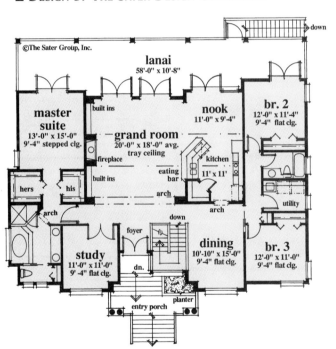

©The Sater Group, Inc.

lanai
58'-0" x 10'-8"

master suite
13'-0" x 15'-0"
9'-4" stepped clg.

built ins

nook
11'-0" x 9'-4"

br. 2
12'-0" x 11'-4"
9'-4" flat clg.

grand room
20'-0" x 18'-0" avg.
tray ceiling

fireplace

built ins

kitchen
11' x 11'

eating bar

arch

hers

his

arch

arch

utility

foyer

down

dining
10'-10" x 15'-0"
9'-4" flat clg.

br. 3
12'-0" x 11'-0"
9'-4" flat clg.

study
11'-0" x 11'-0"
9'-4" flat clg.

dn.

entry porch

planter

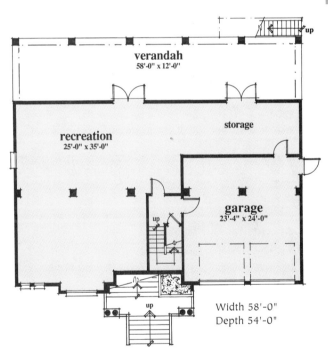

up

verandah
58'-0" x 12'-0"

recreation
25'-0" x 35'-0"

storage

up

garage
23'-4" x 24'-0"

up

Width 58'-0"
Depth 54'-0"

The dramatic arched entry of this cottage borrows freely from its Arts and Crafts past, creating a happy marriage of casual and traditional. The foyer and central hall open to the grand room, with a fireplace flanked by built-ins. The heart of the home is served by a well-crafted kitchen with hard-working amenities. Wrapping counter space, a casual eating bar and a corner walk-in pantry please the cook, while the adjacent morning nook welcomes the entire family. An archway announces the elegant formal dining room, which features a box-bay window. A secluded master suite offers access to the lanai through French doors. The bedroom leads to an opulent private bath through a dressing area flanked by His and Hers walk-in closets. A step-up soaking tub, twin lavatories and a glass-enclosed shower highlight the master bath. Two secondary bedrooms, which share a full bath, reside to the right of the plan.

PLAN 6692

Square Footage: 2,068

■ DESIGN BY POLLARD-HOSMAR ASSOCIATES

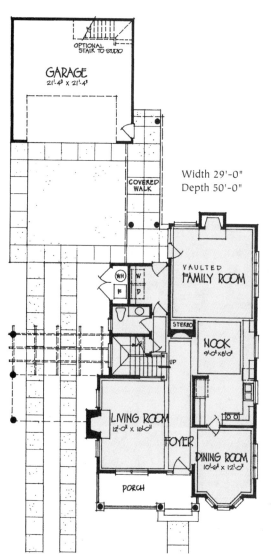

GARAGE
21'-4" x 21'-4"

OPTIONAL
STAIR TO STUDIO

COVERED
WALK

Width 29'-0"
Depth 50'-0"

VAULTED
FAMILY ROOM

STEREO

NOOK
9'-0" x 8'-0"

LIVING ROOM
12'-0" x 16'-0"

UP

FOYER

DINING ROOM
10'-6" x 12'-0"

PORCH

This quaint bungalow home, perfect for a narrow lot, will fit into any neighborhood. From its covered front porch to its covered walk in the rear, this home is filled with amenities. Inside, the foyer is flanked by a formal, bayed dining room on the right and a formal living room with a fireplace to the left. The U-shaped kitchen easily serves the dining room, while not neglecting its adjacent nook. A vaulted family room waits at the rear of the home, offering a second fireplace, a built-in stereo cabinet and backyard access. The sleeping zone is upstairs and includes two family bedrooms sharing a full bath, and a vaulted master suite. Here, the homeowner can be pampered by a large walk-in closet, a private deck and a sumptuous bath complete with a separate tub and shower.

PLAN 8867

First Floor: 1,193 square feet
Second Floor: 789 square feet
Total: 1,982 square feet

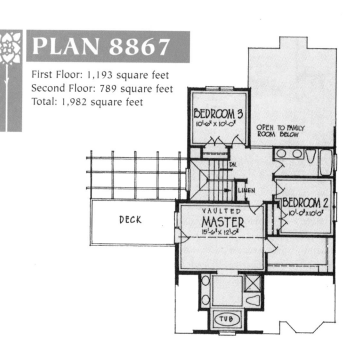

BEDROOM 3
10'-0" x 10'-0"

OPEN TO FAMILY
ROOM BELOW

DN.

LINEN

DECK

VAULTED
MASTER
15'-6" x 12'-0"

BEDROOM 2
10'-0" x 10'-0"

TUB

■ DESIGN BY POLLARD-HOSMAR ASSOCIATES

PLAN 8871

First Floor: 1,210 square feet
Second Floor: 876 square feet
Total: 2,086 square feet
Studio: 276 square feet

Two stories of bungalow bliss! And perfect for a narrow lot, too. With rafter tails, Craftsman-style windows and a covered front porch, this three-bedroom home is designed to please. The entryway is flanked by a vaulted, formal living room on the right and a formal dining room defined by columns on the left. The dining room is connected to the efficient kitchen via a butler's pantry. At the back of the home, a spacious family room features an abundance of windows and a warming fireplace, and a sunny nook offers access to the rear deck. Up an open staircase, two family bedrooms share a full hall bath and a linen closet. Completing this floor, the master suite offers built-in shelves, a walk-in closet and a sumptuous bath. A detached two-car garage also features an upstairs studio which could be an apartment, home office or art studio.

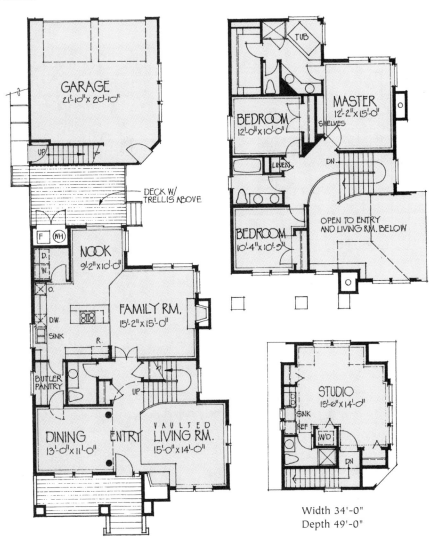

Width 34'-0"
Depth 49'-0"

■ DESIGN BY THE SATER DESIGN COLLECTION

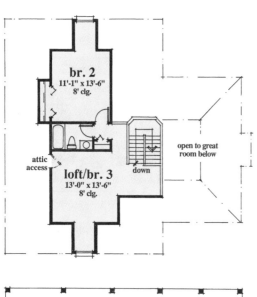

br. 2
11'-1" x 13'-6"
8' clg.

attic
access

loft/br. 3
13'-0" x 13'-6"
8' clg.

down

open to great
room below

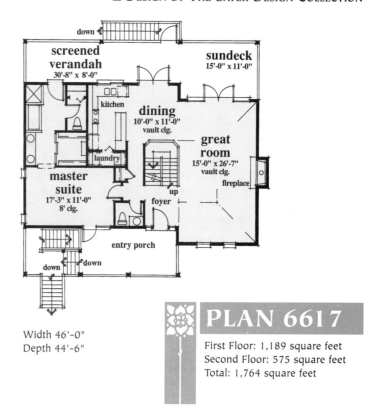

down

screened
verandah
30'-8" x 8'-0"

sundeck
15'-0" x 11'-0"

kitchen

dining
10'-0" x 11'-0"
vault clg.

great
room
15'-0" x 26'-7"
vault clg.

laundry

fireplace

master
suite
17'-3" x 11'-0"
8' clg.

up

foyer

down   down

entry porch

Width 46'-0"
Depth 44'-6"

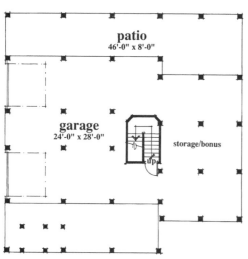

patio
46'-0" x 8'-0"

garage
24'-0" x 28'-0"

storage/bonus

up

PLAN 6617

First Floor: 1,189 square feet
Second Floor: 575 square feet
Total: 1,764 square feet

An abundance of porches and a deck encourage year-round indoor-outdoor relationships in this classic two-story home. The spacious great room with its cozy fireplace and the adjacent dining room both offer access to the screened verandah/deck area. An efficient kitchen and nearby laundry room make chores easy. The private master suite offers access to the verandah and leads into a relaxing master bath complete with a walk-in closet. Bedroom 2 shares the second floor with a full bath and a loft, which may be used as a third bedroom.

© American Home Gallery, Ltd.

■ DESIGN BY DESIGN TRADITIONS

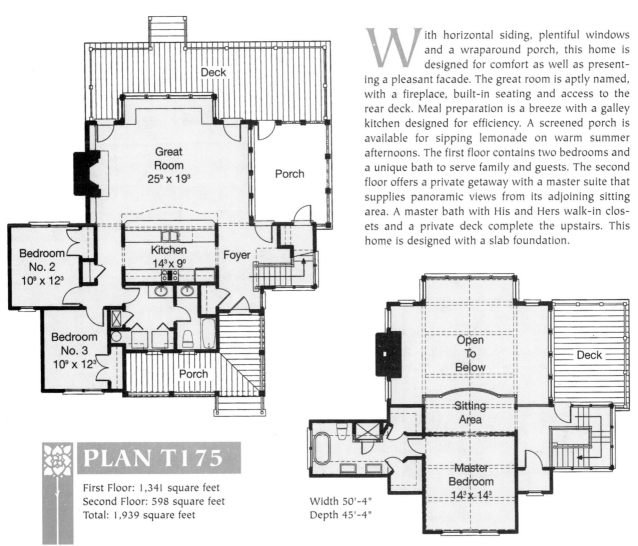

Deck

Great Room
25⁹ x 19³

Porch

Bedroom No. 2
10⁹ x 12³

Kitchen
14³ x 9⁰

Foyer

Bedroom No. 3
10⁹ x 12³

Porch

Open To Below

Deck

Sitting Area

Master Bedroom
14³ x 14³

Width 50'-4"
Depth 45'-4"

With horizontal siding, plentiful windows and a wraparound porch, this home is designed for comfort as well as presenting a pleasant facade. The great room is aptly named, with a fireplace, built-in seating and access to the rear deck. Meal preparation is a breeze with a galley kitchen designed for efficiency. A screened porch is available for sipping lemonade on warm summer afternoons. The first floor contains two bedrooms and a unique bath to serve family and guests. The second floor offers a private getaway with a master suite that supplies panoramic views from its adjoining sitting area. A master bath with His and Hers walk-in closets and a private deck complete the upstairs. This home is designed with a slab foundation.

PLAN T175

First Floor: 1,341 square feet
Second Floor: 598 square feet
Total: 1,939 square feet

■ Design by Alan Mascord Design Associates, Inc.

DINING
10/6 X 12/0+

NOOK
13/10 X 8/4

FAMILY
13/10 X 20/8

2 STORY
LIVING
13/0 X 14/0

DECK

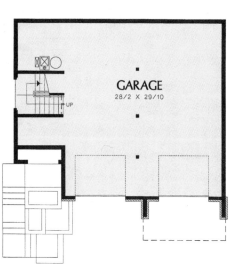

GARAGE
28/2 X 29/10

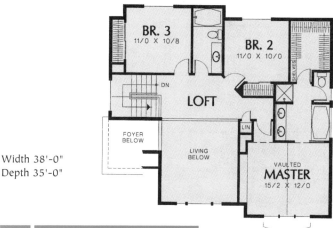

BR. 3
11/0 X 10/8

BR. 2
11/0 X 10/0

LOFT

FOYER BELOW

LIVING BELOW

VAULTED
MASTER
15/2 X 12/0

Width 38'-0"
Depth 35'-0"

PLAN 7469

First Floor: 1,106 square feet
Second Floor: 872 square feet
Total: 1,978 square feet

Though this home gives the impression of the Northwest, it will be the winner of any neighborhood. Craftsman style is evident both on the outside and the inside of this three-bedroom home. From the foyer, the two-story living room is just a couple of steps up and features a through-fireplace. The U-shaped kitchen has a cooktop work island, an adjacent nook and easy access to the formal dining room. A spacious family room shares the fireplace with the living room, is enhanced by built-ins and also offers a quiet deck for stargazing. The upstairs consists of two family bedrooms sharing a full bath and a vaulted master suite complete with a walk-in closet and sumptuous bath. A two-car, drive under garage has plenty of room for storage.

Perfect for a narrow lot, this two-story home has plenty to offer. The entryway opens directly into the two-story great room/dining area, where a built-in media center and a fireplace make this a room to truly relax in. Note the plant shelves that run the width of the home here. The C-shaped kitchen offers plenty of counter and cabinet space and has an adjacent nook with built-in shelves and access to the side porch. Upstairs, two secondary bedrooms share a full hall bath with a dual-bowl vanity while the master bedroom suite features a private bath, a walk-in closet and a secluded deck. A two-car garage enters from the rear and has lots of storage room.

PLAN 7495

First Floor: 860 square feet
Second Floor: 845 square feet
Total: 1,705 square feet

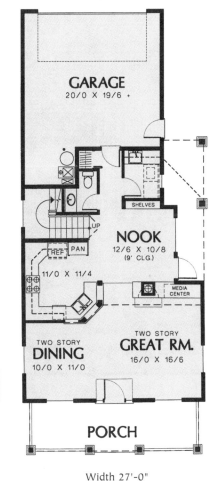

GARAGE
20/0 X 19/6 +

SHELVES

NOOK
12/6 X 10/8
(9' CLG.)

UP

REF PAN

11/0 X 11/4

MEDIA CENTER

TWO STORY
DINING
10/0 X 11/0

TWO STORY
GREAT RM.
16/0 X 16/6

PORCH

Width 27'-0"
Depth 64'-0"

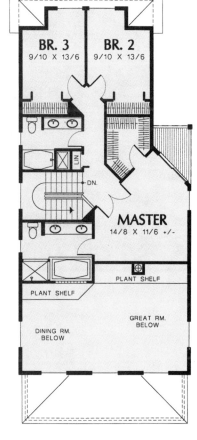

BR. 3
9/10 X 13/6

BR. 2
9/10 X 13/6

LIN

DN.

MASTER
14/8 X 11/6 +/-

PLANT SHELF

PLANT SHELF

DINING RM.
BELOW

GREAT RM.
BELOW

1,701 To 2,100 Square Feet

■ DESIGN BY ALAN MASCORD DESIGN ASSOCIATES, INC.

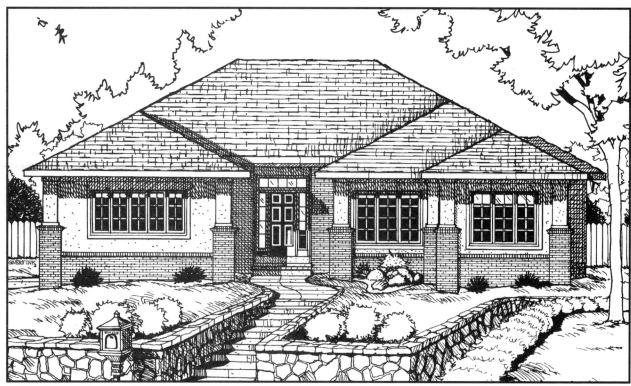

■ Design by Design Basics, Inc.

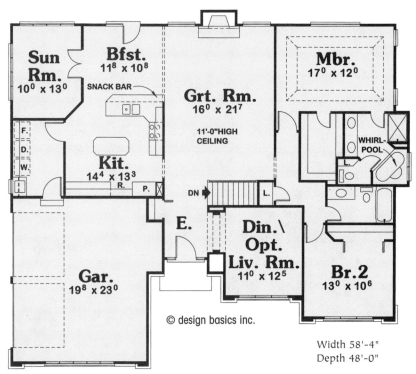

Sun Rm.
10⁰ x 13⁰

Bfst.
11⁸ x 10⁸

SNACK BAR

Grt. Rm.
16⁰ x 21⁷

11'-0" HIGH CEILING

Mbr.
17⁰ x 12⁰

WHIRL-POOL

F
D
W

Kit.
14⁴ x 13³

R.   P.

DN   L.

E.

Din.\ Opt. Liv. Rm.
11⁰ x 12⁵

Br.2
13⁰ x 10⁶

Gar.
19⁸ x 23⁰

© design basics inc.

Width 58'-4"
Depth 48'-0"

Sturdy pillars framing the wall corners give a fine geometric balance to this two-bedroom home. To the right of the foyer is a dining/living room option. Traffic flow is enhanced through two entrances into the kitchen which includes an island counter and snack bar. A large laundry room accommodates a soaking sink and freezer space. A large master suite is enhanced with a vaulted ceiling and other amenities such as a walk-in closet, whirlpool tub and separate shower. Plentiful windows in the sunroom make it a great haven for plants. An alcove in the two-car garage provides space for a workbench.

PLAN 7012

Square Footage: 1,894

■ DESIGN BY HOME PLANNERS

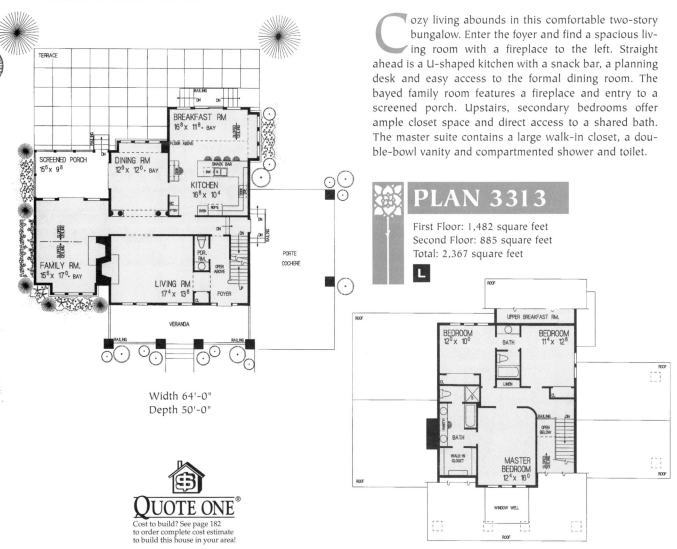

Width 64'-0"
Depth 50'-0"

Quote One®

Cost to build? See page 182
to order complete cost estimate
to build this house in your area!

Cozy living abounds in this comfortable two-story bungalow. Enter the foyer and find a spacious living room with a fireplace to the left. Straight ahead is a U-shaped kitchen with a snack bar, a planning desk and easy access to the formal dining room. The bayed family room features a fireplace and entry to a screened porch. Upstairs, secondary bedrooms offer ample closet space and direct access to a shared bath. The master suite contains a large walk-in closet, a double-bowl vanity and compartmented shower and toilet.

PLAN 3313

First Floor: 1,482 square feet
Second Floor: 885 square feet
Total: 2,367 square feet

L

■ DESIGN BY DESIGN TRADITIONS

PLAN T242

Square Footage: 2,489

This fine bungalow, with its multiple gables, rafter tails and pillared front porch, will be the envy of any neighborhood. A beam-ceilinged great room is further enhanced by a through-fireplace and three sets of French doors to the rear terrace. The U-shaped kitchen features a cooktop island with snack bar and offers a beam-ceilinged breakfast/keeping room which shares the through-fireplace with the great room. Two secondary bedrooms share a full bath, while the master suite is designed to pamper. Here, the homeowner will be pleased with a walk-in closet, a separate tub and shower and access to the rear terrace. The two-car garage has a side entrance and will easily shelter the family fleet.

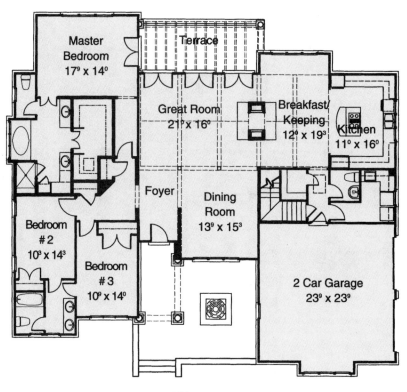

Width 68'-3"
Depth 62'-0"

■ DESIGN BY HOME PLANNERS

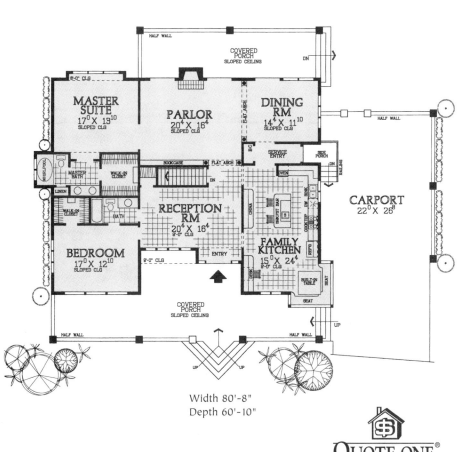

Width 80'-8"
Depth 60'-10"

Quote One®
Cost to build? See page 182
to order complete cost estimate
to build this house in your area!

PLAN 3498

Square Footage: 2,135

You'll savor the timeless style of this charming bungalow design. With pleasing proportions, it welcomes all onto its expansive front porch—perfect for quiet conversations. Inside, livability excels with a side facing family kitchen. Here, an interesting bumped-out nook facilitates the placement of a built-in table and bench seats. A formal dining room rests to the rear of the plan and enjoys direct access to a back porch. The parlor, with a central fireplace, also has access to this outdoor living area. The master bedroom is just a step away from the parlor. It offers large dimensions and a private bath with a walk-in closet, dual lavs and a bumped-out tub. An additional bedroom may also serve as a study.

TERRACE

KITCHEN
12⁰ X 13⁸

COOK TOP   PTRY   OVEN   D   W   LAUNDRY

FAMILY RM
11⁰ X 16¹⁰

SNACK BAR   S   CL

MASTER BEDROOM
14⁰ X 14⁰

GATHERING RM
18² X 16⁰

DINING
10⁴ X 12⁴

NICHE   S

LEDGE ABOVE

LINEN

BATH
SEAT

WALK-IN CLOSET

DN

FOYER

CL

CL

BATH

NICHE   S

STUDY/ OFFICE
12⁴ X 10¹⁰

S   CL

BEDROOM
11¹⁰ X 10¹⁰

BEDROOM
11¹⁰ X 10¹⁰

CL

WHIRLPOOL   SEAT   S

PLANTER

COVERED PORCH

PLANTER

Width 58'-0"
Depth 54'-0"

This attractive bungalow design separates the deluxe master suite from family bedrooms and puts casual living to the back in a family room. The formal living and dining areas are centrally located and have access to a rear terrace, as does the master suite. The kitchen sits between formal and informal living areas, sharing a snack bar with both. The two family bedrooms are found to the front of the plan, with a full bath nearby. A home office or study opens off the front foyer and the master suite.

PLAN 3319

Square Footage: 2,274

L D

QUOTE ONE®
Cost to build? See page 182
to order complete cost estimate
to build this house in your area!

■ DESIGN BY HOME PLANNERS

■ DESIGN BY DESIGN BASICS, INC.

PLAN 7029

Square Footage: 2,167

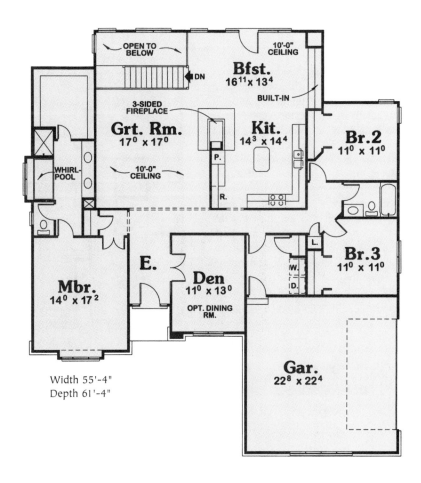

Width 55'-4"
Depth 61'-4"

OPEN TO BELOW

DN

10'-0" CEILING

Bfst.
16¹¹ x 13⁴

BUILT-IN

3-SIDED FIREPLACE

Grt. Rm.
17⁰ x 17⁰

Kit.
14³ x 14⁴

Br.2
11⁰ x 11⁰

10'-0" CEILING

P.

R.

WHIRL-POOL

Mbr.
14⁰ x 17²

E.

Den
11⁰ x 13⁰

OPT. DINING RM.

L.

W. D.

Br.3
11⁰ x 11⁰

Gar.
22⁸ x 22⁴

A Prairie influence is evident in this three-bedroom bungalow. Perfect for a walk-out lot situation, a stairway in the great room leads to the lower level and is open to two-story-high windows with a view to the back. A three-sided stone fireplace brings warmth and light to the spacious island kitchen, breakfast area and great room. Depending on the need, a den or dining room is located just to the right of the entryway. The master suite provides ample closet space and twin lavs across from a whirlpool tub. Separated for privacy, two secondary bedrooms share a full bath.

© American Home Gallery, Ltd.

■ DESIGN BY DESIGN TRADITIONS

A satisfying blend of shingles and wood trim complements a box-bay window and a Palladian-style clerestory on this stylish bungalow. A formal dining room invites planned events, but the grand great room, with a focal-point fireplace, built-in cabinetry and double doors to the rear porch, welcomes any occasion. A split bedroom plan affords seclusion to the master suite, which offers a spacious private bath and a wall of windows for natural light. On the opposite side of the plan, two family bedrooms share a gallery hall and a full bath. This home is designed with a basement foundation.

PLAN T187

Square Footage: 2,721

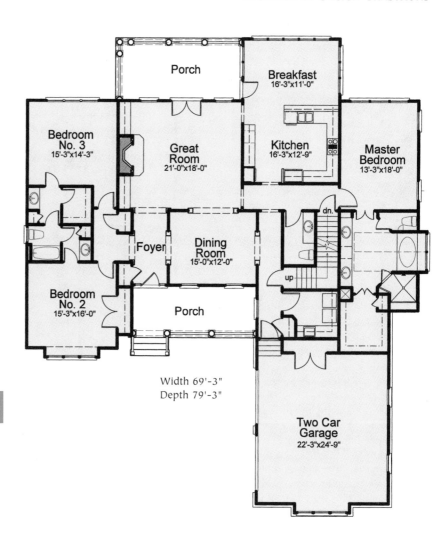

Width 69'-3"
Depth 79'-3"

■ DESIGN BY NORTHWEST HOME DESIGNING INC.

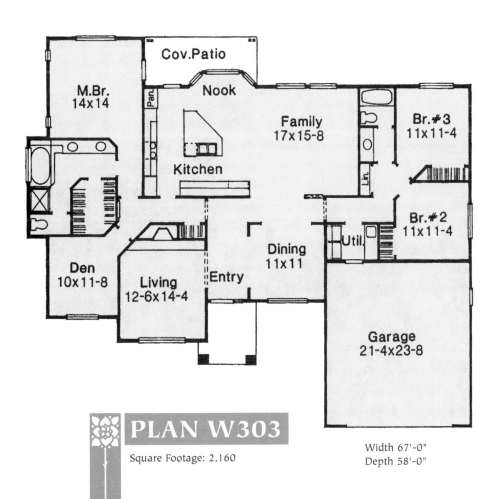

Cov.Patio

M.Br.
14x14

Nook

Pan.

Family
17x15-8

Br.#3
11x11-4

Kitchen

Den
10x11-8

Br.#2
11x11-4

Living
12-6x14-4

Entry

Dining
11x11

Util.

Garage
21-4x23-8

PLAN W303

Square Footage: 2,160

Width 67'-0"
Depth 58'-0"

S iding and shingles combine with gables and window details to give this three-bedroom home plenty of curb appeal. The entryway is flanked by a formal dining room to the right and a formal living room on the left. Directly ahead is a spacious family room with easy access to the island kitchen and bay windowed nook. Split bedrooms provide privacy for the master bedroom suite, with the two secondary bedrooms on the right. The master suite features a walk-in closet and a private bath. A cozy den is nearby for quiet reading, or use it as a home office. A two-car garage easily shelters the family fleet.

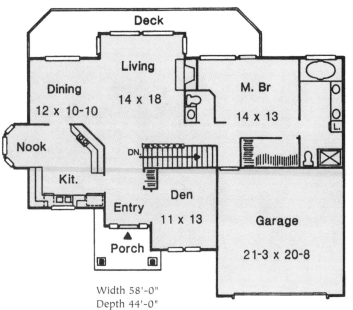

Deck

Living
14 x 18

Dining
12 x 10-10

M. Br
14 x 13

Nook

DN.

Kit.

Den
11 x 13

Entry

Garage
21-3 x 20-8

Porch

Width 58'-0"
Depth 44'-0"

PLAN W316

Main Level: 1,436 square feet
Lower Level: 1,195 square feet
Total: 2,631 square feet

Shingles, gables and Craftsman-style windows all combine to give this home plenty of curb appeal. Inside, a cozy den opens to the right of the foyer, while a wonderful kitchen is to the left. Here, a bayed nook encourages early morning coffee breaks. A spacious living room features a warming fireplace, a wall of windows and access to the rear deck. Located on the main floor, the master bedroom suite offers a walk-in closet, access to the rear deck and a bath with a separate tub and shower and a dual-bowl vanity. Downstairs, two secondary bedrooms share a full bath and access to a large rec room which features its own outdoor deck.

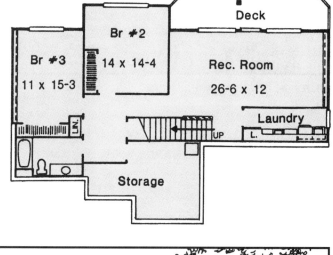

Deck

Br #2
14 x 14-4

Br #3
11 x 15-3

Rec. Room
26-6 x 12

LN.

Laundry

UP

L.

Storage

■ DESIGN BY NORTHWEST HOME DESIGNING INC.

■ DESIGN BY SELECT HOME DESIGNS

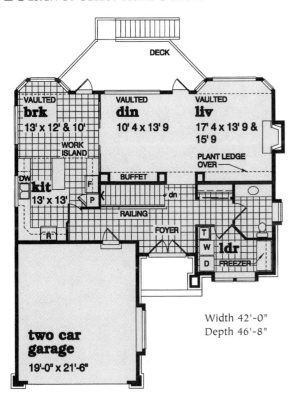

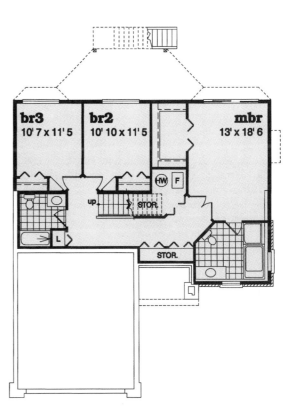

Width 42'-0"
Depth 46'-8"

Beautiful craftsman accents are evident in this design, perfect for a sloping lot. A double-door entry opens off a covered porch to an impressive vaulted foyer. Living areas are to the back and manifest in vaulted living and dining rooms. The living room boasts a bay window and fireplace. Access to the deck sits between the living and dining rooms. The L-shaped kitchen features an island work space and vaulted breakfast bay with deck access. The laundry area is to the front of the house and contains a half bath. Stairs to the lower level are found in the foyer. Sleeping quarters are found below—two family bedrooms and a master suite. The master suite has a walk-in closet and bath with separate tub and shower. Family bedrooms share a full bath.

PLAN Q478

Upper Level: 1,128 square feet
Lower Level: 1,092 square feet
Total: 2,220 square feet

■ DESIGN BY POLLARD-HOSMAR ASSOCIATES

A trio of gables, together with shingles and detailed windows present a Craftsman-style bungalow perfect for any neighborhood. To the left of the foyer is a den/living room that shares a through-fireplace with the formal dining room. The kitchen features a cook-top island and an adjacent sunny nook, both open to the spacious great room. Here, a vaulted ceiling, a bowed-window wall and a second fireplace enhance any gathering. Located on the main level for privacy, the lavish master suite is sure to please. Complete with a coved ceiling, walk-in closet, sumptuous bath and private outdoor deck, this suite is designed to pamper. Downstairs, two family bedrooms share a full bath and a large family room with access to the rear yard.

Width 54'-6"
Depth 54'-0"

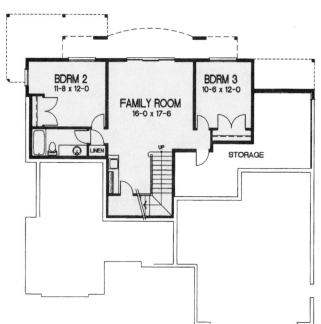

PLAN 8876

Upper Level: 1,813 square feet
Lower Level: 839 square feet
Total: 2,652 square feet

COPYRIGHT LARRY E. BELK

■ DESIGN BY LARRY E. BELK DESIGNS

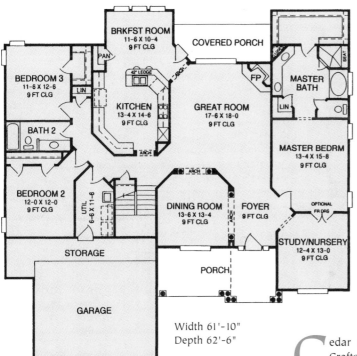

BRKFST ROOM
11-6 X 10-4
9 FT CLG

COVERED PORCH

PAN

BEDROOM 3
11-6 X 12-6
9 FT CLG

LIN

42" LEDGE

KITCHEN
13-4 X 14-6
9 FT CLG

GREAT ROOM
17-6 X 18-0
9 FT CLG

FP

MASTER
BATH

LIN

BATH 2

MASTER BEDRM
13-4 X 15-8
9 FT CLG

ARCH

BEDROOM 2
12-0 X 12-0
9 FT CLG

UTIL
6-6 X 11-6

ARCH

DINING ROOM
13-6 X 13-4
9 FT CLG

FOYER
9 FT CLG

OPTIONAL
FR DRS

STORAGE

PORCH

STUDY/NURSERY
12-4 X 13-0
9 FT CLG

GARAGE

Width 61'-10"
Depth 62'-6"

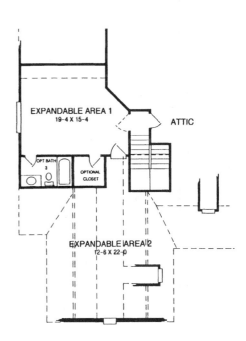

EXPANDABLE AREA 1
19-4 X 15-4

ATTIC

OPT BATH
3

OPTIONAL
CLOSET

EXPANDABLE AREA 2
12-6 X 22-0

PLAN 8158

Square Footage: 2,366

Cedar shingles and brick give this home the flavor of a Craftsman cottage. Inside, an up-to-date floor plan includes all of today's amenities. Nine-foot ceilings throughout give the plan a spacious feel. The dining room is defined by elegant arched openings flanked by columns. A corner fireplace serves the great room with panache. The kitchen features lots of counter and cabinet space along with a walk-in pantry and a snack bar. The master suite includes optional access to a "flex" room that would be perfect as a study or home-office. Two secondary bedrooms share a hall bath. The optional second floor includes space for an additional bedroom, a bath and a large storage area over the garage. Please specify crawlspace or slab foundation when ordering.

■ DESIGN BY POLLARD-HOSMAR ASSOCIATES

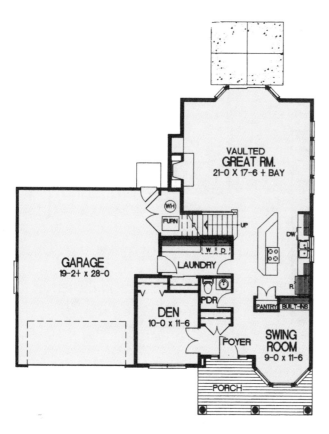

VAULTED
GREAT RM.
21-0 X 17-6 + BAY

WH
FURN
UP
DW
W I D

GARAGE
19-2+ x 28-0

LAUNDRY

PDR

DEN
10-0 x 11-6

PANTRY BUILT-INS
R.

FOYER

SWING
ROOM
9-0 x 11-6

PORCH

Craftsman-style windows, two prominent gables and a smattering of shingles are all elements of a true bungalow home. A swing room with a bay window and built-ins, just to the right of the foyer, is available for use as an office, formal dining or living room or a parlor. The vaulted great room features a second bay—this time with sliding glass doors in it—a fireplace, built-ins and easy access to the kitchen. The sleeping zone upstairs consists of two secondary bedrooms sharing a full bath, a vaulted master bedroom suite with a private bath and a walk-in closet, and a future bonus room. Note the built-ins at the top of the staircase.

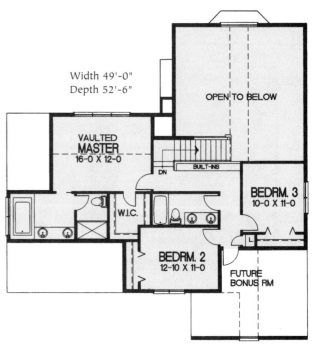

Width 49'-0"
Depth 52'-6"

OPEN TO BELOW

VAULTED
MASTER
16-0 X 12-0

BUILT-INS

DN

BEDRM. 3
10-0 X 11-0

W.I.C.

BEDRM. 2
12-10 X 11-0

FUTURE
BONUS RM

PLAN 8873

First Floor: 1,129 square feet
Second Floor: 871 square feet
Bonus Room: 122 square feet
Total: 2,122 square feet

PLAN 3321

First Floor: 1,636 square feet
Second Floor: 572 square feet
Total: 2,208 square feet

L D

2,101 SQUARE FEET & Up

Cozy and completely functional, this 1½-story bungalow has many amenities not often found in homes its size. The covered porch at the front opens at the entry to a foyer with an angled staircase. To the left is a media room, to the rear the gathering room with fireplace. Attached to the gathering room is a formal dining room with rear terrace access. The kitchen features a curved casual eating area and island work station. The right side of the first floor is dominated by the master suite. It has access to the rear terrace and a luxurious bath. Upstairs are two secondary bedrooms connected by a loft area overlooking the gathering room and foyer.

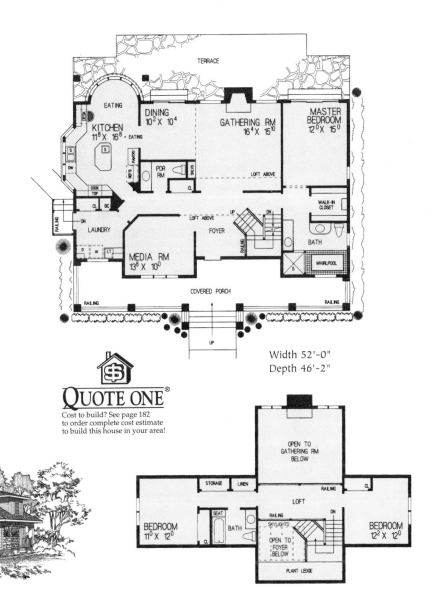

QUOTE ONE®
Cost to build? See page 182
to order complete cost estimate
to build this house in your area!

Width 52'-0"
Depth 46'-2"

REAR ELEVATION

■ DESIGN BY HOME PLANNERS

■ DESIGN BY ALAN MASCORD DESIGN ASSOCIATES, INC.

PLAN 7431

First Floor: 1,389 square feet
Second Floor: 1,049 square feet
Total: 2,438 square feet

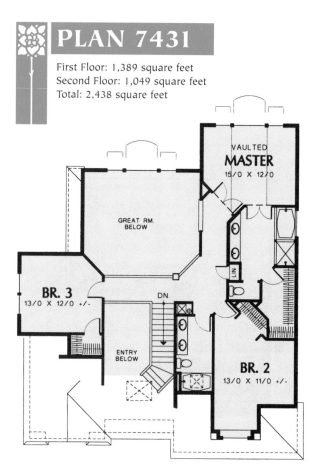

Width 45'-0"
Depth 51'-0"

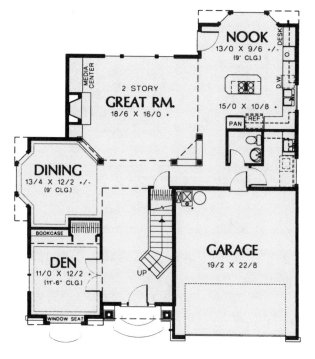

Shingles, stone work and skylights all combine to make this Craftsman house a delight to live in. The pleasure continues inside with a two-story great room acting as the heart of the home. Here a built-in media center flanks a warming fireplace. The L-shaped island kitchen offers an adjacent bayed nook for casual times, while the formal dining room easily accommodates elegant dinner parties. A den with a window seat finishes out the first floor. Nicely open to the lower floor, the upstairs contains two family bedrooms and a lavish, vaulted master suite. Here, a walk-in closet is reached via a luxurious bath that includes twin vanities and a separate shower and tub.

■ DESIGN BY HOME PLANNERS

BEDRM
15⁴ x 11⁸

BEDRM
11⁶ x 11⁰

BATH

LINEN

DN

QUOTE ONE®

Cost to build? See page 182
to order complete cost estimate
to build this house in your area!

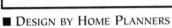

PLAN 3497

First Floor: 1,581 square feet
Second Floor: 592 square feet
Total: 2,173 square feet

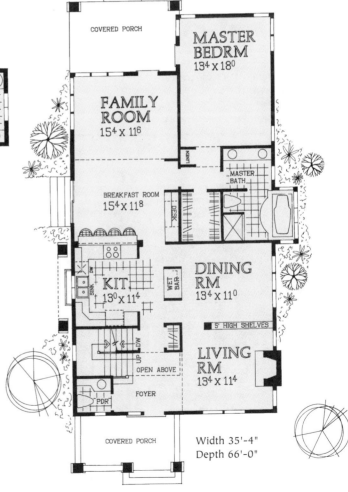

COVERED PORCH

MASTER
BEDRM
13⁴ x 18⁰

FAMILY
ROOM
15⁴ x 11⁶

MASTER
BATH

BREAKFAST ROOM
15⁴ x 11⁸

DESK

WET
BAR

DINING
RM
13⁴ x 11⁰

KIT
13⁰ x 11⁴

SINK

DW

5' HIGH SHELVES

UP DW

OPEN ABOVE

LIVING
RM
13⁴ x 11⁴

PDR

FOYER

COVERED PORCH

Width 35'-4"
Depth 66'-0"

This handsome bungalow is designed for easy living with a floor plan that puts the owner's comfort first. A quaint living and dining room is separated with a half wall of built-in shelves. The large kitchen has an open wet bar to the dining room and a snack bar to the combination breakfast and family room. The extra-large family room has sliding glass doors off the breakfast area and a door opening onto the covered rear porch. The master suite offers privacy and convenience thanks to thoughtful first floor planning. The two spacious bedrooms upstairs share a twin-basin bath.

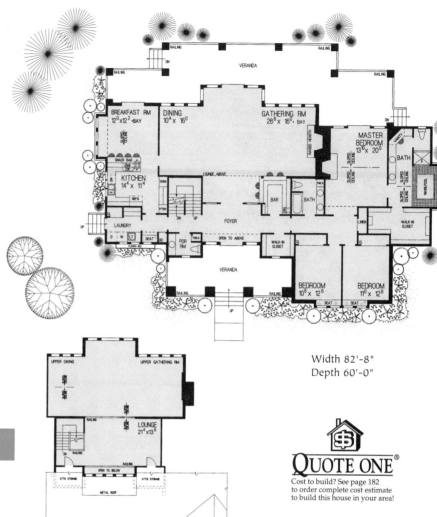

Verandas at both the front and rear of this engaging bungalow provide outdoor enthusiasts with a front row seat to enjoy the changing seasons. To further entice you outdoors, the master bedroom, the breakfast room and the gathering room all have French doors that open onto the rear veranda. During frosty weather, a raised-hearth fireplace warms the combined gathering room and dining room and offers a friendly invitation. Bedrooms are efficiently separated from the living area. A romantic fireplace and a luxurious private bath enhance the master suite. Two family bedrooms share a full bath. The second floor holds a lounge that makes a great getaway for quiet contemplation or study.

Width 82'-8"
Depth 60'-0"

PLAN 3315

First Floor: 2,918 square feet
Second Floor: 330 square feet
Total: 3,248 square feet

L

QUOTE ONE®

Cost to build? See page 182
to order complete cost estimate
to build this house in your area!

■ DESIGN BY HOME PLANNERS

■ DESIGN BY SELECT HOME DESIGNS

PLAN Q528

First Floor: 1,092 square feet
Second Floor: 1,147 square feet
Total: 2,239 square feet

Width 47'-0"
Depth 48'-0"

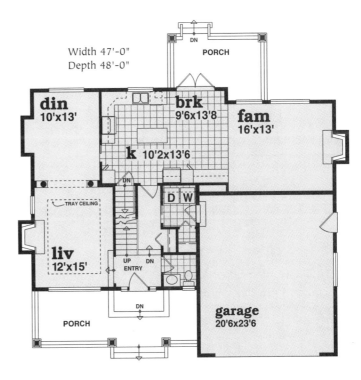

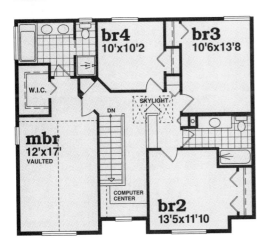

REAR ELEVATION

Shingle siding and a covered front porch add style to this Craftsman design. The interior is arranged thoughtfully and with an eye to varied lifestyles. Formal areas are on the left: a living room with tray ceiling and fireplace, and a formal dining room. A columned entry separates the two. The island kitchen connects directly to the breakfast room and family room with fireplace. Note the double doors in the breakfast room to a rear covered porch. The second floor has space for four bedrooms—one of them a master suite. The master bedroom has a vaulted ceiling and walk-in closet and features a luxury bath with separate tub and shower. Family bedrooms share a full bath.

Width 55'-10"
Depth 63'-6"

PLAN A297

First Floor: 1,758 square feet
Second Floor: 685 square feet
Total: 2,443 square feet

SUITE 2 11'-8" x 14'-8"
OPEN TO BELOW
LIN.
BATH
LOFT
DN
UNFIN. STOR. 9'-6" x 10'-6"
SUITE 3 10'-10" x 12'-6"
W.I.C.
BATH
DN
BONUS ROOM 11'-0" x 17'-8"

PATIO
MASTER SUITE 14'-6" x 14'-0"
BREAKFAST 11'-8" x 9'-4"
FAMILY ROOM 20'-6" x 15'-4"
KITCHEN 13'-0" x 15'-2"
W.I.C.
W.I.C.
UP
P.
PDR.
FOYER
MASTER BATH
DINING ROOM 12'-6" x 12'-6"
LAUNDRY
GARAGE 20'-10" x 22'-6"

With a stone and shingle facade, this three-bedroom home offers plenty of curb appeal. Craftsman-style windows and multiple gables only enhance this appeal. Inside, a formal dining room is located just to the right of the foyer and has easy access to the L-shaped island kitchen. A spacious family room is complete with a warming fireplace flanked by built-ins and French door access to the rear patio. A bayed breakfast area works well with the kitchen's large work island. Situated on the first floor for privacy, the master suite is designed to pamper. With a walk-in closet, separate tub and shower, bayed sitting area and private access to the rear patio, this suite is sure to please. Upstairs are two secondary suites—one with a private bath, and one with unfinished storage—and a large bonus room.

■ Design by Northwest Home Designing Inc.

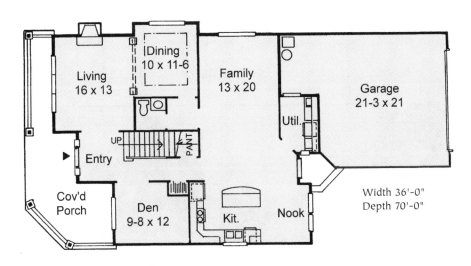

Living 16 x 13

Dining 10 x 11-6

Family 13 x 20

Garage 21-3 x 21

Util.

UP

PANT

Entry

Cov'd Porch

Den 9-8 x 12

Kit.

Nook

Width 36'-0"
Depth 70'-0"

With kind of a country version of Craftsman styling, this fine three-bedroom home is sure to be a family favorite. The two-story foyer opens to the formal living room on the left—complete with a fireplace—and a cozy den on the right. A huge family room shares space with an L-shaped kitchen and a sunny nook. The second floor consists of two family bedrooms sharing a full hall bath, an unfinished bonus room and a comfortable master bedroom suite. Here, the homeowner is encouraged to relax with a sumptuous bath and a walk-in closet.

PLAN W324

First Floor: 1,297 square feet
Second Floor: 838 square feet
Bonus Room: 321 square feet
Total: 2,456 square feet

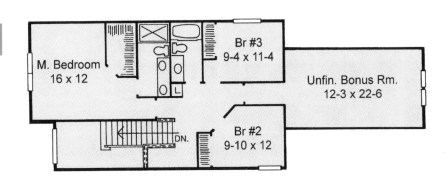

M. Bedroom 16 x 12

Br #3 9-4 x 11-4

Unfin. Bonus Rm. 12-3 x 22-6

DN.

Br #2 9-10 x 12

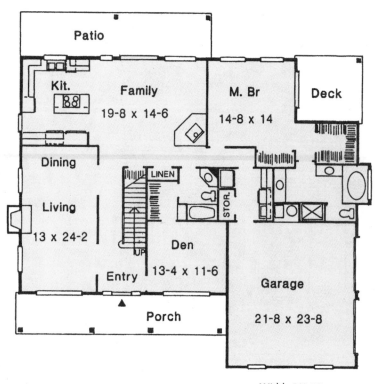

Patio

Kit.

Family
19-8 x 14-6

M. Br
14-8 x 14

Deck

Dining

Living
13 x 24-2

LINEN

STOR.

Den
13-4 x 11-6

Entry

Porch

Garage
21-8 x 23-8

UP

Width 58'-0"
Depth 52'-0"

PLAN W308

First Floor: 1,944 square feet
Second Floor: 618 square feet
Total: 2,562 square feet

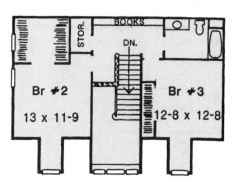

STOR.

BOOKS

DN.

Br #2
13 x 11-9

Br #3
12-8 x 12-8

A gabled dormer is flanked by two shed dormers on this attractive bungalow. Inside, the two-story foyer ushers you into either a cozy den—which can be used as a guest suite with a full bath nearby—or a spacious living room complete with a warming fireplace. The efficient kitchen offers a cooktop work island and easy access to the nearby family room, where a corner fireplace adds ambience to any occasion. Located on the first floor for privacy, the master bedroom suite is sure to please with two closets (one a walk-in!), a separate tub and shower, two vanities and a private deck. The two family bedrooms are upstairs and share a full bath and built-in bookcases.

■ DESIGN BY NORTHWEST HOME DESIGNING INC.

■ DESIGN BY POLLARD-HOSMAR ASSOCIATES

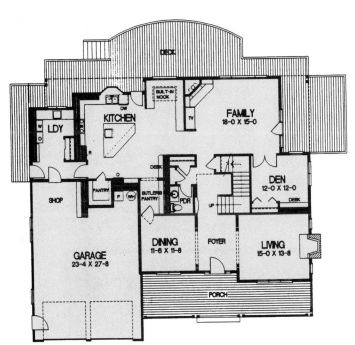

Width 60'-0"
Depth 55'-0"

R after tails, shingles and a pillared porch combine with the Craftsman-styled windows to present an attractive facade to this fine four-bedroom home. Formal areas are to the front, with a living room available just across the hall from the dining room—perfect for after dinner conversation. Casual living takes place at the rear of the home, with a spacious family room offering a corner fireplace, deck access and an adjacent den with a built-in desk. The large kitchen is filled with amenities, such as a huge work island, a walk-in pantry, a bay window over the sink and a built-in nook area. Up the curving staircase, three family bedrooms share a full hall bath. Bedroom 4 also features access to a large bonus room with a skylight. The master suite completes this floor, with a room-sized walk-in closet, lavish bath and a vaulted ceiling.

PLAN 8856

First Floor: 1,878 square feet
Second Floor: 1,592 square feet
Total: 3,470 square feet

■ DESIGN BY SELECT HOME DESIGNS

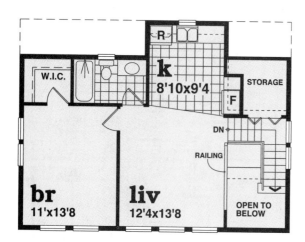

W.I.C.

R

k
8'10x9'4

STORAGE

F

DN

RAILING

OPEN TO BELOW

br
11'x13'8

liv
12'4x13'8

PLAN Q506

First Floor: 768 square feet
Second Floor: 679 square feet
Total: 1,447 square feet

Perfect for a guest apartment, or as an income possibility, this fine Craftsman carriage house will look good in any neighborhood. With rafter tails, a shed dormer, a gabled porch roof and a stone-and-siding facade, the Craftsman style is highly evident. A two-car garage shares space with a laundry room and a half bath, while the main living takes place upstairs. Plenty of storage can be found at the first landing of the stairs. The living room is open to the stairwell, and is adjacent to the petite-yet-efficient kitchen. The bedroom features a walk-in closet.

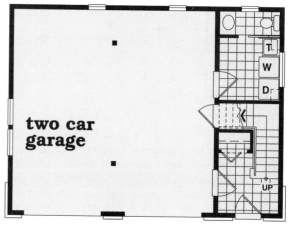

two car garage

T
W
D

UP

Width 32'-10"
Depth 28'-4"

■ DESIGN BY ALAN MASCORD DESIGN ASSOCIATES, INC.

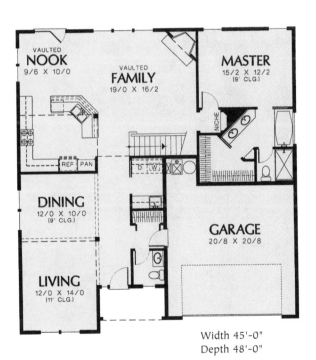

Width 45'-0"
Depth 48'-0"

This highly attractive bungalow exhibits many Craftsman-style features, such as rafter tails, detailed windows and an over-hanging roofline. Inside, the layout is great for entertaining, either formally or casually. The formal dining room is open to the living room, making it a great area for dinner parties and after dinner conversations. Toward the rear of the home, a vaulted family room features a corner fireplace and easy access to the efficient kitchen and vaulted nook. Here, access to the rear yard provides for outdoor dining. The master bedroom suite is situated on the first floor for privacy, and has a walk-in closet and a lavish bath. Upstairs, three bedrooms—or two and a loft—share a full hall bath.

PLAN 7481

First Floor: 1,579 square feet
Second Floor: 788 square feet
Total: 2,367 square feet

When You're Ready To Order . . .

Let Us Show You Our Home Blueprint Package.

Building a home? Planning a home? Our Blueprint Package has nearly everything you need to get the job done right, whether you're working on your own or with help from an architect, designer, builder or subcontractors. Each Blueprint Package is the result of many hours of work by licensed architects or professional designers.

QUALITY

Hundreds of hours of painstaking effort have gone into the development of your blueprint set. Each home has been quality-checked by professionals to insure accuracy and buildability.

VALUE

Because we sell in volume, you can buy professional-quality blueprints at a fraction of their development cost. With our plans, your dream home design costs only a few hundred dollars, not the thousands of dollars that custom architects charge.

SERVICE

Once you've chosen your favorite home plan, you'll receive fast, efficient service whether you choose to mail or fax your order to us or call us toll free at 1-800-521-6797. For customer service, call toll free 1-888-690-1116.

SATISFACTION

Over 50 years of service to satisfied home plan buyers provide us unparalleled experience and knowledge in producing quality blueprints. What this means to you is satisfaction with our product and performance.

ORDER TOLL FREE 1-800-521-6797

After you've looked over our Blueprint Package and Important Extras on the following pages, simply mail the order form on page 189 or call toll free on our Blueprint Hotline: 1-800-521-6797. We're ready and eager to serve you. For customer service, call toll free 1-888-690-1116.

Each set of blueprints is an interrelated collection of detail sheets which includes components such as floor plans, interior and exterior elevations, dimensions, cross-sections, diagrams and notations. These sheets show exactly how your house is to be built.

Among the sheets included may be:

Frontal Sheet
This artist's sketch of the exterior of the house gives you an idea of how the house will look when built and landscaped. Large ink-line floor plans show all levels of the house and provide an overview of your new home's livability, as well as a handy reference for deciding on furniture placement.

Foundation Plan
This sheet shows the foundation layout includ-

SAMPLE PACKAGE

ing support walls, excavated and unexcavated areas, if any, and foundation notes. If slab construction rather than basement, the plan shows footings and details for a monolithic slab. This page, or another in the set, may include a sample plot plan for locating your house on a building site.

Detailed Floor Plans
These plans show the layout of each floor of the house. Rooms and interior spaces are carefully dimensioned and keys are given for cross-section details provided later in the plans. The positions of electrical outlets and switches are shown.

House Cross-Sections
Large-scale views show sections or cut-aways of the foundation, interior walls, exterior walls, floors, stairways and roof details. Additional cross-sections may show important changes in

floor, ceiling or roof heights or the relationship of one level to another. Extremely valuable for construction, these sections show exactly how the various parts of the house fit together.

Interior Elevations
Many of our drawings show the design and placement of kitchen and bathroom cabinets, laundry areas, fireplaces, bookcases and other built-ins. Little "extras," such as mantelpiece and wainscoting drawings, plus moulding sections, provide details that give your home that custom touch.

Exterior Elevations
These drawings show the front, rear and sides of your house and give necessary notes on exterior materials and finishes. Particular attention is given to cornice detail, brick and stone accents or other finish items that make your home unique.

Frontal Sheet

Foundation Plans

Detailed Floor Plans

Exterior Elevations

Interior Elevations

House Cross-Sections

Important Extras To Do The Job Right!

Introducing eight important planning and construction aids developed by our professionals to help you succeed in your home-building project.

MATERIALS LIST

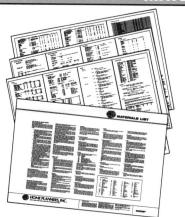

(Note: Because of the diversity of local building codes, our Materials List does not include mechanical materials.)

For many of the designs in our portfolio, we offer a customized materials take-off that is invaluable in planning and estimating the cost of your new home. This Materials List outlines the quantity, type and size of materials needed to build your house (with the exception of mechanical system items). Included are framing lumber, windows and doors, kitchen and bath cabinetry, rough and finish hardware, and much more. This handy list helps you or your builder cost out materials and serves as a reference sheet when you're compiling bids. A Materials List cannot be ordered before blueprints are ordered.

SPECIFICATION OUTLINE

This valuable 16-page document is critical to building your house correctly. Designed to be filled in by you or your builder, this book lists 166 stages or items crucial to the building process. It provides a comprehensive review of the construction process and helps in making choices of materials. When combined with the blueprints, a signed contract, and a schedule, it becomes a legal document and record for the building of your home.

QUOTE ONE®

Summary Cost Report / Materials Cost Report

A new service for estimating the cost of building select designs, the Quote One® system is available in two separate stages: The Summary Cost Report and the Materials Cost Report.

Make even more informed decisions about your home-building project with the second phase of our package, our Materials Cost Report. This tool is invaluable in planning and estimating the cost of your new home. The material and installation (labor and equipment) cost is shown for each of over 1,000 line items provided in the Materials List (Standard grade) which is included when you purchase this estimating tool. It allows you to determine building costs for your specific zip-code area and for your chosen home design. Space is allowed for additional estimates from contractors and subcontractors, such as for mechanical materials, which are not included in our packages. This invaluable tool is available for a price of $110 ($120 for a Schedule E plan) which includes a Materials List. A Materials Cost Report cannot be ordered before blueprints are ordered.

The Summary Cost Report is the first stage in the package and shows the total cost per square foot for your chosen home in your zip-code area and then breaks that cost down into various categories showing the costs for building materials, labor and installation. The total cost for the report (which includes three grades: Budget, Standard and Custom) is just $19.95 for one home, and additionals are only $14.95. These reports allow you to evaluate your building budget and compare the costs of building a variety of homes in your area.

The Quote One® program is continually updated with new plans. If you are interested in a plan that is not indicated as Quote One®, please call and ask our sales reps, they will be happy to verify the status for you. To order these invaluable reports, use the order form on page 189 or call 1-800-521-6797.

CONSTRUCTION INFORMATION

If you want to know more about techniques—and deal more confidently with subcontractors we offer these useful sheets. Each set is an excellent tool that will add to your understanding of these technical subjects.

Plan-A-Home®

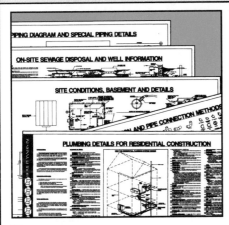

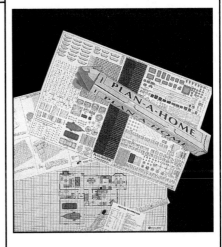

PLUMBING

The Blueprint Package includes locations for all the plumbing fixtures in your new house, including sinks, lavatories, tubs, showers, toilets, laundry trays and water heaters. However, if you want to know more about the complete plumbing system, these 24x36-inch detail sheets will prove very useful. Prepared to meet requirements of the National Plumbing Code, these six fact-filled sheets give general information on pipe schedules, fittings, sump-pump details, water-softener hookups, septic system details and much more. Color-coded sheets include a glossary of terms.

ELECTRICAL

The locations for every electrical switch, plug and outlet are shown in your Blueprint Package. However, these Electrical Details go further to take the mystery out of household electrical systems. Prepared to meet requirements of the National Electrical Code, these comprehensive 24x36-inch drawings come packed with helpful information, including wire sizing, switch-installation schematics, cable-routing details, appliance wattage, door-bell hookups, typical service panel circuitry and much more. Six sheets are bound together and color-coded for easy reference. A glossary of terms is also included.

Plan-A-Home® is an easy-to-use tool that helps you design a new home, arrange furniture in a new or existing home, or plan a remodeling project. Each package contains:

- **More than 700 reusable peel-off planning symbols** on a self-stick vinyl sheet, including walls, windows, doors, all types of furniture, kitchen components, bath fixtures and many more.

- **A reusable, transparent, 1/4-inch scale planning grid** that matches the scale of actual working drawings (1/4-inch equals 1 foot). This grid provides the basis for house layouts of up to 140x92 feet.

- **Tracing paper** and a protective sheet for copying or transferring your completed plan.

- **A felt-tip pen,** with water-soluble ink that wipes away quickly.

Plan-A-Home® lets you lay out areas as large as a 7,500 square foot, six-bedroom, seven-bath house.

CONSTRUCTION

The Blueprint Package contains everything an experienced builder needs to construct a particular house. However, it doesn't show all the ways that houses can be built, nor does it explain alternate construction methods. To help you understand how your house will be built—and offer additional techniques—this set of drawings depicts the materials and methods used to build foundations, fireplaces, walls, floors and roofs. Where appropriate, the drawings show acceptable alternatives. These six sheets will answer questions for the advanced do-it-yourselfer or home planner.

MECHANICAL

This package contains fundamental principles and useful data that will help you make informed decisions and communicate with subcontractors about heating and cooling systems. The 24x36-inch drawings contain instructions and samples that allow you to make simple load calculations and preliminary sizing and costing analysis. Covered are today's most commonly used systems from heat pumps to solar fuel systems. The package is packed full of illustrations and diagrams to help you visualize components and how they relate to one another.

To Order, Call Toll Free 1-800-521-6797

To add these important extras to your Blueprint Package, simply indicate your choices on the order form on page 189 or call us Toll Free 1-800-521-6797 and we'll tell you more about these exciting products. For customer service, call toll free 1-888-690-1116.

D *The Deck Blueprint Package*

Many of the homes in this book can be enhanced with a professionally designed Home Planners' Deck Plan. Those home plans highlighted with a **D** have a matching or corresponding deck plan available which includes a Deck Plan Frontal Sheet, Deck Framing and Floor Plans, Deck Elevations and a Deck Materials List. A Standard Deck Details Package, also available, provides all the how-to information necessary for building *any* deck. Our Complete Deck Building Package contains 1 set of Custom Deck Plans of your choice, plus 1 set of Standard Deck Building Details all for one low price. Our plans and details are carefully prepared in an easy-to-understand format that will guide you through every stage of your deck-building project. This page contains a sampling of 12 of the 25 different Deck layouts to match your favorite house. See page 186 for prices and ordering information.

SPLIT-LEVEL SUN DECK
Deck Plan D100

BI-LEVEL DECK WITH COVERED DINING
Deck Plan D101

WRAP-AROUND FAMILY DECK
Deck Plan D104

DECK FOR DINING AND VIEWS
Deck Plan D107

TREND SETTER DECK
Deck Plan D110

TURN-OF-THE-CENTURY DECK
Deck Plan D111

WEEKEND ENTERTAINER DECK
Deck Plan D112

CENTER-VIEW DECK
Deck Plan D114

KITCHEN-EXTENDER DECK
Deck Plan D115

SPLIT-LEVEL ACTIVITY DECK
Deck Plan D117

TRI-LEVEL DECK WITH GRILL
Deck Plan D119

CONTEMPORARY LEISURE DECK
Deck Plan D120

⬛ *The Landscape Blueprint Package*

For the homes marked with an ⬛ in this book, Home Planners has created a front-yard landscape plan that matches or is complementary in design to the house plan. These comprehensive blueprint packages include a Frontal Sheet, Plan View, Regionalized Plant & Materials List, a sheet on Planting and Maintaining Your Landscape, Zone Maps and Plant Size and Description Guide. These plans will help you achieve professional results, adding value and enjoyment to your property for years to come. Each set of blueprints is a full 18" x 24" in size with clear, complete instructions and easy-to-read type. Six of the forty front yard Landscape Plans to match your favorite house are shown below.

Regional Order Map

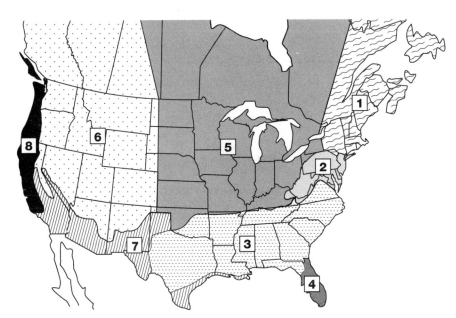

Most of the Landscape Plans shown on these pages are available with a Plant & Materials List adapted by horticultural experts to 8 different regions of the country. Please specify Geographic Region when ordering your plan. See page 186 for prices, ordering information and regional availability.

Region	1	Northeast
Region	2	Mid-Atlantic
Region	3	Deep South
Region	4	Florida & Gulf Coast
Region	5	Midwest
Region	6	Rocky Mountains
Region	7	Southern California & Desert Southwest
Region	8	Northern California & Pacific Northwest

CAPE COD COTTAGE
Landscape Plan L202

GAMBREL-ROOF COLONIAL
Landscape Plan L203

CENTER-HALL COLONIAL
Landscape Plan L204

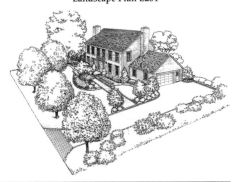

CLASSIC NEW ENGLAND COLONIAL
Landscape Plan L205

COUNTRY-STYLE FARMHOUSE
Landscape Plan L207

TRADITIONAL SPLIT-LEVEL
Landscape Plan L228

Price Schedule & Plans Index

House Blueprint Price Schedule
(Prices guaranteed through December 31, 1999)

Tier	1-set Study Package	4-set Building Package	8-set Building Package	1-set Reproducible Sepias	Home Customizer® Package
A	$390	$435	$495	$595	$645
B	$430	$475	$535	$655	$705
C	$470	$515	$575	$715	$765
D	$510	$555	$615	$775	$825
E	$630	$675	$735	$835	$885
F	$730	$775	$835	$935	$985

Prices for 4- or 8-set Building Packages honored only at time of original order.

Additional Identical Blueprints in same order ....$50 per set
Reverse Blueprints (mirror image) ....$50 per set
Specification Outlines ....$10 each
Materials Lists (available only for those designers listed below):
▲ Home Planners Designs..$50
† Design Basics Designs...$75
◆ Donald Gardner Designs..$50
■ Design Traditions Designs $50
✳ Alan Mascord Designs..$50
● The Sater Design Collection $50
≠ United Design Associates $50
✲ Select Home Designs $50

Materials Lists for "E-F" price plans are an additional $10.

Deck Plans Price Schedule

CUSTOM DECK PLANS

Price Group	Q	R	S
1 Set Custom Plans	$25	$30	$35

Additional identical sets $10 each
Reverse sets (mirror image) $10 each

STANDARD DECK DETAILS
1 Set Generic Construction Details ....$14.95 each

COMPLETE DECK BUILDING PACKAGE

Price Group	Q	R	S
1 Set Custom Plans, plus 1 Set Standard Deck Details	$35	$40	$45

Landscape Plans Price Schedule

Price Group	X	Y	Z
1 set	$35	$45	$55
3 sets	$50	$60	$70
6 sets	$65	$75	$85

Additional Identical Sets.................................$10 each
Reverse Sets (mirror image).............................$10 each

Index

To use the Index below, refer to the design number listed in numerical order (a helpful page reference is also given). Note the price index letter and refer to the House Blueprint Price Schedule above for the cost of one, four or eight sets of blueprints or the cost of a reproducible sepia. Additional prices are shown for identical and reverse blueprint sets, as well as a very useful Materials List for some of the plans. Also note in the Index below those plans that have matching or complementary Deck Plans or Landscape Plans. Refer to the schedules above for prices of these plans. All Home Planners' plans can be customized with Home Planners' Home Customizer® Package. These plans are indicated below with this symbol: 🏠. See page 189 for information. Some plans are also part of our Quote One® estimating service and are indicated by this symbol: 🏠 . See page 182 for more information.

To Order: Fill in and send the order form on page 189—or call toll free 1-800-521-6797 or 520-297-8200.

DESIGN	PRICE	PAGE	CUSTOMIZABLE	QUOTE ONE®	DECK	DECK PRICE	LANDSCAPE	LANDSCAPE PRICE	REGIONS
▲3313	B	157	🏠	🏠			L200	X	1-3,5,6,8
▲3314	B	130	🏠	🏠			L200	X	1-3,5,6,8
▲3315	D	172	🏠	🏠			L200	X	1-3,5,6,8
▲3316	A	32	🏠	🏠			L202	X	1-3,5,6,8
▲3318	B	145	🏠	🏠	D111	S	L202	X	1-3,5,6,8
▲3319	C	160	🏠	🏠	D112	R	L217	Y	1-8
▲3321	C	169	🏠	🏠	D116	R	L209	Y	1-6,8
▲3496	B	127	🏠	🏠			L202	X	1-3,5,6,8
▲3497	B	171	🏠	🏠					
▲3498	B	159	🏠	🏠					
▲3499	B	73	🏠	🏠	D111	S	L283	X	1-8
6617	D	152							
● 6622	C	27		🏠					
6691	C	109							
6692	C	149							
6694	C	133							
† 7012	C	156							
† 7028	C	106							
† 7029	D	161							
† 7030	E	76							
† 7326	D	67							
† 7396	C	102							
7431	C	170							
7445	E	87							
7461	B	41							
✳ 7464	B	125							
✳ 7465	B	99							
7466	B	129							
7467	B	95							
7468	B	131							
7469	B	154							
7470	B	43							
7471	B	35							
7472	B	143							
7473	D	20							
7474	D	81							
7475	C	78							
7476	C	65							
7477	C	33							
7478	C	46							
7479	C	38							
7480	C	51							

DESIGN	PRICE	PAGE	CUSTOMIZABLE	QUOTE ONE®	DECK	DECK PRICE	LANDSCAPE	LANDSCAPE PRICE	REGIONS
7481	C	179							
7482	D	61							
7483	E	16							
7494	C	42							
✳ 7495	B	155							
7497	B	142							
7504	D	70							
7518	C	74							
7521	B	146							
7531	E	86							
◆ 7673	C	112							
◆ 7679	C	113							
◆ 7680	C	54							
◆ 7681	D	37							
◆ 7682	C	138							
◆ 7683	B	111							
◆ 7693	F	89							
◆ 7694	D	59							
◆ 7695	C	137							
◆ 7699	C	140							
◆ 7700	C	116							
◆ 7707	F	88							
8158	C	167							
8258	B	135							
8856	D	177							
8857	C	64							
8858	C	60							
8859	C	62							
8860	C	56							
8861	C	57							
8862	C	63							
8863	C	44							
8864	C	52							
8865	C	39							
8866	B	48							
8867	B	150							
8868	B	47							
8869	B	53							
8870	A	115							
8871	B	151							
8872	C	58							
8873	B	168							
8874	B	117							
8875	B	34							
8876	C	166							
8877	B	147							
8878	C	71							
8978	A	101							
9185	C	100							
✳ 9529	A	103							
✳ 9530	A	98							
✳ 9531	A	105							
✳ 9536	D	69							
✳ 9557	C	15	⌂						
✳ 9590	C	24							
✳ 9591	C	40							
◆ 9637	C	108							
◆ 9641	C	148							
◆ 9693	C	110							
A185	D	82							
A186	D	80							
A201	C	85							
A239	A	124							
A240	B	120							
A241	B	118							
A242	B	123							
A244	B	122							
A250	C	55							
A253	C	75							
A262	C	31							
A296	C	25							
A297	C	174							
A298	D	84							
A301	C	68							
B510	B	128							
B511	B	132							
C119	D	83							
F146	E	28							
J155	D	104							
✳ Q478	C	165							
✳ Q505	A	93							
✳ Q506	B	178							
✳ Q513	B	94							
✳ Q527	B	119							
✳ Q528	C	173							
■ T175	E	153							
■ T176	E	92							
■ T183	E	144							
■ T187	E	162							
■ T242	E	158							
U212	B	134							
≠ V004	C	91							
W300	B	49							
W301	B	50							
W302	C	97							
W303	C	163							
W304	C	139							
W305	C	66							
W306	C	79							
W307	C	45							
W308	C	176							
W309	B	136							
W310	C	36							
W311	E	22							
W312	D	26							
W313	B	141							
W314	B	121							
W315	D	72							
W316	C	164							
W317	B	114							
W318	B	96							
W320	C	77							
W324	C	175							
W330	B	107							
W331	D	90							
Z052	B	126							

Before You Order . . .

Before filling out the coupon at right or calling us on our Toll-Free Blueprint Hotline, you may want to learn more about our services and products. Here's some information you will find helpful.

Quick Turnaround
We process and ship every blueprint order from our office within two business days. Because of this quick turnaround, we won't send a formal notice acknowledging receipt of your order.

Our Exchange Policy
Since blueprints are printed in response to your order, we cannot honor requests for refunds. However, we will exchange your entire first order for an equal number of blueprints at a price of $50 for the first set and $10 for each additional set; $70 total exchange fee for 4 sets; $100 total exchange fee for 8 sets . . . *plus* the difference in cost if exchanging for a design in a higher price bracket or *less* the difference in cost if exchanging for a design in lower price bracket. One exchange is allowed within a year of purchase date. **(Sepias are not exchangeable.)** All sets from the first order must be returned before the exchange can take place. Please add $18 for postage and handling via regular service; $30 via Priority Service; $40 via Express Service.

About Reverse Blueprints
If you want to build in reverse of the plan as shown, we will include an extra set of reverse blueprints (mirror image) for an additional fee of $50. Although lettering and dimensions will appear backward, reverses will be a useful aid if you decide to flop the plan.

Revising, Modifying and Customizing Plans
The wide variety of designs available in this publication allows you to select ideas and concepts for a home to fit your building site and match your family's needs, wants and budget. Like many homeowners who buy these plans, you and your builder, architect or engineer may want to make changes to them. Some minor changes may be made by your builder, but we recommend that most changes be made by a licensed architect or engineer. If you need to make alterations to a design that is customizable, you need only order our Home Customizer® Package to get you started. As set forth below, we cannot assume any responsibility for blueprints which have been changed, whether by you, your builder or by professionals selected by you or referred to you by us, because such individuals are outside our supervision and control.

Architectural and Engineering Seals
Some cities and states are now requiring that a licensed architect or engineer review and "seal" a blueprint, or officially approve it, prior to construction due to concerns over energy costs, safety and other factors. Prior to application for a building permit or the start of actual construction, we strongly advise that you consult your local building official who can tell you if such a review is required.

About the Designers
The architects and designers whose work appears in this publication are among America's leading residential designers. Each plan was designed to meet the requirements of a nationally recognized model building code in effect at the time and place the plan was drawn. Because national building codes change from time to time, plans may not comply with any such code at the time they are sold to a customer. In addition, building officials may not accept these plans as final construction documents of record as the plans may need to be modified and additional drawings and details added to suit local conditions and requirements. We strongly advise that purchasers consult a licensed architect or engineer, and their local building official, before starting any construction related to these plans.

Local Building Codes and Zoning Requirements
At the time of creation, our plans are drawn to specifications published by the Building Officials and Code Administrators (BOCA) International, Inc.; the Southern Building Code Congress (SBCCI) International, Inc.; the International Conference of Building Officials; or the Council of American Building Officials (CABO). Our plans are designed to meet or exceed national building standards. Because of the great differences in geography and climate throughout the United States and Canada, each state, county and municipality has its own building codes, zone requirements, ordinances and building regulations. Your plan may need to be modified to comply with local requirements regarding snow loads, energy codes, soil and seismic conditions and a wide range of other matters. In addition, you may need to obtain permits or inspections from local governments before and in the course of construction. Prior to using blueprints ordered from us, we strongly advise that you consult a licensed architect or engineer—and speak with your local building official—before applying for any permit or beginning construction. We authorize the use of our blueprints on the express condition that you strictly comply with all local building codes, zoning requirements and other applicable laws, regulations, ordinances and requirements. **Notice:** Plans for homes to be built in Nevada must be re-drawn by a Nevada-registered professional. Consult your building official for more information on this subject.

Foundation and Exterior Wall Changes
Most of our plans are drawn with either a full or partial basement foundation. Depending on your specific climate or regional building practices, you may wish to change this basement to a slab or crawlspace. Most professional contractors and builders can easily adapt your plans to alternate foundation types. Likewise, most can easily change 2x4 wall construction to 2x6, or vice versa.

Disclaimer
We and the designers we work with have put substantial care and effort into the creation of our blueprints. However, because we cannot provide on-site consultation, supervision and control over actual construction, and because of the great variance in local building requirements, building practices and soil, seismic, weather and other conditions, WE CANNOT MAKE ANY WARRANTY, EXPRESS OR IMPLIED, WITH RESPECT TO THE CONTENT OR USE OF OUR BLUEPRINTS, INCLUDING BUT NOT LIMITED TO ANY WARRANTY OF MERCHANTABILITY OR OF FITNESS FOR A PARTICULAR PURPOSE.

Terms and Conditions
These designs are protected under the terms of United States Copyright Law and may not be copied or reproduced in any way, by any means, unless you have purchased Sepias or Reproducibles which clearly indicate your right to copy or reproduce. We authorize the use of your chosen design as an aid in the construction of one single family home only. You may not use this design to build a second or multiple dwellings without purchasing another blueprint or blueprints or paying additional design fees.

How Many Blueprints Do You Need?
A single set of blueprints is sufficient to study a home in greater detail. However, if you are planning to obtain cost estimates from a contractor or subcontractors—or if you are planning to build immediately—you will need more sets. Because additional sets are cheaper when ordered in quantity with the original order, make sure you order enough blueprints to satisfy all requirements. The following checklist will help you determine how many you need:

____ Owner

____ Builder (generally requires at least three sets; one as a legal document, one to use during inspections, and at least one to give to subcontractors)

____ Local Building Department (often requires two sets)

____ Mortgage Lender (usually one set for a conventional loan; three sets for FHA or VA loans)

____ TOTAL NUMBER OF SETS

Have You Seen Our Newest Designs?

Home Planners is one of the country's most active home design firms, creating nearly 100 new plans each year. At least 50 of our latest creations are featured in each edition of our New Design Portfolio. You may have received a copy with your latest purchase by mail. If not, or if you purchased this book from a local retailer, just return the coupon below for your FREE copy. Make sure you consider the very latest of what Home Planners has to offer.

Yes! Please send my FREE copy of your latest New Design Portfolio.

Offer good to U.S. shipping address only.

Name _____

Address _____

City_____State_____Zip _____

HOME PLANNERS, LLC
Wholly owned by Hanley-Wood, Inc.
3275 WEST INA ROAD, SUITE 110
TUCSON, ARIZONA 85741

Order Form Key

| TB65 |

Toll Free 1-800-521-6797

Regular Office Hours:
8:00 a.m. to 8:00 p.m. Eastern Time, Monday through Friday
Our staff will gladly answer any questions during regular office hours. Our answering service can place orders after hours or on weekends.

If we receive your order by 4:00 p.m. Eastern Time, Monday through Friday, we'll process it and ship within two business days. When ordering by phone, please have your charge card ready. We'll also ask you for the Order Form Key Number at the bottom of the coupon.

By FAX: Copy the Order Form on the next page and send it on our FAX line: 1-800-224-6699 or 1-520-544-3086.

Canadian Customers
Order Toll-Free 1-800-561-4169

For faster service and plans that are modified for building in Canada, customers may now call in orders directly to our Canadian supplier of plans and charge the purchase to a charge card. Or, you may complete the order form at right, adding 40% to all prices and mail in Canadian funds to:

The Plan Centre 60 Baffin Place
Unit 5
Waterloo, Ontario N2V 1Z7

OR: Copy the Order Form and send it via our Canadian FAX line: 1-800-719-3291.

The Home Customizer®

"This house is perfect...if only the family room were two feet wider." Sound familiar? In response to the numerous requests for this type of modification, Home Planners has developed **The Home Customizer® Package**. This exclusive package offers our top-of-the-line materials to make it easy for anyone, anywhere to customize any Home Planners design to fit their needs. Check the index on page 186-187 for those plans which are customizable.

Some of the changes you can make to any of our plans include:

- exterior elevation changes
- kitchen and bath modifications
- roof, wall and foundation changes
- room additions and more!

The Home Customizer® Package includes everything you'll need to make the necessary changes to your favorite Home Planners design. The package includes:

- instruction book with examples
- architectural scale and clear work film
- erasable red marker and removable correction tape
- ¼"-scale furniture cutouts
- 1 set reproducible, erasable Sepias
- 1 set study blueprints for communicating changes to your design professional
- a copyright release letter so you can make copies as you need them
- referral letter with the name, address and telephone number of the professional in your region who is trained in modifying Home Planners designs efficiently and inexpensively.

The price of the **Home Customizer® Package** ranges from $645 to $985, depending on the price schedule of the design you have chosen. **The Home Customizer® Package** will not only save you 25% to 75% of the cost of drawing the plans from scratch with a custom architect or engineer, it will also give you the flexibility to have your changes and modifications made by our referral network or by the professional of your choice. Now it's even easier and more affordable to have the custom home you've always wanted.

ORDER TOLL FREE!
For information about any of our services or to order call 1-800-521-6797 or 520-297-8200. Plus browse our website: www.homeplanners.com

---

BLUEPRINTS ARE NOT RETURNABLE

**For Customer Service,
call toll free 1-888-690-1116.**

HOME PLANNERS, LLC
Wholly owned by Hanley-Wood, Inc.
3275 WEST INA ROAD, SUITE 110
TUCSON, ARIZONA 85741

THE BASIC BLUEPRINT PACKAGE
Rush me the following (please refer to the Plans Index and Price Schedule in this section):

_____ Set(s) of blueprints for plan number(s) _____. $_____
_____ Set(s) of sepias for plan number(s) _____. $_____
_____ Home Customizer® Package for plan(s)_____. $_____
_____ Additional identical blueprints in same order @ $50 per set. $_____
_____ Reverse blueprints @ $50 per set. $_____

IMPORTANT EXTRAS
Rush me the following:

_____ Materials List: $50 (Must be purchased with Blueprint set.)
$75 Design Basics. Add $10 for a Schedule E-F plan Materials List. $_____
_____ **Quote One®** Summary Cost Report @ $19.95 for 1, $14.95 for each additional, for plans _____ $_____
Building location: City _____ Zip Code _____
_____ **Quote One®** Materials Cost Report @ $110 Schedule A-D; $120 Schedule E for plan_____ $_____
(Must be purchased with Blueprints set.)
Building location: City _____ Zip Code _____
_____ Specification Outlines @ $10 each. $_____
_____ Detail Sets @ $14.95 each; any two for $22.95; any three for $29.95; all four for $39.95 (save $19.85). $_____
❏ Plumbing ❏ Electrical ❏ Construction ❏ Mechanical
(These helpful details provide general construction advice and are not specific to any single plan.)
_____ Plan-A-Home® @ $29.95 each. $_____
DECK BLUEPRINTS
_____ Set(s) of Deck Plan _____. $_____
_____ Additional identical blueprints in same order @ $10 per set. $_____
_____ Reverse blueprints @ $10 per set. $_____
_____ Set of Standard Deck Details @ $14.95 per set. $_____
_____ Set of Complete Building Package (Best Buy!)
Includes Custom Deck Plan _____.
(See Index and Price Schedule)
Plus Standard Deck Details $_____
LANDSCAPE BLUEPRINTS
_____ Set(s) of Landscape Plan _____. $_____
_____ Additional identical blueprints in same order @ $10 per set. $_____
_____ Reverse blueprints @ $10 per set. $_____
Please indicate the appropriate region of the country for Plant & Material List. (See Map on page 185): Region _____

POSTAGE AND HANDLING	1-3 sets	4+ sets
Signature is required for all deliveries. **DELIVERY** (Requires street address - No P.O. Boxes)		
•Regular Service (Allow 7-10 business days delivery)	❏ $15.00	❏ $18.00
•Priority (Allow 4-5 business days delivery)	❏ $20.00	❏ $30.00
•Express (Allow 3 business days delivery)	❏ $30.00	❏ $40.00
CERTIFIED MAIL If no street address available. (Allow 7-10 days delivery)	❏ $20.00	❏ $30.00
OVERSEAS DELIVERY Note: All delivery times are from date Blueprint Package is shipped.	fax, phone or mail for quote	

POSTAGE (From box above) $_____
SUB-TOTAL $_____
SALES TAX (AZ, CA, DC, IL, MI, MN, NY & WA residents, please add appropriate state and local sales tax.) $_____
TOTAL (Sub-total and tax) $_____

YOUR ADDRESS (please print)

Name _____

Street _____

City _____State_____Zip _____

Daytime telephone number (_____) _____

FOR CREDIT CARD ORDERS ONLY
Please fill in the information below:
Credit card number _____
Exp. Date: Month/Year _____
Check one ❏ Visa ❏ MasterCard ❏ Discover Card ❏ American Express

Signature _____

Please check appropriate box: ❏ Licensed Builder-Contractor
❏ Homeowner

ORDER TOLL FREE!
1-800-521-6797 or 520-297-8200

Order Form Key
TB65

Helpful Books & Software

Home Planners wants your building experience to be as pleasant and trouble-free as possible. That's why we've expanded our library of Do-It-Yourself titles to help you along. In addition to our beautiful plans books, we've added books to guide you through specific projects as well as the construction process. In fact, these are titles that will be as useful after your dream home is built as they are right now.

ONE-STORY

1 448 designs for all lifestyles. 860 to 5,400 square feet. 384 pages $9.95

TWO-STORY

2 460 designs for one-and-a-half and two stories. 1,245 to 7,275 square feet. 384 pages $9.95

VACATION

3 345 designs for recreation, retirement and leisure. 312 pages $8.95

MULTI-LEVEL

4 214 designs for split-levels, bi-levels, multi-levels and walkouts. 224 pages $8.95

COUNTRY

5 200 country designs from classic to contemporary by 7 winning designers. 224 pages $8.95

MOVE-UP

6 200 stylish designs for today's growing families from 9 hot designers. 224 pages $8.95

NARROW-LOT

7 200 unique homes less than 60' wide from 7 designers. Up to 3,000 square feet. 224 pages $8.95

SMALL HOUSE

8 200 beautiful designs chosen for versatility and affordability. 224 pages $8.95

BUDGET-SMART

9 200 efficient plans from 7 top designers, that you can really afford to build! 224 pages $8.95

EXPANDABLES

10 200 flexible plans that expand with your needs from 7 top designers. 240 pages $8.95

ENCYCLOPEDIA

11 500 exceptional plans for all styles and budgets—the best book of its kind! 352 pages $9.95

AFFORDABLE

12 Completely revised and updated, featuring 300 designs for modest budgets. 256 pages $9.95

ENCYCLOPEDIA 2

13 500 Completely new plans. Spacious and stylish designs for every budget and taste. 352 pages $9.95

VICTORIAN

14 160 striking Victorian and Farmhouse designs from three leading designers. 192 pages $12.95

ESTATE
15 Dream big! Twenty-one designers showcase their biggest and best plans. 208 pages. $15.95

LUXURY
16 154 fine luxury plans-loaded with luscious amenities! 192 pages $14.95

COTTAGES

17 25 fresh new designs that are as warm as a tropical breeze. A blend of the best aspects of many coastal styles. 64 pages $19.95

BEST SELLERS

18 Our 50th Anniversary book with 200 of our very best designs in full color! 224 pages $12.95

SPECIAL COLLECTION

19 70 Romantic house plans that capture the classic tradition of home design. 160 pages $17.95

COUNTRY HOUSES
20 208 Unique home plans that combine traditional style and modern livability. 224 pages $9.95

CLASSIC

21 Timeless, elegant designs that always feel like home. Gorgeous plans that are as flexible and up-to-date as their occupants. 240 pages. $9.95

CONTEMPORARY

22 The most complete and imaginative collection of contemporary designs available anywhere. 240 pages. $9.95

EASY-LIVING

23 200 Efficient and sophisticated plans that are small in size, but big on livability. 224 pages $8.95

SOUTHERN

24 207 homes rich in Southern styling and comfort. 240 pages $8.95

Design Software   ## Outdoor Projects

SUNBELT

25 215 Designs that capture the spirit of the Southwest. 208 pages $10.95

WESTERN
26 215 designs that capture the spirit and diversity of the Western lifestyle. 208 pages $9.95

ENERGY GUIDE
27 The most comprehensive energy efficiency and conservation guide available. 280 pages $35.00

BOOK & CD ROM

28 Both the Home Planners Gold book and matching Windows™ CD ROM with 3D floorplans. $24.95

3D DESIGN SUITE

29 Home design made easy! View designs in 3D, take a virtual reality tour, add decorating details and more. $59.95

OUTDOOR

30 42 unique outdoor projects. Gazebos, strombellas, bridges, sheds, playsets and more! 96 pages $7.95

GARAGES & MORE

31 101 Multi-use garages and outdoor structures to enhance any home. 96 pages $7.95

DECKS

32 25 outstanding single-, double- and multi-level decks you can build. 112 pages $7.95

Landscape Designs

| EASY CARE | FRONT & BACK | BACKYARDS | BEDS & BORDERS | BATHROOMS | KITCHENS | HOUSE CONTRACTING | WINDOWS & DOORS |

  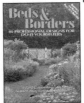    

33 41 special landscapes designed for beauty and low maintenance. 160 pages $14.95

34 The first book of do-it-yourself landscapes. 40 front, 15 backyards. 208 pages $14.95

35 40 designs focused solely on creating your own specially themed backyard oasis. 160 pages $14.95

36 Practical advice and maintenance techniques for a wide variety of yard projects. 160 pages. $14.95

37 An innovative guide to organizing, remodeling and decorating your bathroom. 96 pages $9.95

38 An imaginative guide to designing the perfect kitchen. Chock full of bright ideas to make your job easier. 176 pages $14 .95

39 Everything you need to know to act as your own general contractor...and save up to 25% off building costs. 134 pages $14.95

40 Installation techniques and tips that make your project easier and more professional looking. 80 pages $7.95

| ROOFING | FRAMING | VISUAL HANDBOOK | BASIC WIRING | PATIOS & WALKS | TILE | TRIM & MOLDING |

41 Information on the latest tools, materials and techniques for roof installation or repair. 80 pages $7.95

42 For those who want to take a more-hands on approach to their dream. 319 pages $19.95

43 A plain-talk guide to the construction process; financing to final walk-through, this book covers it all. 498 pages $19.95

44 A straight forward guide to one of the most misunderstood systems in the home. 160 pages $12.95

45 Clear step-by-step instructions take you from the basic design stages to the finished project. 80 pages $7.95

46 Every kind of tile for every kind of application. Includes tips on use installation and repair. 176 pages $12.95

47 Step-by-step instructions for installing baseboards, window and door casings and more. 80 pages $7.95

Additional Books Order Form

To order your books, just check the box of the book numbered below and complete the coupon. We will process your order and ship it from our office within 48 hours. Send coupon and check (in U.S. funds).

YES! Please send me the books I've indicated:

☐ 1:VO	$9.95	☐ 25:SW	$10.95
☐ 2:VT	$9.95	☐ 26:WH	$9.95
☐ 3:VH	$8.95	☐ 27:RES	$35.00
☐ 4:VS	$8.95	☐ 28:HPGC	$24.95
☐ 5:FH	$8.95	☐ 29:PLANSUITE	$59.95
☐ 6:MU	$8.95	☐ 30:YG	$7.95
☐ 7:NL	$8.95	☐ 31:GG	$7.95
☐ 8:SM	$8.95	☐ 32:DP	$7.95
☐ 9:BS	$8.95	☐ 33:ECL	$14.95
☐ 10:EX	$8.95	☐ 34:HL	$14.95
☐ 11:EN	$9.95	☐ 35:BYL	$14.95
☐ 12:AF	$9.95	☐ 36:BB	$14.95
☐ 13:E2	$9.95	☐ 37:CDB	$9.95
☐ 14:VDH	$12.95	☐ 38:CKI	$14.95
☐ 15:EDH	$15.95	☐ 39:SBC	$14.95
☐ 16:LD2	$14.95	☐ 40:CGD	$7.95
☐ 17:CTG	$19.95	☐ 41:CGR	$7.95
☐ 18:HPG	$12.95	☐ 42:SRF	$19.95
☐ 19:WEP	$17.95	☐ 43:RVH	$19.95
☐ 20:CN	$9.95	☐ 44:CBW	$12.95
☐ 21:CS	$9.95	☐ 45:CGW	$7.95
☐ 22:CM	$9.95	☐ 46:CWT	$12.95
☐ 23:EL	$8.95	☐ 47:CGT	$7.95
☐ 24:SH	$8.95		

Additional Books Sub-Total $_____
ADD Postage and Handling $___3.00___
Sales Tax: (AZ, CA, DC, IL, MI, MN, NY & WA residents, please add appropriate state and local sales tax.) $_____
YOUR TOTAL (Sub-Total, Postage/Handling, Tax) $_____

YOUR ADDRESS (Please print)

Name _____

Street _____

City _____ State_____ Zip _____

Phone (_____) _____—_____

YOUR PAYMENT
Check one: ☐ Check ☐ Visa ☐ MasterCard ☐ Discover Card
☐ American Express
Required credit card information:

Credit Card Number _____

Expiration Date (Month/Year) _____/ _____

Signature Required _____

 Home Planners, LLC
Wholly owned by Hanley-Wood, Inc.
3275 W. Ina Road, Suite 110, Dept. BK, Tucson, AZ 85741

TB65

Canadian Customers
Order Toll-Free 1-800-561-4169

RESOURCES

■ MANUFACTURERS

Arts & Craftsman
43 E. 10th St.
New York, NY 10003
(212) 353-1244
Arts and Crafts-style, handmade furniture.

Bradbury & Bradbury Art Wallpapers
P.O. Box 155
Benicia, CA 94510
(707) 746-1900
www.bradbury.com (website)
Turn-of-the-century wallpapers inspired by William Morris, with Art Nouveau florals, Glasgow roses, Viennese geometrics and Craftsman-inspired motifs.

Craftsman Hardware Company
P.O. Box 161
Marceline, MO 64658
(660) 376-2481
Hand-crafted hardware of copper, brass or bronze.

Designs In Tile
P.O. Box 358
Mount Shasta, CA 96067
info@designsintile.com (email)
www.designsintile.com (website)
An Art Tile Studio specializing in custom, hand-decorated ceramic tiles and murals.

Ephraim Faience Pottery
P.O. Box 792
Brookfield, WI 53008
(888) 704-POTS (7687)
Hand thrown, hand decorated Art Pottery.

International Wood Products
7312 Convoy Court
San Diego, CA 92111
(800) 468-3667
www.iwpdoor.com (website) .
Custom hardwood doors

Mica Lamp Co.
517 State Street
Glendale, CA 91203
(818) 241-7227
Copper lamps with unique Mica shade panels made of the same natural materials used at the turn-of-the-century.

Notting Hill Decorative Hardware
P.O. Box 1376
Lake Geneva, WI 53147
(414) 248-8890
dustman@nottinghill-usa.com (email)
www.nottinghill-usa.com (website)
High-end line of hardware for cabinetry and furniture in the Arts & Crafts to Art Nouveau styles.

■ HOUSES TO VISIT

The Ahwahnee
Yosemite National Park, CA 95389
(209) 372-1407
Designed by Gilbert Stanely Underwood in 1925. The Ahwahnee, whose name derives from an Indian word meaning "deep, grassy meadow," is a large 150,000-square foot luxury hotel.

Craftsman Farms
2352 Rte. 10 West (Parsippany)
Box 5
Morris Plains, NJ 07950
(973) 540-1167
Once owned by Gustav Stickley; now open to public, April-November, Wed., Thurs. 12-3pm, Sat., Sun. 1-4pm; large museum shop available with mail order catalog.

The Gamble House
4 Westmoreland Place
Pasadena, CA 91103
(626) 793-3334
www.bfc.usc.edu/bosley/gamble.html
Charles and Henry Greene's undisputed masterpiece and the only one of their "ultimate bungalows" regularly open to the public.

Heginbotham House
(Heginbotham Library)
539 South Baxter Street
Holyoke, CA 80734
(970) 854-2597

Frank Lloyd Wright Home and Studio
951 Chicago Avenue
Oak Park, IL 60302
(708) 848-1976
Wright's first residence; open to public seven days a week, 9-5. Guided tours three times daily on weekdays and every 10-15 minutes on weekends. Mail-order catalog and giftshop.

■ ANTIQUE MARKETS

Outdoor Antique and Collectible Market
Veterans Stadium
Lakewood Boulevard and Conant Street
Long Beach, CA
(213) 655-5703
Third Sunday of every month.

Fairgrounds Antique Market
1826 West McDowell Street
Phoenix, AZ
(602) 247-1004
Third weekend of every month.

Ann Arbor Antiques Market
Washtenaw Farm Council Grounds
Ann Arbor, MI
(734) 662-9453
Third Sunday of the month, April through October, and the second Sunday in November.

Burlwood Antique Center
Route 3
Meredith, NH
(603) 279-6387
Daily, May through October.

Georgia Antique Fair
Interstate 75 and Aviation Boulevard
Atlanta, GA
(404) 872-1913
Begins the Friday before the second Saturday of every month.